c77240

DIASPORA CRITICISM

DIASPORA CRITICISM

Sudesh Mishra

EDINBURGH UNIVERSITY PRESS

© Sudesh Mishra, 2006

Transferred to Digital Print 2011

Edinburgh University Press Ltd
22 George Square, Edinburgh

Typeset in 11/13 pt Monotype Bembo
by Servis Filmsetting Ltd, Manchester, and
printed and bound in Great Britain by
CPI Antony Rowe, Chippenham and Eastbourne

A CIP record for this book is available from the British Library

ISBN-10 0 7486 2105 9 (hardback)
ISBN-13 978 0 7486 2105 7 (hardback)
ISBN-10 0 7486 2106 7 (paperback)
ISBN-13 978 0 7486 2106 4 (paperback)

The right of Sudesh Mishra
to be identified as author of this work
has been asserted in accordance with
the Copyright, Designs and Patents Act 1988.

Contents

Preface

A genre is never ultimately about etymology. When Martin Baumann rebukes James Clifford for encouraging a metaphorical use of diaspora by not bothering about the provenance and coinage of the term (Baumann, 1997: 395), he is unable to see that genre designations bear little relation to the question of etymology. Statements on the etymological origins of a term may indeed participate in the genre, but no genre is really ever regulated by the strictures of etymologists or by the definitions found in dictionaries. The singularity of a genre nomination is really independent of the question of root meanings. Emanating from a diverse range of sources and arenas, generic statements frequently confound the whole issue of origins, roots and beginnings. Root meanings do not give birth to a genre; rather, a genre is made up of the dynamic procession of statements (some entering, some exiting) participating at the relational scene of the nomination. The total statement implied by the designation exists outside this relational order. The etymology of the designation, *novel* ('new', 'unusual' or 'of a kind not seen previously'), for instance, tells us very little about the participatory statements that engender the genre of the novel over the *longue durée*. Derived from *diaspeirein*, which is Greek for 'scattering' or 'sowing' (*speirein*) and originally used to account for the botanical phenomenon of seed dispersal (hence *dia* completely + *speirein* sow), the root meaning of diaspora, similarly, sheds little light on the archive that has emerged around the critical discourse. Diaspora is related to the question of dispersion certainly, but the genre not only exceeds the etymological question but also includes counter-statements or statements that concern matters not strictly connected to the subject of dispersion. A daunting number of works form participatory statements at the scene of the genre of diaspora criticism.

Since it would have been impossible for me to comment on each and every one, my choice of material has been influenced by a simple rule of citation. I have given preference, in short, to those works that form recurrent features or are mentioned with some regularity by those participating in the critical debate. Needless to say, this bears absolutely no relation to the issue of intellectual worth *per se*. Rather, it is meant to indicate the disproportionate impact some works have had on the critical genre. Paul Gilroy's *The Black Atlantic*, Stuart Hall's 'Cultural Identity and Diaspora', James Clifford's 'Diasporas' and William Safran's 'Diasporas in Modern Societies: Myths of Homeland and Return' are four cases in point.

No intellectual work is ever a solitary endeavour. Many friends and colleagues, past and present, here and abroad, have contributed to my thinking on the subject: Vijay Mishra, John O'Carroll, Ian Gaskell, David Punter, Nicholas Royle, Angela Smith, John Drakakis, Kishor Chetty, Seona Smiles, John Frow, Ron Goodrich, Ann McCulloch, Sarah Flattley, Sanjay Srivastava, K. S. Maniam, Syd Harrex, Raj Huilgol, Rick and Sue Hosking, Justin Clemens, Arvind Krishna Mehrotra, Vinay Lal, Dipesh Chakrabarty, Gyan Prakash, Ashis Nandy, Julian Wolfreys, Chandra Dulare, Subramani, Peter Davis, Maurice O'Connor, Som Prakash, Adesh Pal, Larry Thomas, Arlene Griffen, James Procter, Rajendra Chetty, Purushottama Bilimoria, David Sornig, Taliessin Raeburn, Ewen Jarvis, Michael Meehan, Satendra Nandan, Jenny Lee, Tony Romanella and Satendra Nandan. I am grateful to them. I am also grateful to the Institute of Citizenship and Globalisation at Deakin University for taking an interest in my work and to the Department of English and Cultural Studies at Melbourne University for hosting me for six months.

To Margaret, who was there when I was elsewhere, and to Mira, who was everywhere I happened be, I want to thank for the gift of love.

The cover photograph of two sisters was influenced by Wittgenstein's view on features and family faces which forms such a crucial aspect of the book's argument.

for Vijay Mishra
jahajibhai

we carry so many homelands
on the shoulders of a single earth
– *Zbigniew Herbert*

1

Prologue to a Generic Event

Event, Witness, Statement

Long before we can speak of a genre, a genus and therefore a taxonomy, still more one affiliated to that hugely capacious category called criticism, literary, cultural or some other, we must possess the training, the fortunate timing, to witness an event, as it happens, across the tremulous horizon of discourse. Clearly the subject encountering an event, the witness, is also the one who vouches for it, and may be understood as a witness in the related juridical sense of the term. The very act of witnessing installs the attestant, the one present in the raw face of the occurrence, as the subject of the vouched-for event. This same witness is entrusted with the task of enunciating the event in the first instance, since there is no event as such without a corresponding attestant. Similarly, the witness *qua* witness exists only in relation to the event and ceases to exist with the latter's disappearance. The attestant is obliged by the very predicate that constitutes it as subject to formulate one or a number of enunciative statements[1] to frame the eventful entity. It matters little that these statements are overblown conceits, litotes, ironic disavowals, sly innuendoes, casual asides or flagrant untruths, whether they are audaciously forthright or cunningly oblique, for without exception they serve as event-marking testimonies, emanating from the *testis*. In *Remnants of Auschwitz: The Witness and the Archive*, Giorgio Agamben comments on the forked sense of the witness in Latin:

> In Latin there are two words for witness. The first word, *testis*, from which our word testimony derives, etymologically signifies the person who, in a trial or lawsuit between two rival parties, is in the position of a third party (*tertis*). The second word, *superstes*, designates a person who

> has lived through something, who has experienced an event from beginning to end and therefore can bear witness to it. (Agamben, 1999: 17)

At this point it is sufficient to say that the vouched-for event, the one we can actually *bear* to witness in the face of subliminal pleasure or terror, is a mediated happening whereas the event as raw occurrence bears upon it the (question) marks of an incomprehensible purity.

Considering the event in terms of the sublime *now* of the avant garde, Jean-François Lyotard observes:

> That it happens 'precedes,' so to speak, the question pertaining to what happens. Or rather, the question precedes itself, because 'that it happens' is the question relevant as event, and it 'then' pertains to the event that has just happened. The event happens as a question mark 'before' happening as a question. It happens is rather 'in the first place' is it happening, is it, is it possible? Only 'then' is any mark determined by the questioning: is this or that happening, is it this or something else, is it possible that this or that? (Lyotard, 1989: 197)

The question mark is the point at which thought is 'disarmed' (Lyotard, 1989: 197), it is the mark before any remarking, the premonitory sign before any signification. *Is it happening* introduces the possibility that *nothing is happening, nothing happens*, and so thought undoes itself, the witness doubts his senses. Only later is it possible to say that this or that is happening and whether it is this or some other. For Lyotard the question mark relates to the yet-to-be-determined character of the event. Since it is anticipatory, a presentiment, it marks a non-mark, an abyss of sorts. But it is equally possible, I think, to conceive of the question mark as marking too much, as abounding in multiples to the point of madness, thereby rendering thought-as-cognition impossible. The mark is semantically overcharged. In this scheme (or the lack thereof), thought is not peering into the abyss of itself but floundering inside a heady clamour. Language fails because there is, paradoxically, too much language. A state of commotion prevails within the system of signs. In the face of utmost horror, to risk an analogy, nothing may be said because there is too much to say. The din of possibilities at the scene of pure happening – pure because the event may not be extracted, will not *eventuate* – renders impossible the singularity of the event and, by extension, the act of attesting to its occurrence. In this sense, then, the pure event is a cognitive (though not philosophical) impossibility. At once cacophony and delirium, it is devoid of 'the subjectivity and objectivity of what happens' (Deleuze, 1995: 5). Incapable of being witnessed, it withholds its name. It is a species of glossolalia, a saturnalia of tongues, where neither the speaker nor the receiver has any purchase on sense.[2] The witnessed event or the event *proper* is already a nomination, a statement, though of a rudimentary sort, and holds within it the seeds of other statements, opinions, predicates. When newsreaders speak of the Asian Tsunami, we know they are adverting to an event whose eventfulness is dependent on a host of other factors that are being stated, not stated, understated, overstated and counter-stated in relation to the caption: the inexorable force of the tsunami, its link to a primary causal event (earthquake), the special place it now occupies in the calendar of natural disasters, the terrible toll it has exacted on human and other forms of life, its impact on the tourist industry and on various intra-national forms of civil strife, its theological reckoners and apologists, its connections to global warming and its multiple 'impact' sites (Sri Lanka, Thailand, Banda Aceh, Andaman Islands, Maldives and India), its deformation of fragile littoral ecologies and circumvention of prognostic technologies, and so forth. The eventfulness of an event is bound up with the flow of discursive matter around the bare datum of the nomination. Once witnessed, the event incites other statements to justify the nomination. As a matter of fact the transience or longevity of the nomination is entirely dependent on the magnetic capacity of an event to attract statements.[3]

Speaking of the compulsive nomination of 9/11 as (major) event, Derrida says that it

> remains ineffable, like an intuition without concept, like a unicity with no generality on the horizon or no horizon at all, out of range for a language that admits its powerlessness and so is reduced to pronouncing mechanically a date, repeating it endlessly, as a kind of ritual incantation, a conjuring poem, a journalistic litany or rhetorical refrain that admits to not knowing what it's talking about. (Borradori, 2003: 86)

Although the statement, 9/11, as recurring mantra, may not know what it's talking about (and to be sure it does not), it persists in talking nonetheless without the benefit of this knowledge, and this talking, this mesmerising recitation of a date in its curt algebraic form, is, to my mind, graphically overdetermined. Graphically because, in this instance, we are in the province of the sign pictorial rather than the sign abstract; and this sign is televisionary, since technology permits us to see together from great distances, as well as telepathic, for modern mediascapes[4] have trained us to decipher each other's minds from afar. Where Derrida reads repetition as betokening the emptiness of the concept, as 'neutralising, deadening, distancing a traumatism' (Borradori, 2003: 87), I prefer to read it as the symptom of an insufferable excess in speculative signification as it pertains to the spectacle itself. Every repetition – the vertiginious presentation and representation of the assault on the twin towers – offers the becoming-memory of a *différance* (them not us, though they are deferrable to any number of geo-fanatical sites) and an overabundance of supplementary takes on the same memory. For it is proper to ask: what is a Palestinian's view of 9/11 as opposed to a New Yorker's? Or what's a stock-broker's perspective on the event as distinct from a peasant's? Where does a cinematic mediation of 9/11 stop and the non-cinematic begin? Drawing on Heidegger's proposition that *ein Ereignis* (or what we have called the pure event) resists systemic appropriation, in part at least, Derrida insists that there is something irreducibly pre-discursive about that which counts as an event because, as he points out, language stands dumbstruck before it. It may be possible to advance a contrary opinion which argues that, in its raw occurrence, the event is a remorseless brimming over of signs – a chaos-cosmos of sorts. Not ineffability but non-extractability. The former condition relates to the unspeakable paucity of signs whereas the latter relates to their intolerable surfeit. Nothing happens – which is how Derrida understands the pure event (Derrida, 1992: 199) – because too much happens. The language of the pure event, affective or otherwise, is always too much with us. Too sublimely over-charged, it says too much, too soon, and all at once. Which is why in his bid to announce the pure event of God's death, Nietzsche's madman – and all madmen exist inside the maelstrom of the pure event – admits to the unsayability of what he says:

> Here the madman fell silent and looked again at his listeners; and they too were silent and stared at him in astonishment. At last he threw his lantern on the ground, and it broke and went out. 'I come too early,' he said then; 'my time has not come yet. This tremendous event is still on its way, still wandering – it has not yet reached the ears of man'. (Nietzsche, 1976: 96)

When language is in the midst of anarchy, when disquieted by newness, heteroglossia[5] runs riot, turning into glossolalia, cognition falters, comprehension fails. It is, therefore, not a question of the absence of a horizon or context, but of altogether too much horizon (vertigo) and too much context (nausea), for the instrument of appropriation – the discursive statement – to cope with. This is precisely the point at which the attestant enters.

The attestant is able to bear witness and it is this ability that allows it to generate statements, to wrest from the indecipherable big bang of too-much signification a relation, an utterance, a description, a swag of statements, appellations, explications, even a harvest of axioms and motifs. Yet this bearing witness turns the tumultuous, unstable horizon of the pure event, its teeming cornucopia, its semantic turmoil and semiotic glut, into something else: an ensemble and a category and, indeed, an order. This is the paradoxical law of bearing witness to an event, its non-accessibility in the pure carnivalesque form. For once the event is witnessed, the unbearably semiotic dissolves in the space of the legibly symbolic, which space the statement or an array of statements transforms into a scene, an order, a regularity of sorts. By semiotic I refer to a disorganisation of precursory sign-traces that goes by the name of pure event, and by symbolic to the representable sign arrangements that define a witnessed event. Alain Badiou remarks that 'what composes an event is always extracted from a situation, always related back to a singular multiplicity, to its state, to the language connected to it, etc. In fact . . . an event is nothing but a part of a given situation, nothing but a *fragment of being*' (Badiou, 2004: 98). And it is exactly this fragment, and the act of excerpting a fragment, that makes for the event proper. Dostoyevsky captures something of this notion in the opening paragraph of 'The Double' which tracks the consciousness of Yakov Peterovich Golyadkin in the process of waking up:

> It was little before eight o'clock in the morning when Titular Councillor Yakov Peterovich Golyadkin woke from a long sleep, yawned, stretched, and finally opened his eyes completely. He lay motionless in bed, however, for a couple of minutes more, like a man who is not yet quite sure whether he is awake or still asleep, and whether what is happening around him is real and actual or only the continuation of his disordered dreams . . . But a moment later he leapt from bed with one bound, probably because he had at last stumbled upon the idea round which his scattered thoughts, not yet reduced to order, had been revolving. (Dostoyevsky, 2003: 127)

The emergent idea on the verge of order is what distinguishes disordered dreams from the proper event. The pure event has no harness and certainly no harnessable limits. It is what Deleuze, referring to Platonic theories of dimension, calls 'pure becoming without measure, a veritable becoming-mad, which never rests. It always eludes the present, causing future and past, more and less, too much and not enough to coincide in the simultaneity of a rebellious matter' (Deleuze, 1990: 2).[6] Neither a rule nor an order, it is a misrule, a jumble of agitated, overabundant, non-harvestable sign-senses. Sign-senses subsist between words and things. Although emanating from the proposition, they are independent of it. (That I can speak of the pure event from an impure site – an obvious aporia – tells us something about the capacity of language to overreach itself, to slip into the too-garrulous or too-silent non-place of the spectre.) The vouched-for event, on the other hand, succumbs to the delimiting procedure that involves testimony, the issuing of *expressible* yet heterogeneous statements, which is to say, statements in keeping with the phantasmal rules of a proposition, a protocol or an etiquette. The pure event is an untameable excreta of sign-senses (and must always remain so), while the procedures of incorporation that summon the event proper, sundering it absolutely from its pure state, lead to a formation, to an articulation, to something approaching a congruity, a contiguity and an order. And since the law of incorporation is based on structures of repetition and resemblance, for we must be able to decipher the echo, the insinuation, no matter how faint, of a precedent or directive, as well as radical acts of departure, for no new event is worthy of its name, is newsworthy, unless it breaches the limits of all previous events, all prior marks, we are obliged to speak of a scene of enunciative statements. Enunciative statements are past-dependent in that they have to be *re-cognised*,[7] present-discontinuous inasmuch as they say something other than what's in the past and the immediate present, and future-oriented, since by saying this 'something other' they foreshadow the scene of future statements. In any case, even a heterotopia, such as the one in Jorge Luis Borges that provokes Michel Foucault to laughter, must echo the possibility of a table, of tabulation, even if remotely and mockingly, before shattering the 'locus' or 'residence' that 'holds together' a series of common nouns (Foucault, 1991a: xviii):

> This passage quotes a 'certain Chinese encyclopaedia' in which it is written that 'animals are divided into: (a) belonging to the Emperor, (b) embalmed, (c) tame, (d) sucking pigs, (e) sirens, (f) fabulous, (g) stray dogs, (h) included in the present classification, (i) frenzied, (j) innumerable, (k) drawn with a very fine camelhair brush, (l) *et cetera*, (m) having just broken the water pitcher, (n) that from a long way off look like flies.' (Foucault, 1991a: xv)

In this heterotopia the impossibility of generic cohabitation is determined, in the first instance, by the possibility, the potential existence, of the indexical, alphabetical or numerical list itself. For, clearly, what the egregious siding of things does is to shatter the *nomos* of the *taxis*, the law (syntax) of arrangement. Yet, it has to be said, no matter how abstractly or emptily, the heterotopia is doomed to re-cite the list even in the midst of derangement. The law is instituted at the heretical scene of its violation.

Out of the asystemic logorrhoea of the pure event, out of the intolerable semiotic babble, which is never *here* in this sentence except perhaps symptomatically, for otherwise it – the sentence – must slide into vertigo and madness, arises the event proper, which as a witnessed event, as a fragment of being extracted from a situation, aspires to the condition of the statement. And the statement, if we remain true to Foucault's startling definition, appears in the domain between the linguistic sentence and the referent. It is at the intersection where statements share a common residence, a scene and a habitus, that the impure event subscribes to the order of arrangement, to the perpetually contestable propriety of cohabitation. And these statements may be primary non-discursive (i.e. linguistic) sentences mutating into statements or referents sliding into statements, or they may be statements annexed from other events (proximate or distant), disciplines, archives, tracts, and pressed into the service of a new event. Moreover, the so-called 'intersection of common residence' is at once historical, since each event comes with its own durational aura (and duration is not regulated clock time but any meaningful segment suspended above chronology), and transhistorical, since any given event may be deformed and reformed, deranged and rearranged, dispersed and salvaged though acts of citation across innumerable temporalities. Be that as it may, what we are speaking of is a distributive and attributive ordering of *values-as-statements* that cannot dispense with the 'scene' or at least the phantasmal reference to a scene. The scene is where all kinds of statements enter into some form of sociality and it is this sociality – understood as the participatory relationship between diverse actors (statements) – that generates the scene. A scene is not a territory, which suggests enclosures, limits and borders. It is a simulated locus generated by the act of performative *participation* and not by any claims to membership. A scene is *staged* when there is a society of two or more statements acting out a scene. It is 'invoking the reply which makes any scene "move"' (Barthes, 1990: 76). While Roland Barthes is predominantly concerned with the theatre of love and the theatricality of lovers, what he says is on the whole relevant to the scene of the statement as well. Barthes writes that the scene is based on 'an exchange of reciprocal contestations' and depends on 'the practice of a language of which they [the lovers, the participants, the statements] are co-owners [co-sharers]; *each one in his turn*, says the scene, which means: *never you without me*, and reciprocally' (Barthes, 1990: 204). Since statements hail from scenes other than the one they inhabit, what's inside is invariably outside and what's outside is potentially within the scene. (Derrida describes this situation as participation without belonging.) But this externality is forgotten in the reciprocity of statements making a scene.

In any case, I am speaking loosely of the classificatory procedures involved in the engendering of events-as-beings[8] through modalities of dispersion, juxtaposition, indexation, measurement, difference, division, analogy, antagonism, similitude, alignment, segmentation, sedimentation, whether of body (matter) or of spirit (ether). I am referring to the strange attraction[9] of irregular statements, of all that appears discontinuous, evasive and restive in statements, to the same eventful *domicile*, above and beyond all the divergent, maverick and recalcitrant paths a statement may take before, during and after residence. I mean to employ the term 'domicile' in an enriched sense here, as referring to the Latin *domus*, 'home', but also to *domicilium*, 'dwelling', which is derived from the Old English *dwellan*, 'to lead astray, delay' but finds its current sense in Middle English, 'to remain in place'. It is now possible to say that the statement, for that's what holds my attention at this point, 'remains in place' as testament to the impure event, and yet 'delays' and 'leads astray', since the event proper is a metonymic fragment for countless roads not taken, for those nameless unquantifiable spectral[10] potentialities, for all that may never be vouchsafed. 9/11 is no more and no less than a metonym for all the possibilities and impossibilities – in the self and its other – of sorrow, ire, satisfaction, gift (death), horror, retribution, justice, motivation, awe, epiphany, violence, belief, compassion, blindness, malice and hypocrisy – which is to say for all that, in the final analysis, evades the statement, eludes testimony.

The fortunate sociality of statements attesting to an event brings into being a metonymic fragment that finds residence in what I have described as the scene. At this stage, the metonymic fragment is more than the minimal statement (since a scene supposes the participation of two or more statements) yet less than an exemplar. At any rate, as a result of the constitutive 'lack' that characterises all metonymic systems, the fragment postpones the knowledge of its own partiality by straying in the direction of the supplement, its relational, dissenting and rhizomatic other. It is the movement of supplementarity that allows for the unstable processes of incorporation, accreditation, ostracism and disavowal of values-as-statements at the relational scene of the event. Derrida notes that the

> play, permitted by the lack or absence of a centre or origin, is the movement of *supplementarity*. One cannot determine the centre and exhaust totalisation because the sign which replaces the centre, which supplements it, taking the centre's place in its absence – this sign is added, occurs as a surplus, as a *supplement*. The movement of signification adds something, which results in the fact that there is always more, but this addition is a floating one because it comes to perform a vicarious function, to supplement a lack on the part of the signified. (Derrida, 1978: 289)

We need only think of the forever-unfolding scenes of Freudian psychoanalysis and Marxist political economy, where statements are constantly formulated, exhausted, revived and banished, to understand how this works. It should be by now clear that metonymic fragments account for the operation of most taxonomic categories, and the generic event is no exception.

The Generic Event

Not all events are equally eventful. The parsimony or profusion of enunciative statements *over time* determines the eventfulness of an event; while never actually quantifiable, the more eventful the event the greater the number of active statements circulating at its scene. An eventful event reverberates; it brings statements under the umbrella of a nomination. Eventfulness, however, is not simply a matter of dramatic intensity and narrative density (since an event may attract a throng of lively statements over a fleeting moment); it is also a matter of durability or, at least, the aura of durability. An eventful event is able to keep attracting and discarding statements (and all statements are transformative of the event as basic datum) over a substantial span of time. No doubt ideology motivates the over- or under-deployment of all eventful statements since power of one kind or another (economic, sexual, military, institutional, disciplinary and so on) underwrites all statements *as values*, past, present and future, but I take this fact as already embedded in my understanding of the statement. Whenever an event gathers about it that quality of time-tested eventfulness that permits it to operate as an *exemplar* (which is a special type of metonymic fragment), we witness the rise of a generic event. But the exemplar cannot, of course, hold itself up as an example since whatever procedures it deploys gains visibility only in relation to other exemplars. A genre, after all, is never a singularity (except in the form of an overarching nomination) since it is made up of more than one – one and an other. In this sense, there is no founding novel since the novel as a generic event comes about in an exemplifying series, without end or beginning. Tzvetan Todorov has something akin in mind when he claims that 'the question of origins cannot be separated from the terrain [scene] of the genres themselves' (Todorov, 1990: 15). And since each exemplar must stand in relation to some other in a haphazard process, the generic event neither generates nor conforms to universal laws. One exemplar may substitute another, but without clarifying any fixed codes. What Lyotard says about philosophical discourse holds equally true for the exemplar in that it too lives by the fundamental rule – the rule of the rule, the law of the law – 'that it must be in search of its rule' or 'its rule is that what is at stake is its rule' (Lyotard, 1989: 394). The exemplar is simultaneously searching and 'waiting for its criterion' (Lyotard, 1989: 394). To be sure, since each exemplar stands in a metonymic relationship to its others, what distinguishes one generic event from other such events are the features that participate at the *scene of exemplification*, each restlessly circling the elusive, unpresentable law that incites it and justifies its place in the scene. As Derrida argues in a discussion of Kant's *Critique of Judgment*, exemplarity is not concerned with making present the law it struggles to exemplify, but with its effects, since this law 'incites [the example] from its place of hiding' (Derrida, 1992: 191). Respect is, thus, 'aimed at persons only insofar as they offer an example of the moral law, which never shows itself but is the cause of that respect' (Derrida, 1992: 190). Or, to put it another way, respect incites statements on moral law without disclosing the total or ideal statement behind the incitement. One could think of this incitement of the law in relation to the forever-elusive essence of one or another generic category. As Frederic Jameson notes in *The Political Unconscious*, some literary critics speak of 'the essence or meaning of a given genre by way of the reconstruction of an imaginary entity – the "spirit" of comedy or tragedy, the melodramatic or epic "worldview", the pastoral "sensibility" or the satiric "vision" . . .' (Jameson, 1989: 107). Here the law – as spirit, vision, worldview or sensibility – incites one or another example without ever showing itself to either the exemplar or the critic. With reference to the special case of James Joyce, Maurice Blanchot comments that the genre (and he is thinking of the novel here) comes about not 'by engendering monsters, formless, lawless works lacking in rigour, but by provoking nothing but exceptions to itself, that constitute law and at the same time suppress it.' In short, 'we could never recognise the rule except by the exception that abolishes the rule, or more precisely, dislodges the centre of which a certain work is the uncertain affirmation, the already destructive manifestation, the momentary and soon-to-be-negative presence' (Blanchot, cit. Todorov, 1990: 14–15). What Blanchot fails to clarify, but which point forms a clandestine part of his argument, is that the simultaneous constitution and abolition of the rule leaves the rule itself outside the order of representation. If what is constituted is *at the same time* abolished and abolished the moment it is constituted, then finally it can be neither constituted nor abolished; it is an unpresentable law that facilitates and subverts both movements at once: suppressing while constituting and constituting while suppressing. It is this same unpresentable law that drives all metonymic categories to the supplement. The question of the generic event is, consequently, never a settled one, for that would lead to its termination. Death, after all, is the failure of supplementarity; or perhaps its finest moment. As a matter of fact, since an exemplar seeks to justify its place in the scene of the genre by pursuing and being pursued by an unpresentable law, it remains outside the law – an outlaw. It seeks to be other than what it is and suppresses the other in order to be what it is. Clearly metonymic exemplars bring to the scene of exemplification strains of lawlessness, of errantry[11] that, ironically, safeguards the generic event from degeneration and certain death.

Exemplary statements participate at the scene of exemplification without belonging to it. This is because the 're-mark' or the repeatable trait or characteristic that 'is absolutely necessary for and constitutive of what we call art, poetry or literature' (Derrida, 1992: 229) participates in all exemplars but belongs *essentially* to none *in particular*. Derrida seems to be offering a radical representation of Ludwig Wittgenstein's principle of family resemblances, where the members of a family possess no common *features* and yet share a *face*; consequently the face, belonging simultaneously to all and none, exists outside the order of relationality and representation. In an article entitled 'Universals and Family Resemblances', Renford Bambrough provides the following illustration of Wittgenstein's principle:

> Let us suppose that 'the Churchill face' is strikingly and obviously present in each of the ten members of the Churchill family, and that when a family group photograph is set before us it is unmistakable that these ten people all belong to the same family. It may be that there are ten features in terms of which we can describe 'the family face' (high cheekbones, cleft chin, dark hair, dimpled cheeks, pointed ears and ruddy complexion). It is obvious that the unmistakable presence of the family face is compatible with the absence from each of the ten members of the family of one of the ten constituent features of the family face. It is also obvious that it does not matter if it happens that the feature which is absent from the face of each individual member of the family is present in every one of the others. The members of the family will then have no *feature* in common, and yet they will all unmistakably have *the Churchill face* in common. (Bambrough, 1968: 190–1)

Similarly, for Derrida, the re-mark participates without belonging:

> Every text participates in one or several genres, there is no genreless text, there is always a genre and genres, yet such participation never amounts to belonging. And not because of an abundant overflowing or a free, anarchic and unclassifiable productivity, but because of the trait of participation itself, because of the effect of the code and of the generic mark. In marking itself generically, a text unmarks itself [*se démarque*]. If remarks of belonging belong without belonging, participate without belonging, then *genre-designations cannot be simply part of the corpus.* (Derrida, 1992: 230)

If they are not part of the corpus, then genre designations remain aloof from the statements that participate at the relational scene: the nomination, to be precise, is never affected by what occurs in its name. (In the concluding chapter, I discuss the immutability of genre designations in the context of Saul Kripke's thesis on rigid designators.) This may go some way towards explaining why the scene of exemplification (or the relational scene) is devoid of a systemic or unified body (corpus). It is the partial, performative arena where the example is caught up in the paradoxical and relational movement of constitution and abolition *at the same time*. Consequently, the total statement is never realised.

At this stage, it would be prudent to limit my understanding of the generic event, or the genre as we may now call it, to aesthetic and social scientific categories of writing, and to critical discourse in particular, for our topos, that which I am striving to conjure into visibility here, goes by the name of diaspora criticism. In so naming this event, even at this premature stage, I am preparing to bear witness to it, and have already, in some measure, borne witness to it, since gestures of nomination achieve in the raw the promise, the obligation to the future, that marks the nominated object. I may be close to repeating an axiom when I say that all acts of naming are promissory in one form or another. Indeed the process of bearing witness to a genre, of stating what it is and is not, entails the act of engendering the exemplar. What distinguishes an exemplar is the fortunate sociality of event-generating elements or statements. Event-spawning statements perform at least four simultaneous actions. First, they echo a prior (not in a chronological sense) order, no matter how faintly, erringly or aberrantly; second, they cannibalise other orders, whether past or present, whether fortuitously or through meticulous argument; third, they renew, recruit or expel whatever order or archive deemed to be anachronistic or antagonistic; and, fourth, they surpass all such orders by (lawlessly, relentlessly) pursing an unpresentable law through a peculiar relational process. The durability and currency of a particular genre – understood in terms of the shared scene of its various exemplars – rests entirely on the capacity of the latter to perform all four actions in time.[12] And the desire and drive to perform is clearly predicated on the eternal dissatisfaction that haunts the exemplars; and haunts, too, the witnesses.[13] Any sign of inertia is fatal to the exemplar and ultimately to the genre. As the *Britannica World Language Dictionary* (International Edition, 1959) reminds us, in a certain philosophical sense, an event may refer to 'anything that occurs, usually manifesting changes and lasting only a relatively short time: thus opposed to *object*, which endures.' It follows that the durable event has within it a certain restorative strain – a life-maintaining mutability – that permits it to exfoliate, to shed all statements that betray symptoms of exhaustion. Within the scene of the dynamic genre, we witness a series of minor epistemic turns and tremors (as opposed to severe ruptures that distinguish one event from another), that keeps it one step ahead of whatever (statement or exemplar) is obsolescent or effete in its temporal habitus. This habitus or scene may be quite different from the time of the event's initial appearance (its durational quality), but that point I have already noted. What I want to say here is that in the region of the internal epistemic tremor there is a notable intensification of all the four statement-related actions described above, but particularly of the two actions of incorporation (of new statements) and purgation (of moribund ones), since the genre is under intense pressure to overcome its own fast-approaching death. In the aftermath of an internal epistemic tremor the genre may shift its terms of reference but without renouncing its name. If the scene of exemplification is transformed as a consequence, then the transformation is bound to be, more or less, dialectical; and dialectics, as Deleuze explains, is 'the art of conjugation' where 'it is the task of language

. . . to establish limits and to go beyond them. Therefore language includes terms which do not cease to displace their extension and which make possible a reversal of the connection in a given series . . .' (Deleuze, 1990: 8). What never alters is the pursuit of the always unpresentable law that justifies the singularity of the designation – which is why we speak of *this* genre and not some other. All dialectical manoeuvres, all possible transformations of the scene, are already present in the nomination. The two epistemic tremors of Kleinian object relations theory, with its stress on the social ego rather than instinctual energies, and Lacanian neo-Freudianism with its renewed but radically different – poststructuralist and semiotic – emphasis on id-based drives, may be seen as scene-transforming points in Freudian psychoanalysis. In this regard, we may speak of the two scenes of exemplification within the genre of Freudian psychoanalysis.

The argument so far has been as follows. A proper event is an already witnessed entity and, in its most rudimentary form, consists of a minimal statement: 9/11 or Asian Tsunami or Postmodernism. The eventfulness of an event is determined by its capacity, over time, to recruit timely statements and to jettison untimely ones. When an event attains that pitch of eventfulness that transforms it into an exemplar, we witness the rise of a genre or genre-like category. Not all events, of course, undergo this sort of transformation. All exemplars are made up of statements that perform the four simultaneous actions described previously. Exemplars exist only in relation to other exemplars, but without attesting to any universal or transcendent principle. In fact, it is the process of seeking and suppressing an unpresentable law (i.e. the statement in its impossible totality), or at least the critical process of attributing this motivation to the various exemplars, that creates the shared scene of exemplification. Exemplars perpetually exist in a condition of supplementarity. A genre is no more and no less than the repertoire of statements at the relational scene of exemplification; and this scene enjoys a nomination that demands no proof.[14] Clearly there is no *generic* name without the scene since it is the heteroglossic encounter between statements and exemplars that makes for the nomination in the first instance. A nomination minus the scene is always an extra-generic nomination. Since they operate metonymically, exemplars are subject to the indefatigable process of supplementation. And it is through the logic of supplementation that one exemplar surpasses another's argument while compensating for an insufficiency (and all metonyms are insufficient) in the latter.

Diaspoetics

The genre of diaspora criticism, for that's my ongoing example, sustains itself by recognising and repeating certain methodological manoeuvres derived from contemporary theory (philosophy, human geography, cultural, race and ethnic studies, border theory, literary studies, structuralism, deconstruction, social anthropology, postmodernism, postcolonialism and so on); through selectively incorporating the archives of other disciplinary genres (migration or citizenship studies, ethnography, film studies, history, musicology, population studies and economics); by recruiting and transforming a quasi-biblical description – diaspora[15] – into a modern critical practice; and by *staging* a series of statements about travelling communities that, in a sly combinatory manner, surpasses all the previous orders of bearing witness to migratory events and mobile subjects. The meta-critical activity of talking about this site, of engendering the genre as a secondary critical witness bearing witness to the testimony of other witnesses, other critics, who actually engender the event (diaspora) and themselves as its subjects (diasporists) through a diversity of statements, I would like to, without any further delay, call *diaspoetics*. Diaspoetics is the meta-critical art, the *techne*, of witnessing the witnesses of the event called diaspora criticism.[16] Its method is a bringing forth (*techne*) and holding up to scrutiny all statements and exemplars, whether arborescent (rooted) or rhizomorphic (routed), that end up vouching for it. Its mode of operation is that of an intervention, the interposition of a non-witnessing witness or, rather, of a witness who attests to the act of bearing witness, but its behaviour is incontestably that of a supplement. For not only does it add to (and subtract from) the scene of the event, thus servicing its constitutive metonymic drive, but it subversively overreaches it as well.

I have referred to a vestigial durational quality that characterises the emergence of an event, for there is a temporal horizon of some description from which the event is extracted, which is not the same as saying it is limited to this horizon, since I have made it amply clear that exemplars are spatially staged rather temporally placed at the relational scene of exemplification. It is this scene that allows us to speak of Rushdie, Rabelais, Dickens and Sterne in the same breath when discussing aspects of the novel form. Exemplars bring together eventful statements that are habitually transportable, transhistorical and transformative. The eventful statement succeeds in traversing multiple temporal dimensions, modifying itself at the slightest contact with other eventful statements, and yet without ever dispensing with the shared scene of exemplification. Even when epistemic tremors transform the shared scene of exemplification, the nomination stays intact. Otherwise it would be impossible to bear witness to the extant events of cultural materialism and evolutionary biology in the twenty-first century, an era decidedly remote from that familiar to the founders of these discursive practices: Marx and Darwin. (Marxian or Darwinian axioms may be transferable to other genres but this action will have little impact on these initial sites, except by the way of return.) Exemplars are driven towards an unpresentable law that incites from its place of hiding, thereby giving rise to an incessant flow of effects and examples. All exemplars are metonymic types futilely dreaming of the total statement that reveals, once and for all, the corpus of the generic law.

While it is imprudent to speak of diaspora criticism as a major generic event, it is possible to bear witness to a certain durational quality surrounding its emergence. It is admissible, in other words, to claim that this critical event was wrested from a teeming epistemological situation in the 1980s and 1990s and continues to attract a flurry of exemplars. To be sure, I am not in the least concerned with the amorphous mass of diaspora-style commentary that came and went, namelessly, narcissistically or under different banners, prior to this period. I am not in the position, for that would be an untenable one, to bear witness to the amorphous, chaotic, tumultuous, overdetermined situation – the pure event – out of which arose the impure genre of diaspora criticism. I am concerned rather with the strange attraction, the fortunate sociality of theoretical statements that, despite their promiscuity and non-consanguinity, testify to, and thereby generate, the exemplars of diaspora criticism. To nominate the durational horizon of this event as the 1980s and 1990s (and now extending into the first decade of the new millennium) is to identify a sudden garrulity of a discursive kind around the eventful entity – diaspora – that was formerly lacking, or, if present, present in a quasi-discursive, non-eventful manner. This garrulity and gregarity had much to do with the publication of Sheffer's *Modern Diasporas in International Politics* in 1986, Gilroy's *The Black Atlantic* in 1993, the launching of the transnational journal, *Diaspora*, in 1991, and the participation in the debate of other significant periodicals such as *Public Sphere*, *Cultural Anthropology*, *Critical Inquiry*, *Social Text*, *Positions*, *Daedalus* and *Textual Practice*. These institutional fora, together with the individual interventions of foundational witnesses such as Gabriel Sheffer, William Safran, Walker Conner, Daniel and Jonathan Boyarin, Roger Rouse, Khachig Tölölyan, James Clifford, Robin Cohen, Steven Vertovec, Stuart Hall, Paul Gilroy, Kobena Mercer, Rey Chow, Aihwa Ong, R. Radhakrishnan, Avtar Brah, Martin F. Manalansan IV, Brent Hayes Edwards and Vijay Mishra, among others, created the scene of garrulity and sociality for the emergence of generic exemplars. There was, to be sure, no shared scene of exemplification and, consequently, no exemplars prior to this period.

It is my opinion that the genre of diaspora criticism has, so far, witnessed three scenes of exemplification – or two epistemic tremors or riffs (limit-transforming repetitions) – in its metonymic drive towards the unpresentable law of the total statement. These scenes do not constitute neat temporal blocks. Rather, they intersect across the same temporal axis and some participants (such as Vijay Mishra and Stanley Tambiah) end up contributing to more than one. In the first scene, which may be labelled the *scene of dual territoriality*, the emphasis falls on divided terrains as exemplars seek to account for diasporic subjects, cultures and aesthetic effects in terms of the subjective split between the geo-psychical entities of here and there, of hostland and homeland. In a move that is reminiscent of structuralism's reliance on stable coordinates, the home and host territories are seen as cohesive tensional entities. This position is premised, it seems, on a reading of the homeland state as classically auto-centred, racially self-evident and ideologically homogenised. Suspended between two such terrains (living without belonging in one, belonging without living in the other), diasporas are seen to represent a new species of social formation. For diasporists participating in the first scene of exemplification, there is a straightforward correlation between territorial-nationalistic and psychological-ideological (dis)locations.[17] It is exactly this move, this mapping of the geopolitical onto the psycho-subjective, which spawns a series of classificatory statements about diasporas in general. Roughly, there are three sets of statements interacting at the scene of exemplification. The first set seeks to identify the new *being* (psychic identity) of an uprooted ethnic cluster as it vacillates between homeland (the absent topos) and hostland (the present topos), the second set undertakes to tabulate the peculiar *characteristics* of this cluster, while the third, targeting the constitutive role played by memory in identity formations, attributes to the diaspora a departure (from an implied or designated norm) on the *plane of consciousness*. Strains and symptoms of this consciousness may be found in the diaspora's social, cultural and aesthetic practices.[18] In their privileging of determinate territorial loci, first scene participants take an overwhelmingly aborescent view of diasporic formations. The main contributors to this scene are Gabriel Sheffer, Walker Conner, William Safran and Robin Cohen. Chapter 2 is devoted to an analysis of this first scene of exemplification.

The fundamental proposition sustaining the scene of dual territoriality was soon found to be groundless and this moment of identification created an epistemic riff that dialectically transformed the first scene without dangerously affecting the nomination. This second scene may be described as the *scene of situational laterality*. The exemplars participating here take issue with the idea of bounded terrains and the constitutive role played by the tensional split between homeland and hostland in diasporic subject constitution. In *The Black Atlantic*, which comprises this scene's privileged exemplar, Paul Gilroy writes against 'national and nationalistic perspectives' because 'neither political nor economic structures of domination are simply co-extensive with national borders' (Gilroy, 1993: 9). Endeavouring to explain the diaspora of the black Atlantic (Africans transported and translocated to the Americas, Caribbean and Europe in the ever-unfolding drama of modernity) in ways that 'transcend both the structures of the nation-state and the constraints of ethnicity and national particularity' (Gilroy, 1993: 19), Gilroy emphasises the 'rhizomorphic, fractal structure of [this] transcultural, international formation' (Gilroy, 1993: 4). In this picture, homogenised, circumscribed and nationalised territories no longer function as privileged referents for identity constitution. Gilroy owes an intellectual debt – one he freely acknowledges – to Stuart Hall's insights on the complexities of cultural identity in black Britain. In a paper first published in 1990 entitled 'Cultural Identity and Diaspora', Hall makes a case for diasporic identities based on what he calls strategic *positioning*. He explains that during the movement of *différance* that drives all signification, 'meaning, in any specific instance, depends on the contingent and arbitrary stop – the necessary and temporary "break" in the infinite semiosis of language.' However, '[t]his does not detract from [Derrida's] . . . original insight. It only threatens to do so if we mistake this "cut" of identity – this *positioning*, which makes meaning possible – as natural and permanent rather than arbitrary and contingent . . .' (Hall, 1990: 229–30). Hall's emphasis on the strategic positional cut as constitutive of identity opened up the possibility for future commentators (such as Gilroy, Mercer, Clifford and Brah) to think of diasporas in terms of lateral, peripatetic and multipolar (as distinct from linear, fixed and bipolar) positionalities. It follows that the whole question of diasporic identity ends up being linked to situation-specific *becoming*, or the middle passage (milieu) in the active sense, rather than to the tensional pressures exercised by bipolar nation-states.[19] Drawing on Hall's and Gilroy's insights, James Clifford refers to the lateral axes of dissemination – rhizomorphic routes in preference to arboreal roots – as distinct from dualistic concepts of origin and return: symbolic, psychological or actual. Arguing against teleologies of origin and return, he observes that 'multi-locale diasporas are not necessarily defined by a specific geopolitical boundary' and that they betray a 'principled ambivalence about physical return and attachment to land' (Clifford, 1994: 304–5). Entering the fray on the side of hybridity, Mishra thinks of this ambivalence in relation to what he calls the 'semantics of the hyphen' (Mishra, 1996a: 433) whereby the diasporic subject is simultaneously sundered from and sutured to its various psycho-territories. Here the subject rhizomatically experiences, at the one and the same time, the double movement of deterritorialisation and reterritorialisation. For Deleuze and Guattari, the rhizome upholds the principle of an asignifying rupture:

> Every rhizome contains lines of segmentarity according to which it is stratified, territorialised, organised, signified, attributed, etc., as well as lines of deterritorialisation down which it constantly flees. There is a rupture in the rhizome whenever segmentary lines explode into a line of flight, but the line of flight is part of the rhizome. These lines always tie

> back to one another. That is why one can never posit a dualism or a dichotomy, even in the rudimentary form of good and bad. (Deleuze and Guattari, 1987: 9)

Deriving their argument from such versions of poststructuralist thought, the participants at the scene of situational laterality assume a dogmatically decentred view of diasporic movements and subjectivity. Indeterminacy supplants stable points of geo-psychical recognition. Chapter 3 focuses on the crucial contributors to this second scene of exemplification.

The third scene, which may be dubbed the *scene of archival specificity*, while both critiquing and enlisting the exemplars of the two previous scenes, dispenses with the more generalist paradigms in favour of an interrogative specificity. Instead of drawing on an assortment of diasporic clusters to frame a general theory of diasporas, the third scene participants perform an archaeology on specific diasporas. As Mishra puts it: 'To understand diasporas necessitates tempering [*sic*] with idealist notions of the exemplariness of diasporas in the modern world' (Mishra, 2001: 29). Unhappy with 'the idealist scenarios endorsed by some diaspora theorists', he recommends a much more rigorous archive-based interrogation of 'individual diasporic histories' (Mishra, 2001: 28). This recommendation inaugurates the second epistemic riff within the genre. Mishra's own work, for instance, involves charting the historically-motivated differences and discontinuities between the old and the new Indian diasporas. The old or exclusivist diasporas that came about during the time of plantation capital exist in a discontinuous and yet overlapping relationship with the new or border diasporas that are a feature of migratory flows in the era of advanced capital. Exemplars in the third scene include Martin Manalansan's work on queer Filipinos in New York, Donna Gabaccia's detailed account of Italian dispersion over the *longue durée*, Brent Hayes Edwards' revisionist take on the black Atlantic and Martin Baumann's micro analysis of religious identity formations among Hindu Trinidadians. Chapter 4 provides an in-depth account of the principal participants in this scene.

No matter what the exemplar or the scene of exemplification, diasporists have built their theories around a fundamental, if prodigiously understated and scantily inspected, economic premise. Khachig Tölölyan, for instance, thinks of modern diasporas as 'exemplary communities of the transnational moment' (Tölölyan, 1991: 5). Aihwa Ong, too, describes dispersed communities in terms of transnationality. She explains:

> *Trans* denotes both moving through space or across lines, as well as changing the nature of something. Besides suggesting new relations between nation-states and capital, transnationality also alludes to the *trans*versal, the *trans*actional, the *trans*lational, and the *trans*gressive aspects of

> contemporary behaviour and imagination that are incited, enabled, and regulated by the changing logics of state and capitalism. (Ong, 1999: 4)

By limiting themselves to transnational modes and temporality, Tölölyan and Ong mean to draw a distinction between the classical 'ethno-diasporas' – Jews, Greeks, Parsis and Armenians – and large-scale dispersal of significant ethnic clusters witnessed in the time of advanced capital. This distinction has appealed to a wide range of diasporists. Ian Chambers, for instance, claims that the 'chronicles of diasporas – those of the black Atlantic, of metropolitan Jewry, of mass rural displacement – constitute the ground swell of modernity' (Chambers, 1994: 16). Before taking exception to idealist notions of exemplarity, Mishra too conceived of diaspora as 'the exemplary condition of late modernity' (Mishra, 1996a: 426). After sorting through the general confusion regarding periodisation, Chapter 5 contends that for diasporists there are at least three distinct historical moments corresponding to the emergence of diasporas: classical, the (early) modern and the late (advanced) modern. Diasporists are mostly concerned with the last of these moments, but they rarely dissect the economic assumptions underpinning many of their assertions. In other words, they decline to investigate the actual workings of transnational capital, that is to say capital delinked from the material realms of production. Are we really in the middle of a metamorphic stage in the history of capital? Has post-Fordist speculative capital based on market predictions and exchange rates mechanism – the spectral economy – finally replaced the humdrum systems of surplus value production and accumulation? Is it true that floating financial capital no longer relies on classically anchored modes of production for its daily proliferation? Is the labour theory of value, consequently, defunct? What is the connection between delinked capital *and* hypermobile populations *and* hybrid cultural productions? Is this connection mimetic or symptomatic? Is Arjun Appadurai correct in identifying 'fundamental disjunctures between economy, culture, and politics' (Appadurai, 1996: 33) in the global system? By avoiding such base-level questions, diasporists fail to clear sufficient ground for many of their assertions about globalisation, modernity and transnationalism. Chapter 5 takes a close look at these three crucial pillars of diaspora criticism.

Suggesting that diaspora criticism has turned into an immense culture industry ceaselessly *defining* an object – diaspora – without becoming in any way *definite*, Chapter 6 affords a short account of those works that profess titular or eponymous belonging without participating in the genre. Where the three scenes of exemplification were distinguished by a certain methodological focus, theoretical rigour and dialectical consistency, a simple titular mention is now sufficient for some studies to count as potential 'exemplars'. The current proliferation of extra-generic studies points to the paradox that haunts the law that incites the genre from its place of hiding. In its desire to fix limits and to attain the definitional moment of the total statement, diaspora criticism keeps overstepping set limits, rules and definitions. As the rule is the want of a rule and the limit the want of a limit, it follows that the nomination, the generic rubric, is increasingly being treated as empty and promiscuous. When this happens – and it usually happens to a genre at an advanced stage – it becomes possible for a breathtaking array of projects to share in the nomination *without any recourse to generic memory* and *without the burdensome responsibility of participation*. Such emptily 'nominal' studies, sundered as they are from the three scenes of exemplification, *belong without participating* in the genre. And since participation without belonging best describes what occurs in a genre, the reversal of this order may, in all likelihood, intimate the first symptom of an approaching exhaustion.

Notes

1. My understanding of the enunciative statement coincides with Foucault's: 'A statement is not confronted (face to face as it were) by a *correlate* – or the absence of a *correlate* – as a proposition has (or has not) a referent, or as a proper noun designates someone (or no one). It is linked rather to a "referential" that is made up not of "things", "facts", "realities", or "beings", but of laws of possibility, rules of existence for the objects that are named, designated, or described within it, and for the relations that are affirmed or denied in it' (Foucault, 1992: 91).
2. Commenting on Paul's first Letter to the Corinthians, Agamben writes: 'The "speaking in tongues" (*lalein glōssē*) of which Paul writes refers to an event of speech – glossolalia – in which the speaker speaks without knowing what he says ("no man understandeth him; howbeit in the spirit he speaketh mysteries" [1 Corinthians 14:2])' (Agamben, 1999: 114).
3. The philosopher Donald Davidson has analysed events in terms of the dispersion of simultaneous argument places in sentence formations. Eventfulness, accordingly, relates to the possibilities and potentialities of predication in any given statement (Davidson, 1996: 81–95).
4. Coined by Arjun Appadurai, mediascapes 'refer both to the distribution of the electronic capabilities to produce and disseminate information (newspapers, magazines, television stations, and film production studios), which are now available to a growing number of private and public interests throughout the world, and to the images of the world created by these media. These images of the world involve many complicated inflections, depending on their mode (documentary or entertainment), their hardware (electronic or pre-electronic), their audiences (local, national, or transnational), and the interests of those who own and control them. What is most important about these mediascapes is that they provide (especially in their television, film, and cassette forms) large and complex repertoires of

images, narratives, and ethnoscapes to viewers throughout the world, in which the world of commodities and the world of news and politics are profoundly mixed. What this means is that many audiences throughout the world experience the media themselves as a complicated and interconnected repertoire of print, celluloid, electronic screens, and billboards. The lines between the realistic and the fictional landscapes they see are blurred, so that the further away these audiences are from the direct experiences of metropolitan life, the more likely they are to construct imagined worlds which are chimerical, aesthetic, even fantastic objects, particularly if assessed by the criteria of some other perspective, some other imagined world' (Appadurai, 1996: 35).

5. I use heteroglossia in the sense suggested by M. M. Bakhtin, that is as representing the diversity of social voices and stratified utterances that make up the compositional unity of a narrative system (Bakhtin, 1981: 260–75).
6. Deleuze gives this extraordinary example to illustrate his point: '*Alice* and *Through the Looking-Glass* involve a category of very special things: events, pure events. When I say "Alice becomes larger," I mean that she becomes larger than she was. By the same token, however, she becomes smaller at the same time. She is larger now; she was smaller before. But it is at the same moment that one becomes larger than one was and smaller than one becomes. This is the simultaneity of becoming whose characteristic is to elude the present. Insofar as it eludes the present, becoming does not tolerate the separation or the distinction of before and after, or of past and future. It pertains to the essence of becoming to move and to pull in both directions at once. Alice does not grow without shrinking, and vice versa' (Deleuze, 1990: 1).
7. Re-cognition describes the process where two statements are alike but non-identical; similarly, re-citation describes the act of echoing a precedent while simultaneously diverting from it.
8. I understand 'being' in the Heideggerian sense as pertaining to all existential entities. As such, I resist Deleuze's understanding of events as incorporeal entities or extra-beings, based on the simple and no doubt simplistic assertion that whatever eludes the proposition is simultaneously generated by it and cannot evade – precisely in the moment of evasion – a certain mode of beingness.
9. In chaos theory 'strange attractors' are forces, at once aleatory and deterministic, that give rise to natural systems such as the weather.
10. Derrida defines the spectre as a becoming-body, neither body nor spirit but potentially both (Derrida, 1994: 6).
11. 'The "perpetual mutability" *(in inconstantia constans)* which animates me, far from squeezing all those I encounter into the same functional type (not to answer my demand), violently dislocates their false community: errantry does not align – it produces iridescence: what results is the nuance' (Barthes, 1990: 103).
12. Let me clarify at once that by durability and currency I am referring to asystemic patterns of dispersion and recurrence rather than to linear notions of longevity. In his important work, *The Architext: An Introduction*, Gérard Genette makes this observation: '. . . [T]he argument of duration must be handled carefully: the longevity

of the classical forms (epic, tragedy) is not a sure indication of transhistoricity, given the conservatism of the classical tradition and its ability to sustain mummified forms for centuries . . . A more significant criterion than longevity would be the capacity for dispersion (among diverse cultures) and for spontaneous recurrence (without the stimulus of a tradition, revival, or "retro" style)' (Genette, 1992: 215).

13. Derrida notes that it is the law's inaccessibility that 'bars the gate to genealogical history' while stimulating 'desire for the origin and genealogical drive . . .' (Derrida, 1992: 197).
14. Genette makes the point that no one act of generic nomination is more sound than another: 'In the classification of literary species as in the classification of genres, no position is essentially more "natural" or more "ideal" – unless we abandon the literary criteria themselves, as the ancients did implicitly with the modal position. There is no generic level that can be decreed more "theoretical," or that can be attained by a more "deductive" method, than the others: all species and all subgenres, genres, or supergenres are empirical classes, established by observation of the historical facts or, if need be, by extrapolation from those facts – that is, by a deductive activity superimposed on an initial activity that is always inductive and analytical, as we have seen in the charts (whether explicit or implicit) of Aristotle or Frye, where the existence of an empty compartment (comic narrative; extroverted-intellectual) helps one discover a genre ("parody," "anatomy") otherwise condemned to invisibility' (Genette, 1992: 214).
15. Nico Israel notes that 'Diaspora . . . has traditionally possessed a specifically religious and spiritual significance. According to the *OED*, the word's original usage was in the Septuagint (third to second century B. C. Greek) translation of the Old Testament book of Deuteronomy, chapter 28, when the postexodus Moses, after informing the Israelites of the many good things that will transpire if they are faithful and observant, warns them of the dire consequences [removal from all earthly kingdoms] of disobedience . . . In the context of its appearance in Deuteronomy, this diasporic removal is associated with a curse, with a perpetual otherness amid others, with blindness, madness, and defeat (Deut. 28: 28), with a spreading that weakens. (In fact, the Hebrew word *Za'avah*, rendered *diaspora* in Greek, denotes not so much a "removal" as a "fleeing in terror."). Although generally homologous with loss, the word "diaspora," like "exile," has accrued a positive resonance as well, bespeaking a sense of tenacity, resistance, and preservation of faith during the worst of circumstances. Generally applied to the experience of the Jews – the mutation of diaspora to "the Diaspora" is a fairly recent one – the description has seemed apposite to the experiences of other minority groups at different points in their histories as well: to Christians, to Muslims, to the Irish, to African Americans, and, most recently, to postcolonial migrants' (Israel, 2000: 2–3).
16. Todorov makes the important point that while '*historical* existence of genres is signalled by discourse on genre,' this 'does not mean that genres are simply metadiscursive notions and not discursive ones' (Todorov, 1990: 17).
17. Elsewhere I have demonstrated how any account of *dis*location is simultaneously an account of *this* location (Mishra, 2002a: 136–45).

18. Steven Vertovec has commented that diaspora refers variously to a 'social form', to a 'type of consciousness' and to a 'mode of cultural production' (Vertovec, 1997: 277–8).
19. In the early part of his paper, Hall distinguishes strategic commonality of identification (being) from arbitrary discontinuities of the self (becoming), without discounting the political relevance of both these modes of subject formation.

2

The Scene of Dual Territoriality

The School of 1986

In his prefatory remarks to *Modern Diasporas in International Politics*, Gabriel Sheffer notes that the research papers brought together in the volume take as their primary focus 'the relations between the homelands and host countries' in order 'to re-examine the international and trans-state aspects of diaspora activities' (Sheffer, 1986: Preface). Suspecting that the twelve contributing scholars (not excluding the editor) were on the brink of inaugurating 'a new field of study', Sheffer accepts the task of generating a series of statements that would define and demarcate the scope of the project:

> The theoretical questions dealt with in this volume include: reasons for solidarity between diasporas and homelands; the problems of dual authority and loyalty; the importance and magnitude of the economic-political dimension of diaspora relations with host countries and homelands; the mobilisation and manipulation of political power, and the effectiveness of diaspora activities and their influence on national and international systems. (Sheffer, 1986: Preface)

Later, in what ostensibly serves as a prolegomenon to the collection, he explains that the papers were 'researched according to a general framework' where stress was placed 'not on distinct studies of particular diasporas, but rather on the comparative aspect of their experience and behaviour' since the idea was 'to develop a valid theory' of global diasporas (Sheffer, 1986: 14). While not entirely accurate (since some of the essays are indeed distinct studies of specific diasporas), Sheffer's remarks make it clear that the papers were brought into fruitful juxtaposition according to a given framework in order to evolve a valid theory around the nominated object – namely diaspora. While the influence of the holdall framework on theoretical outcomes is plainly of concern, what interests me in particular are the generic statements gleaned tactfully from the eleven exemplars that gather around the nomination to form the first scene of exemplification. For what is being summoned into visibility here, more or less premeditatively and self-consciously, is a genre of criticism that departs significantly from kindred domains of study:

> In fact, for some time scholars have been studying the politics of ethnic, religious and racial groups in pluralistic societies to the point where these fields are emerging as a recognised sub-field of political sciences. However, most of these studies have dealt primarily with the domestic implications of ethnic pluralism in the West, or with state policies vis-à-vis minorities in the Eastern Bloc or in Third World countries. This category includes studies that emphasise ethnic (or religious, or racial) integration, as well as studies that focus on the regulation or management of domestic conflicts in which ethnic groups are involved. Yet, the various trans-state networks which are based on ethnic solidarity, connections and affinities (which in turn command powerful loyalties, control significant political and economic resources, and exercise influence on political states and on their international relations) have not been sufficiently examined. Thus, this volume tackles a neglected aspect of ethnic politics, namely, the international dimension of the ethnic question. (Sheffer, 1986: 2).

Instead of positing an intra-national or policy-based approach to the subject of ethnic minorities in different countries, Sheffer sees his project as correcting an oversight by attending to 'trans-state networks' distinguished by complex ethnic ties and solidarities. This shift in perspective, though ingeniously simple, institutes the fundamental 'break' in methodology between earlier studies and the present one. The methodological discontinuity, to be sure, gives rise to a new critical practice that makes (through acts of nomination) as well as takes (by means of a changed analytical apparatus) a new kind of object or, rather, a new type of social species: namely modern diasporas. Sheffer is attentive to the handful of previous studies on historical diasporas,[1] of which John Armstrong's 'Mobilised and Proletarian Diasporas' (1976) is theoretically the most audacious, but treats them as incidental proto-generic events rather than as genuine instigators of a new domain of enquiry. (The present study maintains a distinction between proto-generic instances retrospectively incorporated into exemplars and pre-generic ones not subject to such incorporation.) This tactical incorporation permits him and his associates to selectively salvage the outcomes of the earlier research while insisting on a radical break from past methodologies. In fact, it is quite possible to argue that Armstrong's prototypical description of diaspora as 'any [minority] ethnic collectivity which lacks a territorial base within a given polity' (Armstrong, 1976: 393) is the spectre that haunts the entire genre of diaspora criticism.

Having instituted the rupture at one fell stroke, Sheffer draws liberally from assorted case studies to issue a series of classificatory statements aimed at facilitating the new genre. Not unexpectedly, this procedure requires him to pinpoint the exact 'scope of the modern diaspora phenomenon' (Sheffer, 1986: 3), beginning with the minimal overarching definition:

> Modern diasporas are ethnic minority groups of migrant origins residing and acting in host countries but maintaining strong sentimental and material links with their countries of origin – their homelands. (Sheffer, 1986: 3)

Construing the diaspora project in terms of a 'complex triadic relationship between ethnic diasporas, their host countries and homelands' (Sheffer, 1986: 1), Sheffer comes up with an extended typology – professedly operational and unfinished – that sets the benchmark for appraising the modern variety of this social phenomenon:

> Ethnic diasporas are created either by voluntary migration (e.g., Turks to West Germany) or as a result of expulsion from the homeland (e.g., the Jews and the Palestinians) and settlement in one or more countries. In these host countries the diasporas remain minority groups (the Anglo-Saxon segment in Canada for example will therefore be excluded from the present study). In their host countries diasporas preserve their ethnic, or ethnic-religious identity and communal solidarity. This solidarity serves as the basis for maintaining and promoting constant contacts among the diasporas' activist elements. These contacts have political, economic, social and cultural significance for the diasporas, their host countries and homelands. This is also the basis for the organised actions of the diasporas. One of the purposes of these actions is to create and increase the readiness and ability of the diasporas to preserve a continuous interest in, and cultural, economic and political exchanges with their homelands. Organised diasporas deal with various aspects of their cultural, social and political needs in a way that either complements or conflicts with the activities of the host government. The emergence of diaspora organisations provides the potential for conflicting pressures and for the development of dual authority and dual loyalty patterns and problems. In order to avoid undesirable conflicts with the norms or laws established by the dominant group in their host countries, the diasporas

> accept certain rules of the game of these countries. At certain periods, however, real or alleged dual loyalties which are generated by the dual authority patterns may create tensions between elements in the host country and the diaspora. This sometimes leads to the intervention of homelands on behalf of their diasporas, or in the affairs of the diasporas themselves. And finally, and most importantly, the capability of diasporas to mobilise in order to promote or defend their interests or the interests of their homelands within their host countries will result in the formation of either conflictual or cooperative triadic networks involving homeland, diaspora and the host country. These triadic relations are now an integral part of international politics and influence the behaviour of all parties involved. (Sheffer, 1986: 9–10)

The foregoing paradigm is built on several related statements or moves. The first move identifies three apparently stable entities – a homeland, a hostland and an ethnically unified diaspora – and defines the new project as the triadic relations[2] between the two territories and a displaced collective ethno-national subject. Strangely, none of these entities are composed of miscellaneous elements that, either potentially or in practice, unsettle the stability attributed to them. Drawing on the 'pull and push factors' popularised by economic historians and sociologists, the second move distinguishes between two types of diasporas, voluntary (attracted to the hostland) and involuntary (expelled from the homeland), but insists, for the sake of delimitation, on the minority status of these groups in their hostlands. It is presumably this minority status that, according to the third move, lends the diaspora a cohesive ethno-national or ethno-religious identity; it presumably also facilitates a sanguine reading of intra-group solidarity. But the collective subjectivity of a diaspora, if we must think in such holistic terms, might not be the result of some psychological response to its minority status. It might just as well be the outcome of modern forms of governmentality. Benedict Anderson's work, for instance, has shown us how the 'bound seriality' of ethnic categories has its origins in the census and electoral systems that created distinctive grids for ethno-national and other forms of identification (Anderson, 1998: 117–33).[3] Somewhat dubiously, then, this macro subject of displaced ethnicity is predicated on the cohesion – implicitly auto-ideological – of the multitudinous micro subjects, rendered as ethnically marked individuals, that make up the mosaic as well as on the subjective integrity of the individual agents themselves. It comes therefore as no surprise to find that (in what spells the fourth move), hailed ideologically either by the homeland (not spoken of in terms of dominant group norms) or the hostland (founded on the norms of a dominant group rather than on complex hegemonic principles of fabricated consent), the diasporic entity responds – and this response has economic, cultural and political determinants – as a homogeneous macro subject, inspiring the pattern of dual loyalty to dual authorities that marks it out from other kinds of social formation. After this, the so-called triadic network may be broken down in the ensuing manner: (a) the diaspora is at different times for or against the hostland; (b) the hostland is at different times for or against the diaspora (though usually the latter); (c) the diaspora is at different times for or against the homeland (though usually former); and (d) the homeland is at different times for or against the diaspora. In this diagram, the homeland and the hostland feature tacitly as antagonistic agents (since they are never for each other) and the ethnic diaspora is the macro subject constituted dualistically in the zone of tension. Furthermore, while this is hardly made explicit, the hostland features as a synonym for the modern nation-state, and is rendered in juridical or secular-liberal terms, whereas the homeland is viewed *viscerally* as a terrain (which may or may not be a nation-state) charged with surplus signification and encumbered with unfathomable affects. The homeland, in other words, furnishes the site for a theory of nationalism concerned primarily with what Ernest Gellner describes as 'the re-emergence of atavistic instincts of *Blut and Boden* in the human breast' (Gellner, 1991: 128). In any case, what we have here is an ethnically coherent macro subject spawned in the tension between bipolar territories. Whether its relationship to these territories is one of antagonism or cooperation, the deracinated macro subject is never seen to be internally fissured.

Sheffer's exemplar draws on and sets off a string of related exemplars. Forming a raft of competing statements and comparative instances of the diaspora phenomenon, these exemplars strive to work within the general or, more accurately, generalised framework with the purpose of substantiating its evasive definitional law. I propose to dwell at some length on Walker Conner's article, 'The Impact of Homelands Upon Diasporas', since it remains the most cited exemplar from this early study, but first I want to provide an overview of the way the dual territorial framework is deployed in some of the other case studies, beginning with Myron Weiner's 'Labour Migrations as Incipient Diasporas'. In his article, Weiner seeks to describe how various nation-states, especially those in the Persian Gulf and western Europe, deal with foreign workers who comprise 'incipient' diasporas of Indians, Koreans, Turks, Algerians and so on. Weiner keeps faith with the triadic relations schema by sandwiching labour migrants between sending (homeland) and receiving (hostland) countries. His main assertion is that the assignment of temporary status to the worker fosters an 'illusion of impermanence' shared by the host society, the home society as well as the guest labourer, when the ground reality is starkly different:

> Few host governments are prepared to admit that the foreign workers will remain and that their children, or at least most of them, will not return home. The home country does not want to lose its nationals and certainly does not want to lose remittances. And the parents themselves often continue to dream of returning 'home' and do not want their children to 'lose' their identity or give up their citizenship. (Weiner, 1986, 64–5)

If we were to recast this statement in the light of Louis Althusser's ideological interpellation thesis,[4] we could say that the workers strike up an imaginary relation to the myth of return in direct contradiction to their actual status as permanent minority members of a foreign polity. And this myth is sponsored assiduously by the home territory for practical economic reasons (remittances) and the host territory for invidious political ones as it seeks to mollify the racial terrors of the ethno-national majority. In any case, the dual territorial framework for identifying ethnic diasporas remains, more or less, intact.

Taking up the conspicuously daunting topic of diasporas and languages, Jacob M. Landau squanders the perfect opportunity to query the dual territorial schema by restricting his study to those 'subjects with a direct bearing upon diaspora–host country–home country relations in their linguistic contexts' (Landau, 1986: 76). Within this constrictive framework he manages to advance some tentative typological observations pertaining to a slew of demographic and linguistic factors that contribute to the cultural accommodation or estrangement of diasporas in the host country or, conversely, to their continuing ethno-linguistic identification with a home territory. Unfortunately the more radical questions are neither posed nor answered. The likelihood that languages may themselves become impossibly hybridised or syncretised in the encounter between located and dislocated subjects is never entertained. In the case of Fiji, for instance, the encounter between Indian languages (Hindi and Urdu predominantly but also Tamil and Gujarati), indigenous Fijian dialects (Bauan, Lauan, etc.) and colonial English has resulted in borrowings and counter-borrowings across these language systems. If subjectivity is produced through certain modes of discursive interpellation, as Jacques Lacan would have it, then, at least in a certain trans-ideological sense, the whole issue of cultural alienation and location, home and host, may simultaneously pertain to all or none of the speakers of these languages.

Of course there is considerable merit in stressing the bipolar territorial relations of ethnic diasporas when it comes to specific entities united by a common ideological purpose, as is the case of Palestinians brutally ejected from their home territories through the creation of the state of Israel. Locked as they are in a remorseless battle with the people of Israel to establish a nation-state out of territorial remnants and leftovers, the plight of the Palestinians testifies to the strife caused by the actualisation of theological homecomings where the terminal point of one diaspora is, ironically and acrimoniously, the starting point of another.[5] The dual territorial paradigm, however, turns less attractive when employed for assessing the historically complex dispersal of Chinese, Indian or African populations. Yet the three scholars writing on these mega-diasporas insist on being hamstrung by the dual territorial schema. Despite the magnificent survey of the Indian diaspora where he takes pains to distinguish between the historical phases of population dissemination – ancient, colonial and modern – while being sensitive to regional, motivational, caste and vocational distinctions that inform the ethnic mosaic, Arthur W. Helweg insists on stressing the formative role played by India vis-à-vis the hostland in the consciousness of its diaspora:

> For non-residents, India is their cultural homeland, but the meaning of India as an ethnic home varies for different groups. For those in East Africa, India is the place of return as for retirement, the home of their kinsmen, the location of their ancestral land, the source of their culture and the reason for their extensive, present-day networks. For others, such as those of indenture origins in Trinidad, India evokes in them an emotional feeling and nothing more. (Helweg, 1986: 115)

While he proceeds to demonstrate how ties between India and the hostland come to be established via trade networks, the entertainment industry (Bollywood film and video culture in particular) and religious and spouse-finding tours, Helweg shies away from the question insinuated by the last part of his statement. If the coolie diaspora displays nothing more than an emotional feeling for India, then what precisely is this affect sundered from any thought of a bounded homeland territory? One answer may be that for certain clusters (Trinidadian or Guyanese 'East' Indians, for instance) *milieu effects* such as the dholak, the charpoy or a household deity serve as deterritorialised cultural markers rather than as metonymic signs of an absent geopolitical order. It is worth pointing out that 'milieu' refers to rhizomorphic middles or mid-points (*mi* 'mid' plus *lieu* 'place') rather than to causal beginnings or teleological ends.[6] As I have shown elsewhere, *bidesias* (or songs of estrangement) as sung by coolie women in Fiji's plantations were not principally concerned with issues of translocation to Fiji or dislocation from India: 'Neither Fiji nor India, the proper place of location [for the singer] is ontological suffering, a performative *emotion* the genre of the *bidesia* endows with the spatiality of a *form*' (Mishra, 2002a: 141). Such contrapuntal readings subvert the straitjacket into which the dual territorial schema inserts diasporic entities; they also open up the possibility of forms of relationship other than the geopolitical or national.

If Helweg is unwilling or unable to pursue the subversive possibilities concealed in some of his observations, Milton J. Esman simply closes them off:

> Diaspora politics involves tri-lateral relationships between: (a) a home government, in this case China; (b) a host government in countries where the diasporas reside; and (c) the diaspora communities. (Esman, 1986: 132)

As an afterthought Esman adds the fourth category of 'transnational economic networks which are a vital component of the contemporary overseas Chinese phenomenon' (Esman, 1986: 132). Even so, he is predominantly concerned with the popular perception of the Chinese diaspora as servicing an ethnically exclusive set of interests or, more worryingly, as the willing instruments of the People's Republic of China. In the article 'Black America as a Mobilising Diaspora', written with Armstrong's thesis on proletarian and mobilised diasporas in mind, Locksley Edmondson, too, walks the well-trodden path of dual territoriality:

> . . . [W]henever we posit the idea of a 'diaspora' as a unit of analysis, this involves not simply matters of internal relevance to a given diasporic group but also necessarily embraces the dynamics of that group's external relationships, especially with its 'homeland.' In other words, the condition of Black America as an African diaspora is but a starting point for comprehending ultimately Black American orientation towards and interactions with the African continental homeland. But while essentially concerned with the network of relationships established directly by the diaspora with the homeland, as well as with the capacity of the diaspora to influence host country policies toward the homeland, the enquiry is obliged to proceed beyond these frontiers to encompass other international orientations of the diaspora especially when relevant to the issues of African advancement and racial uplift in the wider sphere of international relations. (Edmondson, 1986: 166–7)

The last statement suggests that the African diaspora in North America is not averse to lobbying on behalf of continental Africans in the wider international sphere, and therefore outside the border of the American hostland, but this does not intimate a radical break from the dual territorial framework used in the interpellation of diasporas as unique social formations. Like Esman with regard to the Chinese, Edmondson perceives African Americans as an ethnically unified macro entity posited in terms of a decisive dislocation from the homeland. Conceived in a 'general continental [rather] than specific ethno-national sense' due to '[c]ultural uprooting and loss of direct ties with particular homeland cultural groups and political systems' (Edmondson, 1986: 175–6), this greater homeland induces in the diaspora a considerable measure of emotional, ideological and economic concern. That African Americans are able to act on this concern by intervening on behalf of the homeland in the international arena testifies to the peculiar power they wield as a significant minority in a superpower hostland. By no means does it subvert the terms of reference set up by the dual territorial framework.

Walker Conner

Territorial binarisms influence the nomination, identification and evaluation of diasporic entities in nearly all the case studies compiled in *Modern Diasporas in International Politics*, and most famously in Walker Conner's 'The Impact of Homelands Upon Diasporas'. In this exemplar, Conner draws a distinction between homelands and states and assesses the status of diasporas in relation to the coincidence or non-coincidence in a physical territory of the two conceptions. For Conner, the state is a political entity with regulatory powers over a geographical territory whereas the homeland, cast in supra-rational genealogical terms such as the motherland, the fatherland and the ancestral land, is 'imbued with an emotional, almost reverential dimension' (Conner, 1986: 16). While his cartography of the homeland is wonderfully intricate as well as insightful, it is fundamentally based on the serial displacement of a sign that remains intact throughout its peregrinations. Defining diaspora as broadly 'that segment of a people living outside the homeland' (Conner, 1986: 16), and by implication inside a hostland of sorts, Conner sees homeland identification or what he terms 'homeland psychology' (Conner, 1986: 28) as the overriding factor in distinguishing diasporas from non-diasporas. Maintaining that 'the populated world is subdivided into a series of perceived homelands to which, in each case, the indigenous ethno-national group is convinced it has a profound and exclusive proprietary claim,' he asserts:

> In such an environment, diasporas are viewed at best as outsiders, strangers within the gates. They may be tolerated, even treated most equitably, and individual members of the diaspora may achieve highest office. Their stay may be multigenerational, but they remain outsiders in the eyes of the indigenes, who reserve the inalienable right to assert their primary and exclusive proprietary claim to the homeland, should they so desire. (Conner, 1986: 18)

This remark opens an unsavoury can of worms. Conner appears to be equating the indigenous ethno-national group (viewed in decidedly hegemonic terms) with the proprietary claimants of the emotional homeland which, in turn, seems to coincide with the political state. The equation may hold true in some instances (such as Fiji or Tonga), but it is hardly applicable across the board. In Australia, for instance, there is an indigenous ethno-national group – the Aborigines (to continue speaking in familiar macro terms) – whose claims to ownership of a homeland, or several homelands, runs up against the political state regulating the homeland territory. It could be argued that the community of Anglo-Celts that founded Australia as a liberal bourgeois nation-state generated a separate myth of the homeland (of which the swagman, the convict and the digger are three genealogical founders) by negating, substituting and expropriating visions of the homeland espoused by the indigenous minority. Since this 'imposed' homeland is coterminous with the political state, it puts in doubt the precise status of the indigenous population. Does it constitute an internally displaced cluster, even an anomalous diaspora?

Conner is not blind to the pitfalls of his definition since, further into the essay, he succeeds in teasing out the intricacies of the homeland and state categories. However, his main purpose is to pinpoint diasporas as ethnic segments living outside the homeland. This entails accounting for the complex variations in the state–homeland dichotomy. At one stage he comments that 'political borders of states have been superimposed upon the ethnic map with cavalier disregard for ethnic homelands'; consequently, '[m]ost states contain several homelands, and their land borders regularly dissect others' and that this 'lack of coincidence between borders of states and homelands' may encourage intrastate as well as interstate conflicts (Conner, 1986: 20). It is suggested that arbitrary borders have led to the forcible transformation of non-travelling ethnic communities into diasporas. A further variation in the state–homeland dichotomy is afforded by 'the homeland state – that is, a state which the ethnopolitical myth links closely to a specific people and its homeland'. Conner observes that public policies in this instance may 'reflect concern with maintaining the ethno-national purity of the homeland' (Conner, 1986: 21). Analysing the policies of the homeland state in the context of the *Gastarbeiter* (or guest worker) presence in Sweden and Germany, he notes that they do not testify to 'a cosmopolitan trend away from homeland and homeland-state psychology':

> The influx [of guest workers] originated almost without premeditation, on the naïve assumption that the states could benefit without cost, because the foreign workforce would expand and contract (disappear) simultaneously with demand. Even before it became evident that such was not the case and that large numbers of workers might become permanent residents, hostility towards the alien presence arose. (Conner, 1986: 25)

In Conner's opinion, it is the hostility evident within the homeland state that turns the guest workers – be they Turks or Algerians or Filipinos – into a segment of people living outside the homeland. And this definition may be understood in the obvious corporeal sense of displacement from a primordial homeland (or primordium) and in the more subtle ideological sense of disavowal by another.

Conner then undertakes to gauge the status of diasporas in the 'multi-homeland state that has not adopted the ethno-political myth of a homeland state' and which advocates 'the disappearance of the various ethno-national identities in favour of a single statewide one' and encourages 'the erosion of homelands into an undifferentiated statewide territory' (Conner, 1986: 27). He discovers that compatriotism does not necessarily sublimate the homeland psychology:

> Basque and Catalan ethno-nationalism has grown more violent in response to the increased immigration of Castillians. Corsicans have responded similarly to French incursions. An emotional Quebecois slogan proclaiming we must be 'Masters in Our Home' reflects the reaction to Anglophones within Quebec Province. (Conner, 1986: 28)

This, in turn, gives rise to the summary remark that 'neither homeland states nor multi-homeland states provide healthy environments for diasporas'. Although the latter is manifestly a superior entity, 'the reception accorded to aliens in the homeland is hardly affected by proclamations concerning the rights of citizens, and local xenophobia can surface any time' (Conner, 1986: 29).

But what about the 'immigrant state' that is 'essentially devoid of homelands' such as the United States? Do diasporas fare better there? Riding roughshod over the Amerindian minority by consigning their homelands to reservations, Conner insists that the fundamental feature of the immigrant state 'is that most of the population lives in non-homeland territory' and that 'all legal settlers have an equal claim upon it, regardless of their ethno-national background'. While he is shrewd to the fact that the melting pot fable of America does not always pass muster, since 'the prejudice and bias against "newcomers" have often been great', Conner believes that '[w]here the myth of the immigrant society harmonises rather well with reality, diasporas can come to feel "at home." Their claim is equal to any other's' (Conner, 1986: 29–33). In the aftermath of 9/11, Arab Americans may have reasonable cause to quibble with this sanguine reading of the United States. In any case, it remains a possibility that select groups of ethno-nationals, either because of their power or pedigree or a combination, are in the position to claim exclusive ownership of the homeland psychology in their relationship to one or another territorial fragment (as the welter of popular songs – Georgia, Sweet Home Alabama, California Dreaming, etc. – brimming with provincial nostalgia appears to insinuate) or, correspondingly, to a racialised idea of America that refuses to dovetail with constitutional ideals. Even if his assertions were borne out, Conner is duty-bound to explain what happens to a diaspora when it begins to feel at home, since the category is by definition predicated on a certain experience of the *unheimlich* in the hostland. Furthermore, he sheds no light on how the emotion of being at home is dissimilar, if indeed it is, from homeland identification. Could it be that, as Stuart Hall suggests, 'people who have been dispersed forever from their homelands . . . belong at one and the same time to several "homes" (and to no one particular "home")' (Hall, 1992: 310), thereby creating multiple forms of belonging without precluding the constitutive experience of the *unheimlich* in the abstract? After reassessing sub-homeland states, which he understands as homeland fragments that fall outside the homeland state (Republic of Ireland vis-à-vis Northern Ireland) or homelands dismembered and distributed among other states (Kurdistan or Kashmir), Conner asserts that the purpose of his study was to determine 'how the degree of congruity between ethnic and political borders helps shape ethno-political myths, which in turn, affect the fortunes of diasporas' (Conner, 1986: 38).

In spite of the intricate variations on the homeland–state relations he advances, Conner seldom diverts from the dual territorial schema. Even his pithy description of diasporas as segments of people living outside their homelands summons up the other pole of the binary – hostlands – which forms the psychological or conceptual 'outside' for these dispersed entities. Conner's definition is like the proverbial serpent, perpetually at risk of swallowing its own tail. It may be argued, for instance, that Turks living in the Kurdish regions of Turkey constitute a genuine diaspora since, despite the juridical and military control exerted over these areas by *their* political state, they effectively represent a segment residing inside a hostland. Hegemonic citizenship, it may be inferred, does not automatically instil in the citizen *feelings* of ownership for *all* homelands that come under the jurisdiction of the political state. It may be further inferred that there are two breeds of citizen: a homeland citizen and a non-homeland citizen. Evidently the former has prior emotional and ideological claims over the homeland territory. But the converse case is also possible. If Turkey lays claims to regions settled by Kurds in what is an extended notion of the legitimate homeland state (and withholds from this significant minority, as it does, even the demographic courtesy of a separate ethnic identity as part of this claim), Kurdish subjects of Turkey may experience a subjective split and feel estranged, as citizens of Turkey, from the homeland provinces they physically inhabit. This would, in turn, render them a diaspora. Add to this internal split the fact that the projected map of Kurdistan – as advanced by the Kurdish League Delegation to a conference in San Francisco in 1945 – encroaches on territory overseen by four extant political states (Syria, Iraq, Iran and Turkey) and the constitutive relations between homelands, states and ethnic diasporas turns so complex as to surrender all point.

With the exception of the immigrant state where the status of the diaspora remains murky and undertheorised, the three polities of the homeland state, the multi-homeland state and the sub-homeland state afford different examples of how diasporas get construed as ethnic segments living outside the homeland. No matter what the combination of homeland–state relations and no matter how oddly and erratically the sign 'homeland' operates in a given polity, the diaspora is almost always the hostile other of the homeland psychology and, consequently, doomed to reside in a hostland. Perhaps the most intriguing aspect of the dual territorial schema is the supposed affective relations between territory and subjectivity. It is clearly assumed that the subjectivity of a diaspora, projected as a cohesive ethno-national entity, is overwhelmingly shaped by the relationship it keeps with a home as well as a host territory, and to the exclusivist myths generated by them. These myths are associated with the botanical tropes of immemorial roots – the native as naturally *in place* in the homeland – and ephemeral alien transplantations – the diasporic interloper as *intrinsically out of place* in the native territory. And since the impact of territory on subjectivity is never actually quantifiable, what emerges under the guise of scientific methodology is a clutch of untested speculations. Indeed, what may be an ideology of affects sponsored by nationalist discourses of most varieties, and therefore open to critical scrutiny, is read in obscurantist terms of insider–outsider psychology. To be fair, Conner is concerned with the self-evidential character of nationalistic discursive formations; that is to say, he is interested in critically mapping their status as 'common sense' if by that phrase we mean the ensemble of pre-critical codes and assumptions found within any social organisation (Gramsci, 1971: 323–7). Since blood, soil, lineage, language and ethnicity operate interchangeably in such formations, he makes it his business to plot the lines of flight that converge in such discourses. However, this occurs at the expense of other lines of flight that, perhaps less self-evidentially, cut across nationalistic discursive formations to form other quasi-discursive nodes and possibilities. Modes of subjectivity and cross-subject alliances determined by class, gender, education, religion, sexual preferences, accent and language are tactfully left out. There is a perfectly sound explanation for the oversight. The point is to stress the primacy of dual territorial coordinates in the subjective formation of a new social species; and ethnicity, because of its ostensible roots in specific terrains, is *inherently* an important co-determinant. To pay too much attention to competing factors would unravel the whole dual territorial framework for constructing diasporic subjectivity.

William Safran

William Safran's controversial article, 'Diasporas in Modern Societies: Myths of Homeland and Return', published in the inaugural issue of the journal *Diaspora* (1991), is fundamentally a summary of and a response to the framework devised by the Sheffer-led school. While admitting that the definition of diaspora as a segment of people living outside the homeland is broadly representative of the new critical genre, Safran points out that Conner's account lacks specificity and leaves itself open to metaphoric substitution. Diaspora, he complains, has become too flexible a term and may refer to 'several categories of people – expatriates, expellees, political refugees, alien residents, immigrants, and ethnic and racial minorities *tout court*'. In an attempt to stabilise the nomination, he lists six taxonomical principles that would settle the question of definitional boundaries '[l]est the term lose all meaning':

> . . . I suggest that Connor's [*sic*] definition be extended and that the concept of diaspora be applied to expatriate minority communities whose members share several of the following characteristics: 1) they, or their ancestors, have been dispersed from a specific original 'center' to two or more 'peripheral,' or foreign, regions; 2) they retain a collective memory, vision, or myth about their original homeland – its physical location, history, and achievements; 3) they believe that they are not – and perhaps cannot be – fully accepted by their host society and therefore feel partly alienated and insulated from it; 4) they regard their ancestral homeland as their true, ideal home and as the place to which they or their descendants would (or should) eventually return – when conditions are appropriate; 5) they believe that they should, collectively, be committed to the maintenance or restoration of their original homeland and to its safety and prosperity; and 6) they continue to relate, personally or vicariously, to that homeland in one way or another, and their ethnocommunal consciousness and solidarity are importantly defined by the existence of such a relationship. (Safran, 1991: 83–4)

Safran's taxonomy discloses a notable shift in the attribution of agential force within the triadic network that informs the dual territorial schema. Unlike Conner who argues for the pivotal role of homelands and homeland dwellers in projecting diasporas as dwellers in hostlands, Safran gives prominence to diasporic entities and proceeds to enumerate a host of *features* that sets them apart from other social formations. These features are traceable to determinate psychological processes and reactions and derived from the transformation in the collective ethno-national consciousness brought about by the tensional split between home and host territories. Even the first characteristic of dispersal, which initially appears not to represent the consciousness of diasporas, ends up doing so since it is the diaspora that ascribes (implicitly or otherwise) unequal affective values to 'original' centre and 'peripheral' region. At any rate, Safran adopts the general rhetorical ploy of speaking on behalf of *bloc* diasporas with the intention of casting light on their peculiar ethno-national consciousness *from within*, as it were. One consequence of this ploy is that the causal pressures exerted by homelands and hostlands become significantly less crucial in a constitutive sense. The effect engendered upon the *consciousness* of bloc diasporas becomes far more important in sustaining the generic definition. This awareness, in turn, encourages the ascription to the diaspora of a self-nominating agency or, if you like, of a collective will-to-self-definition. If the category of diaspora is internal to the consciousness of dispersed minorities ('they retain', 'they believe', 'they regard', 'they . . . relate'), then it is possible to give short shrift to a whole host of extra-subjective factors, both 'here' (hostland) and 'there' (homeland), which may nurture the necessary condition for the type of interpellation Safran describes. Finally, then, diaspora consciousness is treated as the active component framed between two relatively passive territories.

Having devised a six-tiered taxonomical chart or *tabula*[7] from Conner's broad-brush definition, Safran sets out to determine which dispersed entities satisfy the specific terms of his classification. In what appears to be an unintended mimicry of poststructuralist genre theory, he begins by alluding to the '"ideal type" of the Jewish Diaspora' (Safran, 1991: 84) and observes that, while meeting some of the conditions of his taxonomy, no other dispersed ethno-national group actually subscribes to this exemplary or normative model.[8] While the precise nature of the definitional law surrounding the ideal type is never made transparent (though it is definitely of a higher order than the enumerated chart), it is clear that all other displaced minority groups come up slightly or considerably short. Although the ideal type that justifies the law of designation remains tantalisingly elusive, it does serve to stimulate discussion on the distance or proximity of other likely contenders to the designated ideal. Not surprisingly, this ploy spawns a ranked hierarchy of ethno-national aspirants to the law that sustains the designation, beginning with the Armenians whose 'diaspora condition resembles that of the Jews most closely':

> Armenian ethnicity and the solidarity of the Armenian community are based on a common religion and language, a collective memory of national independence in a circumscribed territory, and a remembrance of betrayal, persecution, and genocide. Like the majority of Jews, most Armenians live outside the ancestral homeland and have developed several external centers of religion and culture. Like Jews, Armenians have performed a middlemen function in the host societies among which

> they lived . . . The fostering of Armenian language has been important, but this has not prevented Armenians from being fully immersed in the language and culture of the host society. (Safran, 1991: 84)

The inventory goes on to incorporate several other kinships. Curiously, though, what brings about the lack of taxonomical fit between the Armenian diaspora and the Jewish ideal is never actually discussed.

For the rest of the section, Safran uses his *tabula* to discuss conformist and non-conformist diasporas but reserves the right to conscript and exclude particular entities depending on whether or not they exhibit a diaspora-style consciousness. According to the ground rules of the typology, the Poles of Russian Poland and the Austrian province of Galicia fail to qualify because 'they had not been physically removed from their land and could not, therefore, be considered a diaspora'; however, 'the Poles who settled in France between the Polish insurrection of 1830 and the end of World War I . . . could be considered members of a genuine diaspora' since 'they regarded themselves as temporary residents', kept the dream of the homeland alive, cultivated a separate cultural identity, fostered linguistic ties to the mother tongue and 'vowed to fight for the reestablishment of the Polish state' while also fulfilling the role of ' "fighting middlemen" in the service of the causes of their host countries' (Safran, 1991: 85). Likewise, even though 'the Maghrebi and Portuguese *immigrés* in France and the Turkish *Gastarbeiter* in Germany' have not been 'forcibly expelled from their countries of origin' or exposed to 'the political obligation, or the moral burden, of reconstituting a lost homeland or maintaining an endangered culture', they actively nourish a diaspora consciousness and may be included, therefore, in the umbrella species. Safran claims that 'many Maghrebis speak of a "fermeture relative du systéme politique national" and find assimilation impossible so long as *francité* is equated with European and Christian', a feeling bolstered by many French ethno-nationals who 'refer to even those Maghrebis who have forgotten most of their Arabic and who speak and write in French as "*immigrés* de la deuxiéme génération" or as Algerians' (Safran, 1991: 86). The diaspora consciousness of the Portuguese, on the other hand, revolves around their delusional genius for understating 'the poverty of the real Portugal and for projecting a somewhat idealised image of a mystical Portugal and Portuguese civilisation (Lusitanism)'; the Turks, meanwhile, exercise facets of the consciousness by internalising ' "the myth of return" (*Heimkehrillusion*) . . . fostered by German elites and policy-makers' (Safran, 1991: 86) antagonistic to hybrid visions of the Deutschtland.

Needless to say, there are several minorities that simply flunk the litmus test of consciousness at the first level by not qualifying as *dispersed* ethno-national entities. One such case is that of 'the Flemish-speaking Belgians who live in their own communities in Wallonia' among French speakers; these Belgians cannot be described as a bona fide diaspora because 'they have not been exiled or expatriated, and their condition is the result of demographic changes around them'; the Magyars, too, fail to constitute a properly dispersed entity for the reason that they are 'politically [not territorially] detached from the motherland'; even the Gypsies, who comprise 'a "metadiaspora" in their economic rootlessness' and by virtue of their failure to relate to a single originating territory, are left out since 'diaspora consciousness is an intellectualisation of an existential condition' and the Gypsies, it seems, choose not to intellectualise and therefore possess no consciousness full stop:

> The Gypsies have no myth of return because they have no precise notion of their place of origin, no clear geographical focus, and no history of national sovereignty. (Safran, 1991: 86–7)

The Palestinians, on the other hand, satisfy the requirements of the *tabula* in several respects. They have been banished or 'encouraged to flee' from an original locality; '[t]hey have memories of their homeland; their descendants cultivate a collective myth about it; and their ethnic communal consciousness is increasingly defined by – and their political mobilisation has centred around – the desire to return to that homeland.' Nevertheless, they are non-diasporic in the sense that 'the vast majority of Palestinians (i.e., those who have not emigrated to the United States or western Europe) do not live altogether as "strangers in strange lands:" in Jordan, Syria, and Lebanon, they live within the territory of the "Arab nation" (*al umma 'al 'arabiyya*)'. Moreover, 'they have not had to make the kinds of cultural or linguistic sacrifices characteristic of other diasporas: they continue to speak their language and practice their religion' (Safran, 1991: 87). How such an imaginary pan-Arab category essentially differs from other similar categories – the pan-African or the pan-European or the pan-Pacific – is not spelt out, probably because any meticulous analysis along these lines would leave most diasporas out in the definitional cold. Furthermore, since the upkeep of language and religion is a cardinal feature of diasporic behaviour, it behoves Safran to demonstrate how his *tabula* is compromised in a host society that shares the same language and religion as the diaspora. That the upkeep of language and religion is less fraught in such a host society is beyond dispute, but the issue here is 'maintenance' and not the varying degrees of ease and difficulty experienced in the process.

Safran's progressively futile search for diasporas that correspond to the Jewish ideal, which constitutes the law that overrides all laws, does not end with the Palestinians. The Corsican, Indian, Parsi, Chinese, African and Latin American diasporas are all put through the hoops and, despite the innumerable correlations and crossovers, found wanting. Safran regards the Indian diaspora as a 'genuine one' in that it is tri-continental, has an extended history, plays 'an auxiliary (or middleman) role within host societies' and tends to be 'integrationist' as well as 'particularist'. Nonetheless, it falls short of the norm because 'an Indian homeland has existed continuously' and it 'has not been noted for encouraging an "ingathering"' of its peoples. In addition, 'the Indian diaspora status has not always been associated with political disability or even minority status' and the 'homeland myth is not particularly operative where the Indian diaspora is in the majority (as in Fiji) [*sic*] or where it constitutes a large, well-established, and sometimes dominant minority (as in Trinidad and Tobago, Nepal, Guyana, and Sri Lanka)' (Safran, 1991: 88–9). Despite the many similarities with the ideal Jewish type, the Parsis also constitute a flawed diaspora in that 'unlike the Jews, they are not widely dispersed but concentrated in a single area [Bombay]' and 'have no myth of return to their original homeland, Iran, whence they emigrated in the eight century' (Safran, 1991: 89). The Chinese, on the other hand, depart from the ideal type through a dilution of the homeland myth and an attendant enfeebling of diaspora consciousness. This is evident particularly in those host territories

> . . . where legal and political disabilities have been removed and economic opportunities have expanded, so that the knowledge of the Chinese language and the connection with Chinese culture have become weak (as, increasingly, in the United States and Canada); and where the Chinese community has become so dominant that it has been able to secure an institutionally guaranteed status for its culture – in effect, to recreate a Chinese community outside the original homeland, but with more appealing political and economic conditions (as in Singapore). (Safran, 1991: 89)

Safran adds that, in the aftermath of the Vietnam war, many ethnic Chinese 'went from Indochina to France or the United States – just as many dissatisfied Jews went from the Soviet Union to North America or western Europe, instead of Israel, and many blacks went from the West Indies to the United States or Britain, instead of Africa' (Safran, 1991: 89). That such itineraries consisting of serial detours and digressions may put in doubt the whole dual territorial enterprise does not seem to occur to Safran. In the end, whatever cannot be doctored or tailored to fit is left out of the *tabula* instead of calling it into dispute. The upshot is that African Americans flunk the 'maintenance' test because they 'no longer have a clearly defined African heritage to preserve', while Mexican Americans, mindful that the 'poverty and political corruption of Mexico . . . stand in too sharp a contrast with conditions in the United States', embrace an assimilatory policy while recoiling from the homeland myth (Safran, 1991: 90). If poverty and corruption are truly such potent obstacles to the nourishment of a diaspora consciousness, then most third world diasporas residing in the United States would be devoid of a homeland myth. All too precipitously, then, Safran conflates the *imaginary* relations diasporas keep with homelands with the *actual* political and economic conditions of these polities. He also tends to treat the homeland myth exclusively in positive terms.

Near the end of his discussion, Safran puts his case in a nutshell:

> In sum, both diaspora consciousness and the exploitation of the homeland myth by the homeland itself are reflected not so much in instrumental as in expressive behaviour. It is a defense mechanism against slights committed by the host country against the minority, but it does not – and is not intended to – lead its members to prepare for the actual departure for the homeland. The 'return' of most diasporas . . . can thus be seen as a largely eschatological concept: it is used to make life more tolerable by holding out a utopia – or *eutopia* – that stands in contrast to the perceived *dystopia* in which actual life is lived. (Safran, 1991: 94)

The taxonomical justification, then, is entirely dependent on accounting for what is fundamentally elusive and ultimately unquantifiable – expressive behaviour. Yet the law of taxonomy, and therefore of genre, dictates that the expressive behaviour of diasporas submit to a common locus where, isolated from other varieties of social behaviour, they may be numbered, juxtaposed, indexed, relativised, evaluated, compared, contrasted and transvalued in a new spatial arrangement. For, after all, it is through expressive behaviour that one obtains access to a group's ethno-national consciousness. There are two things that warrant attention here. One concerns Safran's project as an exemplar participating with and (sometimes) against other exemplars (Sheffer, Conner, Edmondson, Helweg and so on) at the scene of dual territoriality; the other involves what is internal to the exemplar – that is, the persistent juxtaposing of the expressive behaviour of dispersed ethno-communities in relation to an unattainable ideal. In the first instance, Safran differs from both Sheffer and Conner in suggesting that, while predicated on territorial binaries, what finally distinguishes diasporas from other related formations is a peculiar consciousness *interior* to the ethno-national cluster. In the second case, he posits an ideal Jewish type that, as in Wittgenstein's example of family resemblances, makes possible the order of relationality (i.e. the production of a series of ethno-communal aspirants) while remaining perpetually outside this order. In fact, Safran's article presents a bizarre exercise in self-subversion inasmuch as the *tabula* of six traits advanced with such diligence and authority at the start of the project is gradually eroded by the 'test' cases he subjects to analysis. As if acknowledging this defeat, Safran aborts the study with a series of unanswered (and perhaps unanswerable) queries aimed at clarifying, but inevitably complicating, the whole issue of taxonomy.

Several papers showcased in the early instalments of *Diaspora* make use of the dual territorial framework as propounded by the Sheffer-led school and reworked and rewired by Safran. Noting that his 'Preface' to the inaugural issue serves as a clandestine manifesto of sorts, Khachig Tölölyan, for instance, declares that the new journal will be devoted to 'the traces of struggles over and contradiction within ideas and practices of collective identity, of homeland and nation' (Tölölyan, 1991: 3). What this means essentially is that *Diaspora* will concentrate on teasing out the warps and woofs within the triadic relations informing the dual territorial schema. In an article that appeared a year later, Marian Rubchak employs Antanas J. Van Reenan's concept of 'diasporic mentality' to discuss the Lithuanian diaspora in North America and comments that the phrase alludes to 'the mind-frame of a people with a powerful sense of the Lithuanianness of their own and future generations, who set out to resist assimilation into mainstream America' (Rubchak, 1992: 117). Taking exception to Van Reenan's provocative division of Lithuanian immigrants into prewar assimilationists and postwar non-assimilationists, she commends 'Safran's formula' because it has the capacity to 'embrace the entire Lithuanian immigration, so that both waves could be seen as an extended Other of their *imagined* [i.e. homeland] *community*' (Rubchak, 1992: 125). Rubchak insists that the Lithuanian diaspora is not historically fissured in the manner suggested by Van Reenan and portrays it as 'a dedicated "transnational collectivity" maintaining its connection to the homeland' (Rubchak, 1992: 120). By skirting around the instabilities and asymmetries that actually exist within the Lithuanian ethno-national grouping, this move effectively restores a fundamental cohesion and stability to the triadic network identified by both Sheffer and Safran. Setting his sight on the Ethiopian diaspora stranded in Canada, John Sorenson, too, subscribes cheerfully to the dual territorial framework. He claims that his purpose is to trace 'the conflict between ethnic and national identity', to analyse 'the renegotiation of identity in a diaspora actively concerned with the homeland' and to chart 'myths of homeland and return among one of the world's largest refugee populations . . .' (Sorenson, 1992: 201). By placing himself inside the straitjacket of the dual territorial schema at the outset, Sorenson shuts out any real possibility of testing its feasibility.

Robin Cohen

Robin Cohen's *Global Diasporas: An Introduction* (1997) adopts the by-now-familiar ploy of delineating a new generic domain through the comparative alignment of dispersed ethno-national entities. Writing some eleven years after

Sheffer, Cohen is mindful of the epistemic 'turn' instituted in the intervening years by the likes of Hall, Gilroy, Mercer and Clifford – a turn that initiated what I have dubbed the second scene of exemplification. Treated more fully in the next chapter, this scene of situational laterality is characterised by asynchronous migrations, crabwise detours and overdetermined identities that defeat all attempts to institute a discrete homeland–hostland dichotomy. In this second scene, subjective filiations are viewed as provisional or occurring at the micro-local and heterotopic levels (kinship identifications, ad hoc associations, attachments to milieu items, institutions, adoption of hybrid cultural forms and practices, etc.) rather than at the customary macro level of the homeland or nation-state. Cohen associates this scene with a certain species of postmodern praxis and concedes that it 'fundamentally question[s] the very ideas of "home" and "host"'. He also admits that the 'unidirectional – "migration to" or "return from" – forms of movement are being replaced by asynchronous, transversal flows that involve visiting, studying, seasonal work, tourism and sojourning, rather than whole-family migration, permanent settlement and the adoption of exclusive citizenships' (Cohen, 1997: 127–8). And yet, somewhat puzzlingly, he ends up employing a modified version of the dual territorial framework without bothering to negotiate the incompatibilities between the first and the second scenes of exemplification.

Cohen prepares the ground for his version of the dual territorial schema by questioning Safran's *tabula* which represents diasporas as either subscribing to or departing from an ideal Jewish standard. Taking his cue from the second scene participants (particularly Clifford and the Boyarins), he mounts a compelling case against the ideal type scenario. Although Cohen does not refer to the work in question, the argument for venturing beyond an idealised ethnicist model was first mooted, albeit somewhat tentatively, by George Shepperson in 1976. In his 'Introduction' to *The African Diaspora: Interpretive Essay*, Shepperson observed that

> . . . [t]he application of the Greek word for dispersion, *diaspora*, to . . . Jewish migration from their homeland into all parts of the world not only created a term which could be applied to any other substantial and significant group of migrants, but also provided a concept which could be used to interpret the experiences (often very bitter experiences) of other peoples who had been driven out of their native countries by forces similar to those which dispersed the Jews: in particular, slavery and imperialism. (Shepperson, 1976: 1–2)

Since it comprised an isolated proto-generic instance by being considerably ahead of its time, Shepperson's intervention went largely unnoticed. Two decades later, writing in a similar vein but adopting a more abrasive tone,

Cohen points out that the prototypical Jewish example 'is much more complex and diverse than many assume':

> The religious zealots in the tradition of Ezra and the prophets should not be allowed to appropriate the Babylonian and Sephardic experiences to their cause. Those experiences were distinguished by considerable intellectual and spiritual achievements which simply could not have happened in a narrow tribal society like that of ancient Judaea. The voluntarist component in the history of Jewish migration should not be overlooked. Not all Jewish communities outside the natal homeland resulted from forcible dispersal. Indeed, there is considerable evidence to suggest that the Jews are not a single people with a single origin and a single migration history. (Cohen, 1997: 21)

Since the Jewish case offers several, sometimes contradictory, forms of dispersion, Cohen feels justified in questioning its privileged status in Safran's *tabula* and invites his readers to take stock of the 'changes and expansions of the meaning of the term diaspora as it comes to be more widely applied' (Cohen, 1997: 22). In his opinion there is no valid reason for nominating a superordinate ethno-national standard that endorses the rule of relationality. It is an important objection certainly, but it does not hinder Cohen from employing a modified and expanded version of Safran's *tabula*. If there is a hidden principle that incites generic statements, creating the scene of participation (or what I have dubbed the relational scene), then, for Cohen, it is a principle devoid of any singular ethno-national content. For precisely this reason he dispenses with ethno-national categories in his macro typology. Instead of arranging diasporas in discrete ethno-national compartments, Cohen proposes a quintet of ethnically neutral categories: victim, labour, trade, imperial and cultural. If at first this appears to be a viable, even preferable, typology, it soon becomes clear that the macro order is propped up by the usual ethno-national units:

> The chapters are organised thematically, but in most one or two particular groups have been used as exemplary cases. Thus, when considering the most prevalent concept of diaspora [victim], the Jews have been selected to illustrate the argument. Africans and Armenians are shown to be analogous victim diasporas. The British have been represented as an imperial diaspora, the Indians as a labour diaspora, while the trading diasporas have been typified by the Chinese and Lebanese. Finally, the peoples of the Caribbean abroad are . . . usefully characterised as a cultural diaspora. (Cohen, 1997: x)

Cohen is not unmindful of the risks involved in promoting equivalences between general categories and specific ethno-national diasporas, for he subsequently notes:

> It is important to emphasise at the outset that I am not suggesting a perfect match between a particular ethnic group and a specific type of diaspora. Quite the contrary. I am fully aware that the Jews were not only a victim diaspora, but also one that was periodically successful in trade and commerce and one also that now evinces a high level degree of cosmopolitanism appropriate to our global age. Likewise, the Chinese were indentured labourers (therefore a labour diaspora) as well as a successful trading diaspora. In the case of the Indians, exactly the reverse holds. While they are regarded as archetypes of a labour diaspora, they also have an important mercantile history. (Cohen, 1997: x–xi)

Even if we were to grant that the examples he adduces 'are prompts, models and guides' (Cohen, 1997: xi) and not watertight equations, the decision to continue with the macro designations in the light of such acknowledged contradictions betrays a conservative, if not a defensive, strategy. The exceptions that are internal to the ethno-national archetypes do not, it seems, put in doubt the macro framework or necessitate a redrawing of taxonomic parameters; they merely serve as minority supplements that endanger the rule in a potential sense but in practice fall outside its order. Cohen admits that his ethno-nationalities are more or less hyphenated (victim-trade-cosmopolitan, labour-trade, etc.) but has no intention of letting the 'hyphen' destabilise his macro categories at the level of nomination. He also declines to consider any number of possible micro factors (such as regional, vocational, class, caste, gender and time distinctions) within the specific examples capable of destabilising the equation between ethno-nationalities and diaspora types.

Whatever its typological merit, the quintet of victim, labour, imperial, trade and cultural diasporas that sustains Cohen's macro order fails to justify the classificatory decision taken at the primary level – that is, at the level of differentiating diasporic entities from other social formations. In order to deal with this shortcoming, Cohen turns to Safran's *tabula* for guidance. Where Safran felt the need to broaden Conner's minimal definition of diasporas as segments living outside the homeland and to boost Sheffer's triadic relations schema, Cohen is overcome by the urge to 'tweak' Safran's *tabula* of six key characteristics while supplementing it with several of his own:

> I would amend the first stated feature by adding that dispersal from an original centre is often accompanied by the memory of a single traumatic event that provides folk memory of the great historic injustice that binds

> the group together. I would adapt the penultimate characteristic to allow the case of not only the 'maintenance or restoration' of a homeland, but also its very creation. This will cover the case of an 'imagined homeland' that only resembles the original history and geography of the diaspora's natality in the remotest way. (In some cases – the Kurds and Sikhs come to mind – a homeland is clearly an *ex post facto* construction.) (Cohen, 1997: 23)

One may easily concede the constitutive effects of a single traumatic event on victim diasporas such as the Palestinians or the Armenians, but surely this cannot hold equally for trade and imperial diasporas such as the Chinese and the English. How are these voluntary or 'aggressive' diasporas tormented by memories of a single traumatic event? Imperial diasporas may instigate traumatic events that constitutively haunt victim diasporas (slaves, indentured servants, refugees, etc.) for considerable lengths of time, but whether they can lay claim to their own group-defining trauma is not only doubtful but ethically disturbing. When it comes to definitional matters, Cohen is a lot steadier at the end than at the start:

> Normally, diasporas exhibit several of the following features: (1) dispersal from an original homeland, often traumatically; (2) alternatively, the expansion from a homeland in search of work, in pursuit of trade or to further colonial ambitions; (3) a collective memory and myth about the homeland; (4) an idealisation of the supposed ancestral home; (5) a return movement; (6) a strong ethnic group consciousness sustained over a long time; (7) a troubled relationship with host societies; (8) a sense of solidarity with co-ethnic members of other countries; and (9) the possibility of a distinctive creative, enriching life in tolerant host countries. (Cohen, 1997: 180)

Not wholly persuaded by Safran's *tabula*, Cohen recalibrates some of the more crucial features while adding fresh ones. Indeed, it is a sense of taxonomic deficiency that drives his pursuit of the clandestine law of the genre or, better still, of the total unrealisable statement that sustains the tabulated horizon of relationality. In the process of augmenting Safran's list of six key characteristics to nine, Cohen propagates comparative examples that never culminate in the total statement. For every typological characteristic he advances in support of the rule, there is always an exception. In addition, there is the related problem of internal anomalies and contradictions within the series. To cite one instance: how is it possible for a diaspora with aggressive colonial ambitions (characteristic 2) to reside in a *tolerant* host country (characteristic 9), far less enjoy a rewarding and creative life? Having dispensed with the ideal type of the Jews,

Cohen cannot help but be idealistic in his quest for an ethnically empty definition that has universal currency and applicability. At every turn, however, he is confronted with the paradox of having to refer to ethno-national categories in order to justify his *tabula*. The total statement incites the order of relationality by engendering the very examples that strive and invariably fail to deliver its presence.

In the end, Cohen offers us little more than a cranked up version of the dual territorial framework. There is the same emphasis on a unique ethno-social consciousness distinguished by collective desires (of return) and solidarities (with fellow ethno-nationals) and emanating from the two-way interaction with an idealised or original homeland (absent *topos*) and a non-idealised hostland (present *topos*). Like Sheffer and Safran before him, Cohen does not feel the need to reflect on the pitfalls of representing diasporas as class-neutral, gender-neutral and generation-neutral ethnic blocs that uncritically project home and host countries as homogeneous territorial entities. Since the paradigm is internal to diasporas in that *they* conceive of themselves auto-ideologically in this way, the diasporist is free to treat the triadic relations as a discursive effect that warrants neither defence or apology. It is precisely this assumption that is refuted by the second scene participants and forms the point of departure for many of their genre-resuscitating observations. Cohen's *tabula* has been found handy by a small number of subsequent diasporists, including Kim D. Butler and Darshan Singh Tatla. In *The Sikh Diaspora: The Search for Statehood*, Tatla implements Cohen's nine-point test for identifying diasporic formations. While their exceptionality on one point – that of involuntary departure from the homeland – testifies to the tantalising evasions of the total statement, Tatla is satisfied that the 'overseas Sikh communities fulfil the sufficient conditions of a diaspora, i.e. dispersion, reluctant hosts, contest over homeland and maintenance of an active relationship with their mother country' (Tatla, 1999: 5). Driven by a resolutely ingenuous 'search for a consensus on the definition of diaspora' (Butler, 2001: 190), Butler, for her part, negotiates the earlier typologies provided by Safran and Cohen before coming up with her own five-point *tabula*.[9] One of the strengths of her framework, she claims, is that it 'facilitates a close analysis of the three sites in which diasporas take form: the homeland, the hostland, and the diasporan group itself' (Butler, 2001: 195). Thus, some fifteen years after Sheffer first proposed it, Butler rediscovers the triadic relations schema. In the final assessment, however, Tatla and Butler are unfortunate latecomers to a genre party that has long abandoned the scene of dual territoriality.

It is Sheffer's claim in 1986 to have inaugurated a new domain of study, but in all honesty the credit must go to Armstrong for having initiated the typological mode of comparative analysis for dispersed ethno-national formations.[10] Nearly a decade before the publication of Sheffer's *Modern Diasporas in International Politics*, Armstrong had recommended the development of 'an extended longitudinal framework . . . for adequate comparative investigation of the multiethnic polity'; he had also described diasporas as distinctive ethnic collectivities within such polities (Armstrong, 1976: 393). Separating diasporic ethno-national formations into the two distinct types of mobilised and proletarian (and further dividing the former into the subcategories of archetypal and situational), he had set the benchmark for the principle of 'tabular juxtaposition' (Armstrong, 1976: 403) favoured by most first scene participants. To this end, he had delineated a set of ten basic propositions for identifying, evaluating and contrasting diasporas.[11] Armstrong had described the proletarian diaspora as 'essentially a disadvantaged product of modernised polities' and the mobilised diaspora as 'an ethnic group which does not have a general status advantage, yet which enjoys many material and cultural advantages compared to other groups in the multiethnic polity' (Armstrong, 1976: 393). Within the mobilised category, he had drawn a clear line between archetypal diasporas (such as Jews or Parsis) on account of their dispersal being total and irrevocable, and situational diasporas (such as Chinese and Germans) on the grounds that an active relationship to a territorial base rendered their condition, at least in theory, partial and transitory (Armstrong, 1976: 394). His quest for a comprehensive typology for designating diasporic ethno-national formations was subsequently taken up by first scene participants such as Sheffer, Conner, Safran and Cohen. Unlike his legatees at the scene of dual territoriality, Armstrong approached the issue of typology – or, more accurately, tabular juxtaposition – with an intuitive grasp of the ever-vanishing law of the genre that simultaneously drives the search for and defers the possibility of arrival at the total statement. Remarking that his model of mobilised and proletarian diasporas was fundamentally a heuristic device (i.e. one that discovered its argument through a system of trial and error), Armstrong was both shrewd and prescient enough to add that '[a] typology constitutes, by itself, a limited step toward further theoretical development' (Armstrong, 1976: 393). By the time *Global Diasporas: An Introduction* saw the light of day, the scene of dual territoriality had played itself out. Several years before this point was reached, a new company of actors had already entered the fray and, as it happened, dramatically changed the scene.

Notes

1. The proto-generic diasporists include a significant number of scholars working in the area of African-American Studies, including George Shepperson, Elliott P. Skinner, Joseph. E. Harris and St Clair Drake.

2. What Sheffer calls triadic networks (homeland–diaspora–hostland), I call the dual territorial schema since the diaspora is constituted in the tension between two distinct territories.
3. 'Bound seriality, which has its origins in governmentality, especially in such institutions as the census and elections, is exemplified by finite series like Asian Americans, *beurs*, and Tutsis. It is the seriality that makes a United Ethnicities or a United Identities unthinkable' (Anderson, 1998: 117).
4. 'Ideology', Althusser writes, 'represents the imaginary relationships of individuals to their real conditions of existence' (Althusser, 1971: 122).
5. In his book *Literature, Partition and the Nation State*, Joe Cleary makes this point polemically when he comments that 'a people that flees genocide in one place and is received, whether voluntarily or not, into the homeland of another does not have the right to displace its host community and establish its own state on its territory' (Cleary, 2002: 37).
6. Commenting on the rhizome in *A Thousand Plateaus: Capitalism and Schizophrenia*, Deleuze and Guattari write: 'Let us summarise the principal characteristics of a rhizome: unlike trees or their roots, the rhizome connects any point to any other point, and its traits are not necessarily linked to traits of the same nature; it brings into play very different regimes of signs, and even nonsign states. The rhizome is reducible neither to the One nor the multiple . . . It is composed not of units but of dimensions, or rather directions in motion. It has neither beginning nor end, but always a middle (*milieu*) from which it grows and which it overspills' (Deleuze and Guattari, 1987: 21).
7. *Tabula*, in the sense I employ it here, refers to a set of rules arranged in a tabulated hierarchy and to their inviolability as inscriptions on a tablet.
8. In his 1983 article entitled 'The Jewish Diaspora and the Middleman Adaptation', Walter P. Zenner described the Jewish diaspora as a unique or ideal type 'by virtue of its special features' including '(1) Specialisation of middleman roles, (2) Permanent urban settlement, (3) Maintenance of a separate moral community, (4) Longevity as a diaspora, (5) Lack of a permanent hinterland [and], (6) Worldwide range' (Zenner, 1983: 152–3).
9. These are as follows: '(1) Reasons for, and conditions of, the dispersal; (2) Relationship with the homeland; (3) Relationship with hostlands; (4) Interrelationships within communities of the diaspora; (5) Comparative studies of different diasporas' (Butler, 2001: 195).
10. Zenner's article, though theoretically malnourished, also presents its argument through a mode of comparative juxtaposition of ethno-national clusters (Zenner, 1983: 141–56).
11. Citing Armstrong verbatim, the ten propositions are as follows: '(1) within the multiethnic polity, the mobilised diaspora is temporarily indispensable for the dominant ethnic elite; (2) within the multiethnic polity, the mobilised diaspora depends for security on the dominant ethnic elite; (3) from the internal standpoint, the delicate balance of forces maintaining a mobilised diaspora's position within the multiethnic polity is most apt to be upset by a sharp overall rise in social

mobilisation; (4) in the external relations of the multiethnic polity, the mobilised diaspora is as indispensable (and as transitory) as it is for the internal interests of the dominant ethnic elite; (5) dominant ethnic elite perceptions of mobilised diaspora disloyalty tend to negate the value of the diaspora for external relations; (6) the most potent source of the dominant ethnic suspicion of the mobilised diaspora is the existence of its "homeland" outside the dominant elite's territorial control; (7) in a multiethnic polity where slow mobilisation of the dominant ethnic group results in a persistent need for mobilised diaspora skills, diasporas will tend to succeed one another in advantageous positions; (8) in polities (whether or not multiethnic) where social and economic modernisation has proceeded rapidly and evenly, mobilised diasporas do not perform indispensable activities and are generally not subject to discrimination; (9) in polities where economic and social modernisation has proceeded rapidly and evenly, proletarian diasporas tend to become progressively more distant culturally and in physical appearance from the dominant ethnic group, and to suffer more discrimination; and (10) there is a reciprocal relation between modernisation and diasporas: (a) in polities where modernisation is rapid and even, mobilised diasporas tend to become vestigial and their members are advantaged; whereas proletarian diasporas become increasingly important and their members deprived; (b) in multiethnic polities where modernisation is retarded, mobilised diasporas are temporarily advantaged as a group, but are successively discarded and their members are deprived; whereas proletarian diasporas are vestigial, and their members are no more deprived than the lower strata of the dominant ethnic group' (Armstrong, 1976: 397–408).

3

The Scene of Situational Laterality

The symptoms of a scene-transforming dissensus were already there, anachronistically, as early as 1983. Seeking to build a comparative typology of middleman minorities in a study entitled 'The Jewish Diaspora and the Middleman Adaptation', Walter P. Zenner contends that, unlike other dispersed ethnonationals of the middleman variety such as the Chinese, Indians, Greeks, Armenians and Arabs, the Jews constitute 'a diaspora without a hinterland' (Zenner, 1983: 141). Zenner appears to be using 'hinterland' in three specific ways here: first, as a synonym for the homeland understood viscerally in the suprarational geo-psychic sense; second, as that which is *hinter*land or land physically left 'behind'; and, lastly, as the temporal backwater or archaic reference point for middleman minorities with links to an ancestral peasantry. Since all three senses imply the presence of a prior territorial base, there is the clear imputation that Jews, deprived of a hinterland, lack an originating terrain as well as the three suggested ways of associating with it. According to Zenner, this 'turn' came about in the early Islamic era:

> The formation of the Jews as a dispersed middleman minority without a hinterland occurred in the early Islamic period (9th and 10th Centuries). From that time up until the present, the pattern was practically self-perpetuating. Obviously there were shifts from one dominant occupation to another. Sometimes most Jews in a particular place were craftsmen; at other times, retainers of the nobility, like the Court Jews, were the main group; at still other times, pawnbrokers and dealers in second-hand goods were predominant. This variation in occupations shows the inherent adaptability of the Jews to the different environments, but analytically it

> shows similarities in that the Jews were involved in trade and economic ventures, estranged from the majority populations and its elites, and exhibited a tendency toward self-employment. (Zenner, 1983: 148)

Zenner's emphasis on shifting occupations and contexts is not postulated with reference to a dual territorial schema. As a matter of fact what is being described here is the historically complex series of *vocational identities* – craftsman, retainer, pawnbroker, dealer, etc. – assumed by the Jews depending on their *situational context* and with little regard to the macro ethno-communities of a host or a home territory. Zenner attributes this 'inherent adaptability' of the Jews to the middleman role that 'made it possible for a community to evolve which could transmit its heritage and reproduce itself all over the world, escaping adversity in one area by establishing a centre elsewhere' (Zenner, 1983: 153). While the territorial presence of modern-day Israel and its potential status as hinterland is adroitly side-stepped, Zenner's view of Jewish culture as a transmission without origins or unidirectional territorial ends offers an early alternative to the bipolar territorial framework for describing disaggregated ethno-national entities. Although he is not equipped to express it in the idiom of deconstruction, Zenner perceives the diaspora of the Jews as being characterised by the perpetual decentring of centres and centring of decentres. Having escaped the notice of all the major diasporists, Zenner's account may be said to comprise a pre- rather than a proto-generic instance at the scene of situational laterality.[1]

The Black Britons: Paul Gilroy, Kobena Mercer and Stuart Hall

A year after the appearance of *Modern Diasporas in International Politics* (1986), Paul Gilroy put out *'There Ain't No Black in the Union Jack': The Cultural Politics of Race and Nation*, which included a chapter bearing the title 'Diaspora, Utopia and the Critique of Capitalism'. Wary as well as weary of the pervasive essentialist habit of equating nation with culture, race and ethnicity (and we might add the masculine gender and the heteropatriarchal family), Gilroy scrutinises 'black cultures within the framework of a diaspora as an alternative to the different varieties of absolutism which would confine cultures in "racial", ethnic or national essences' (Gilroy, 1987: 154). He elaborates:

> It bears repetition that 'race', ethnicity, nation and culture are not interchangeable terms. The cultural forms discussed below cannot be contained neatly within the structures of the nation-state. This quality can be used to reveal an additional failing in the rigid, pseudo-biological

> definition of national cultures which has been introduced by ethnic absolutism. Black Britain defines itself crucially as part of a diaspora. Its unique cultures draw inspiration from those developed by black populations elsewhere. In particular, the culture and politics of black America and the Caribbean have become important raw materials for creative processes which redefine what it means to be black, adapting it to distinctively British experiences and meanings. Black culture is actively made and re-made. (Gilroy, 1987: 154)

A few paragraphs later, he adds:

> Analysis of the political dimensions to the expressive culture of black communities in Britain must reckon with their position within international networks. It should begin with where fragmented diaspora histories of racial subjectivity combine in unforeseen ways with the edifice of British society and create a complex relationship which has evolved through various stages linked in different ways to the pattern of capitalist development itself.
>
> The modern world-system responsible for the expansion of Europe and consequent dispersal of black slave labourers throughout Europe and the new world was from its inception an international operation. Several scholars have pointed to its uneasy fit into forms of analysis premised on the separation of its economic and cultural sub-systems into discrete national units coterminous with nation-states . . . The social structures and processes erected over the productive and distributive relations of this system centred on slavery and plantation society and were reproduced in a variety of different forms across the Americas generating political antagonisms which were both international and transnational in character . . . Their contemporary residues, rendered more difficult to perceive by the recent migration of slave descendants into the centres of metropolitan civilisation, also exhibit the tendency to transcend a narrowly national focus. Analysis of black politics must, therefore, if it is to be adequate, move beyond the field of inquiry designated by concepts which deny the possibility of common themes, motives and practices within diaspora history. This is where categories formed in the intersection of 'race' and the nation-state are themselves exhausted. To put it another way, national units are not the most appropriate basis for studying this history for the African diaspora's consciousness of itself has been defined in and against constricting national boundaries. (Gilroy, 1987: 157–8)

The above is an early rendition of a thesis that Gilroy went on to develop more sedulously in *The Black Atlantic: Modernity and Double Consciousness* (1993).

Magisterial in its scope, this later work provides a compelling account of the non-linear circulation of 'black' Atlantic cultures, ideas, politics, commodities, iconographies and peoples which actively contributed to the emergence of that temporal regime called *western* modernity. Gilroy's argument is that this contribution, so integral, momentous and enduring, remains the repressed and unacknowledged underside of modernity. At any rate, what we have above are a series of propositions strikingly at odds with the triadic relations schema. It has been my contention in the previous chapter that exponents of the dual territorial approach guardedly repeat an ideological ploy in representing diasporas as self-marking ethnic minorities sundered from a homeland entity and residing in a host territory belonging *self-evidently* to a dominant ethno-national entity. In so doing, they achieve a degree of tonal dissonance between themselves and their mediation of hegemonic perceptions or ground-level realpolitik. For Gilroy, this tactic is simply wrong-headed as it peremptorily closes off alternatives lived in the real outside absolutist categories of culture, race and nation. Even if one were to attribute the synonymous exchanges between nation, culture, 'race' and ethnicity to discursive subjects (ethno-nationalists) and objects (nation-states) rather than to the academic analyst, the alternative scenarios must remain mute in the face of this attribution. Consequently, it is not the mythical fit between the pseudo-biological categories of nation, race and culture but its marked lack that opens up, for Gilroy, that voluble arena offered by lived alternatives.

This position undermines the mainstays of the first scene of exemplification in the following ways. First, it permits Gilroy to substitute ethno-national categories with colour-coded ones which militate against any easy equivalence between ethnicity, race and nation. 'Black' may have originated as a negative epidermal and racial signifier, now returned dialogically and polemically to the sender, but it is by no means, for Gilroy, a singular ethno-national category. Rather, it is a political category that rouses a communality of passions[2] between, say, the descendants of emigrants from the Indian subcontinent and those of the Caribbean archipelago in their struggle to interrupt the identification of Britain and things British with an epidermal whiteness, and exclusively with Anglo-Saxon *plus* Celtic/Welsh cultures and practices. (The *plus* here underscores the politically subordinate status of Celtic/Welsh cultures in this formulation.) In this respect, Gilroy's position bears out Stuart Hall's assertion that 'the term "Black" was coined as way of referencing the common experience and marginalisation in Britain and came to provide the organising category of a new politics of resistance, among groups and communities with, in fact, very different histories, traditions, and ethnic identities' (Hall, 1988: 27). In a later essay, Hall observed that this new organising category did not imply an annulment of differences (within the multiplicity of black communities) or the instalment of absolute macro ones (between black and white); rather, it advanced a certain homologous[3] or, better, homonymous structure where identity and difference were seen to be interdependent:

> . . . [D]espite the fact that efforts are made to give this 'black' identity a single or unified content, it continues to exist as an identity *alongside a wide range of differences.* Afro-Caribbean and Indian people continue to maintain different cultural traditions. 'Black' is thus an example, not only of the political character of new identities – i.e. their positional and conjunctural character (their formation in and for specific times and places) – but also of the way identity and difference are inextricably articulated or knotted together in different identities, the one never wholly obliterating the other. (Hall, 1992: 309)

In any homonymous structure, as we well know, a term comes to mirror its other on a certain acoustic and graphic plane while semantically diverging from it. Without this paradoxical movement, which occurs simultaneously, no such structure is possible. Gilroy has exactly this sort of dynamic in mind when he speaks of a diaspora of 'Black Britain'. On the one hand this memorable phrase articulates a distinction between black and the pseudo-biological or jingoistic understanding of Britain (as Anglo-Saxon *plus* Celtic/Welsh) and, on the other, it brings to attention a certain homology that jarringly transforms this prior distinction. It also negatively articulates a white Britain that exists in a fragmentary relationship to Britain proper, since the modifier 'white' invariably requires its black other to complement the fractured narrative of Britain. Britain, at any rate, is no longer a free-standing category intrinsically soldered to a white ethno-national majority. The second move breaks up from within the visceral equation between homeland and ethno-nationality that forms the basis for the dual territorial framework. Gilroy goes further. By professing that British blacks comprise a diaspora whose 'cultures draw inspiration from those developed elsewhere', he disavows any notion of a single originating territory, homeland or nation-state for this diaspora. British blacks and their expressive cultures exist in a polygenetic relationship to multiple 'trace'[4] points in the Americas and the Caribbean. They evince hybrid histories and fragmented subjectivities that cannot be anchored to quarantined cultural practices associated with racially centred terrains. Dispersed temporally (inasmuch as its social forms and processes have been variously *reproduced* and reshaped since the time of slavery) and spatially (in that it has multiple cultural habitats), the black diaspora fits no single ethno-national register; in fact, when prefixed to Britain, black turns the former into a category that exceeds a circumscribed territory (the British Isles) and finds its constitutive points all across the Atlantic. In many ways, Gilroy is being cartographically coy here. For it is clear that the constitutive points of (black) Britain extend as far as the Indian and Pacific Oceans where the British Empire had several of its colonies. There is even today, for instance, a small diaspora of Fiji Islanders domiciled in Britain. At any rate, Gilroy radically destabilises the three discrete columns – the homeland, the hostland and ethno-national cluster – propping up the architrave of the first scene. Africa is no longer the primary referent for the black diaspora since it has multiple trace points without origins; Britain, meanwhile, is an internally fractured category not to be neatly equated with any ethno-racial grouping; it is also, by virtue of its black diaspora, culturally and politically derived from points beyond its mapped territory; and, finally, the black diaspora is no unalloyed ethno-national cluster but rather a creolised product of complex transmissions occurring across America, Europe and the Caribbean. Despite his compelling refutation of the triadic relations schema, Gilroy does not upset the applecart of diaspora criticism when it comes to questions of political identity, consciousness and expressive cultures. Identity is doubtless a useful socio-political tool for minority groups struggling to express their grievances from a disempowered position in any given polity; the part played by the expressive arts and cultures in this struggle is also not to be underestimated. That expressive cultures may symptomatically come to represent a peculiar consciousness is, on the other hand, far more worrisome because of the proximity of consciousness, as Foucault reminds us, to impalpable and diffuse categories such as essence, spirit, psyche and soul.[5] Via the backdoor of consciousness, as we have seen in Safran's case, all sorts of intangibles may be reintroduced to justify the nomination and classification (and even the exclusionary practices) of a new social species – to wit, diaspora. An additional drawback is that such an openly phenomenological stance accepts the post-Cartesian position whereby a self-reflexive spirit, capable of taking consciousness as its critical object, stands isolated from inert matter. It is precisely this split that sustains colonialist taxonomy intent on ranking beings, bodies and things according to a sliding scale of consciousness. The point is not to disavow such self-reflexivity (how could one in any case?) but to interrogate its place in discourses of conquest, capitalism, nationalism, slavery and so forth. Identity politics is indebted historically to a particular way of viewing consciousness and to ignore this genealogy is to begin in bad faith.

Korbena Mercer's important article, 'Diasporic Culture and the Dialogic Imagination: The Aesthetics of Black Independent Film', rode hard on the heels of '*There Ain't No Black in the Union Jack*'. Taking his inspiration from Hall, Gilroy, Bhabha, Braithwaite and Bakhtin in particular, Mercer confronts the various stable and univocal categories operating within the dual territorial framework via the black cinematic arts. Decrying the totalising singled-voiced or 'monologic tendency' in some black British films shot in the mimetic or reflective mode, he weighs in favour of a '*dialogic* tendency which is responsive to the diverse and complex qualities of our black Britishness and British blackness' or, in other words, to 'our differentiated specificity as a diaspora people' (Mercer, 1988: 56). Dialogism occurs when incongruous voices and styles press against one another inside a common arena. Mercer derives his concept of the dialogic imagination from Bakhtin's insights into the internal stratification of speech types as found in the genre of the novel:

> The internal stratification of any single national language into social dialects, characteristic group behaviour, professional jargons, generic languages, languages of generations and age groups, tendentious languages, languages of the authorities, of various circles and passing fashions, languages that serve the specific sociopolitical purposes of the day, even of the hour (each day has its own slogan, its own vocabulary, its own emphases) – this internal stratification present in every language of its historical existence is the indispensable prerequisite for the novel as a genre. The novel orchestrates all its themes, the totality of the world of objects and ideas depicted and expressed in it, by means of the social diversity of speech types [*raznorečie*] and by the differing individual voices that flourish under such conditions. Authorial speech, the speeches of narrators, inserted genres, the speech of characters are merely fundamental compositional unities with whose help heteroglossia [*raznorečie*] can enter the novel; each of them permits a multiplicity of social voices and a wide variety of their links and interrelationships (always more or less dialogised). (Bakhtin, 1981: 262–3)

For Mercer, in the wake of Bakhtin's intervention, what is at stake 'is not the expression of some lost origin or some uncontaminated essence in black film language, but the adoption of a critical voice that promotes consciousness of the collision of cultures and histories that constitute our very conditions of existence' (Mercer, 1988: 56). The mimetic mode, unlike the heteroglossic, is incapable of facilitating this project because it is 'a form of cultural mimicry which demonstrates a neocolonised dependency on the codes which valorise film as a commodity of cultural imperialism' (Mercer, 1988: 56–7). Mercer is being uncharacteristically reductive here, since it can be objected that the mimetic mode in the hands of perceptive ex-colonised auteurs such as Satyajit Ray or Ritvik Ghatak may not necessarily serve a commodity function in the sense suggested above. In fact, the understated epical strands in Ray's starkly realist films do exactly the opposite by creating diegetic layers that provoke an encounter of desires, genders, histories, cultures and belief systems. The irony is that Bakhtin himself draws on the comic realist novels of the nineteenth century, and the works of Dickens in particular, for his examples of dialogism and heteroglossia.

There is admittedly a techno-historical connection between the mimetic mode and the film as a commodity of cultural imperialism, but this cannot possibly be construed as a *natural* or fixed relation. Be that as it may, the dialogic mode is preferable because it is already 'inscribed in the aesthetic practices of everyday life among black peoples of the African diaspora . . . which explores and exploits the creative contradictions of the clash of cultures'. Mercer adds:

> Across a whole range of cultural forms there is a '*syncretic*' dynamism which critically *appropriates* elements from the master-codes of the dominant culture and 'creolises' them, disarticulating given signs and rearticulating their symbolic meaning otherwise. The subversive force of this hybridising tendency is most apparent at the level of language itself where creoles, patois, and Black English decentre, destabilise, and carnivalise the linguistic domination of 'English' – the nation-language of master discourse – through strategic inflections, reaccentuations and other performative moves in semantic, syntactic and lexical codes. (Mercer, 1988: 57)

Mimetic films – and this is the overall point – disregard and distort the experiential aesthetics of the black diaspora that is already dialogic in its creolising tendencies. However, the preference for dialogic cinema is not as revolutionary as it first appears, since it surreptitiously returns the mimetic using a different route. Even if we were to concede that the mimetic mode is inseparable from orientalising patterns[6] of realism where the other (body, soul, culture, civilisation, etc.) is a negatively fabricated entity, we would still have to account for the *mimesis* of creolised everyday practices since the dialogic mode, as I understand it, is something of a conduit for these already realised forms. Further, playing the devil's advocate, one could suggest that it is the monologic mode that is best able to engender the desired state of critical contemplation, at least for a black audience, through the cinematic adaptation of Brecht's *Verfremdungseffekt* or estrangement effect. If dialogic, hybrid and creolised practices are so ubiquitously present in the 'everyday life' of the black diaspora, then the electric 'jolt' of critical reflection with regard to self-evident social structures or hegemonic perceptions may be supplied – it is possible to argue – by a monologic framework. Dispatched with estrangement in mind, even stereotypes are capable of breaking up the ideological myths on which they are erected. How? By utilising the lacuna between depiction and parody. At any rate, it seems that Mercer's dislike for the mimetic mode is founded on a perfectly justifiable concern for the persistence of monolithic and universalist categories within British cultural representations:

> Critical dialogism overturns the binarist relations of hegemonic boundary maintenance by multiplying critical dialogues *within* particular communities

> and *between* the various constituencies that make up the 'imagined community' of the nation. At once articulating the personal and the political, it shows that our 'other' is already inside each of us, that black identities are plural and non-unitary, and that political divisions of gender and sexual identity are to be transformed as much as those of race and class. Moreover, critical dialogism questions the monologic exclusivity on which the dominant version of national identity and belonging are based. Paul Gilroy shows how the sense of a mutual exclusivity and logical exclusivity between the two terms 'black' and 'British' is an essential condition for the hegemony of racism over the English collective consciousness. New ways of interrupting this hegemonic logic are suggested by the dialogic movement of creolising appropriation. (Mercer, 59: 1988)

In the manner of Gilroy, then, Mercer relies on a poststructuralist move that sees the other in its various manifestations (race, class, sexuality, gender and so on) as always internal to the self and therefore occupying the same intimate place as the latter. Not only does this move fracture absolutist identity formations but makes differential rifts or dialogic interactions the fundamental ground for thinking about identity in the first instance. For Mercer, it is vital to correct the view of the nation as an imagined *'communion' of subjects without others.*[7] This would entail appreciating the psycho-linguistic role of the other (à la Lacan), and of various others, in *personal* identity constitution and translating it into a *political* consciousness that engages critically with these *intimate* in-dwellers. Such a deliberate ploy would have the effect, it is hoped, of blasting asunder the monologic exclusivity of most nationalised identity formations. If individual subjects are constituted heterogeneously by internal others, then the same rule would hold for ethno-national clusters and, in turn, the macro unities of homeland and hostland. To be sure, if the other inheres in the self, then the self is to some extent its own other; likewise, if the inherent other of 'British' is black, then black is at a certain level subversively British. Critical dialogism is based on an insistent evocation of such inherent heterogeneities; and it is this internality of contamination that nationalist discourses, driven predominantly by an exclusivist or dogmatic design, find it convenient to overlook. In the final analysis, Mercer undermines the triadic relations schema by sagaciously transposing Bakhtin's perceptions about language, narrative and genre onto culture, cinematic representation and identity politics. He advances a radical critique of the dual territorial approach by instituting poststructuralist procedures that present a destabilised account of subjectivity, identity and consciousness. Consequently, he does not stray too far from the abiding concerns of diaspora criticism. In the 1994 study, *Welcome to the Jungle: New Positions in Black Cultural Studies*, Mercer goes a step further by thinking of dispersion in relation to the 'field of desire' (Mercer, 1994: 30) rather than in terms of the politics of absence and loss. With a pronounced nod in the direction of Deleuze and Guattari, he speaks of the black queer diaspora as being caught up in a 'profusion of rhizomatic connections' and maintains that queer cultural practices have expanded 'the forms of identification and belonging that constitute "community", hence multiplying connections across diverse constituencies within a decentred public sphere' (Mercer, 1994: 30). Mercer's remark was to have profound repercussions for diaspora criticism as it foreshadowed a radical 'turn' away from stable sexual-gender categories by introducing the possibility of non-heteropatriarchal forms of sociality. This development, coming as it does several years after the 1988 essay (which, incidentally, reappears as a revised chapter in *Welcome to the Jungle*), has to be read in the context of some crucial interventions that occurred before 1994.

One such intervention was made by no less a person than Stuart Hall. In the justly celebrated article entitled 'Cultural Identity and Diaspora' (1990), Hall assembled his earlier insights into identity politics and culture studies within a diaspora framework. It is, in fact, no coincidence that the three outstanding practitioners of diaspora criticism in Britain, at this point in time, were Hall, Gilroy and Mercer; it is a matter of documentation that Hall mentored Gilroy by affording detailed feedback on the early drafts of *'There Ain't No Black in the Union Jack'* (Gilroy, 1987: 9); Hall is also on record as having examined Mercer's doctoral dissertation (Mercer, 1994: vii). In the acknowledgement pages of their respective books, Mercer and Gilroy defer to Hall's scholarship while exchanging intellectual salutations. One may reasonably suppose that the three men swapped ideas in their common desire to find a route out of hegemonic understandings of nation, territory, race and ethnicity. In my analysis of the first scene of exemplification, I suggested that diasporists used systems of taxonomy to pin down the peculiar species-like consciousness of deracinated ethno-national entities. Gilroy and Mercer, it has been my argument, enter the debate by subverting the one-to-one relations between race, ethnicity, culture, nationality, sexuality and nation; they do not attempt to repudiate consciousness as a valid object of analysis but they do reject its *bounded peculiarity*, if by that it is implied that diaspora consciousness is an autonomous, unsullied and fixed entity. In their focus on subjective dialogism, creolised forms and multi-territories (as symptomatically extrapolated from speech effects and various cultural practices), Gilroy and Mercer underemphasise the stable unities of ethno-national clusters for the good reason that this would repeat those hegemonic moves they are seeking to upset. They do cite examples of new forms of affinities and alliances but these always bear marks of adulteration and occur along vectors that fail to correspond to stable symmetries, cultures and territories. Hence the stress on musical crossovers, queer alliances, subjective hybridity and cultural syncreticism. While he has no explicit quarrel with

Gilroy or Mercer, Hall is more sensitive to reactive uses of stable identity formations (such as those advanced by Aimé Césaire and Léopold Senghor, the founders of the Négritude movement) as well as being alert to the urgent historical grounds for their deployment. Needless to say, he is also acutely aware of the poststructuralist querying of stable identity formations along the lines of *différance* whereby the self is fractured internally by the other and the attainment of an integrated self is postponed by serial supplements that cannot heal the fracture. There is a continual play of reversal and displacement, for the self may swap places with the other in the quest for presence but any attempt to pin down the latter is persistently thwarted by an endless supply of substitutes. In this manner, the self, since it is constituted in relation to an elusive other, also finds no respite from supplements which keep diverting it from the stable moment of pure self-recognition or self-presence. Hall's signal achievement is his discovery of a theoretical standpoint that allows *strategic political stabilities* to subsist within the linguistic-philosophical dynamic of *différance*. He manages to find a way around the restlessness of *différance* by drawing a careful distinction between signification and meaning:

> For if signification depends upon the endless repositioning of its differential terms, meaning, in any specific instance, depends on the contingent and arbitrary stop – the necessary and temporary 'break' in the infinite semiosis of language. This does not detract from . . . [Derrida's] original insight. It only threatens to do so if we mistake this 'cut' of identity – this *positioning*, which makes meaning possible – as a natural and permanent, rather than an arbitrary and contingent 'ending' – whereas I understand every such position as 'strategic' and arbitrary, in the sense that there is no permanent equivalence between the particular sentence we close, and its true meaning, as such. (Hall, 1990: 229–30)

In this manner, Hall comes up with a perspective on cultural identity that makes room for 'compositional unities'[8] based on the meaningful 'cut' across the restive current of discontinuity, hybridity and difference. For Bakhtin, compositional-stylistic unities (authorial speech, narrator's speech, inserted genres, character's speech and so on) are internally heterogeneous and permit destabilising multiplicities to enter the novel; however, as he clarifies, upon entering the novel they 'combine to form a structured artistic system, and are subordinated to the higher stylistic unity of the work as a whole, a unity that cannot be identified with any single one of the unities subordinated to it' (Bakhtin, 1981: 262). In other words, the novel is composed around the play of stylistic fractures and weavings, whereby one set of heterogeneities comprises a unity which forms a part of another set of heterogeneities, and so on until we invoke the 'work' whose unity cannot be reduced to any of the multiform unities within it. Although his argument is with Derrida, Hall has a similar concept in mind. Utilising the idea of the strategic positional cut in the infinite semiosis of language (or *différance*), he posits diasporic cultural identity around the twin vectors of *being* and *becoming* or 'the vector of similarity and continuity' and 'the vector of difference and rupture' (Hall, 1990: 226). *Being* is past-directed and refers to a sense of collective identification reflecting the 'common historical experiences and shared cultural codes which provide us, as "one people", with stable, unchanging, and continuous frames of reference and meaning, beneath the shifting divisions and vicissitudes of our actual history' (Hall, 1990: 223), whereas *Becoming* alludes to the discordant, polymorphous detours of the sign where '[w]e cannot speak for very long, with any exactness, about "one experience, one identity", without acknowledging its other side – the ruptures and discontinuities which constitute, precisely, the Caribbean's "uniqueness"' (Hall, 1990: 225). In this second sense, cultural identity is future-directed and, as Hall writes elsewhere, 'not founded on the notion of some absolute, integral self' or 'some fully closed narrative of the self' (Hall, 1987: 45):

> Difference . . . persists – in and alongside continuity. To return to the Caribbean after any long absence is to experience again the shock of the 'doubleness' of similarity and difference. Visiting the French Caribbean for the first time, I also saw at once how different Martinique is from, say, Jamaica: and this is no mere difference of topography or climate. It is a profound difference of culture and history. And the difference *matters*. It positions Martiniquains and Jamaicans as *both* the same *and* different. Moreover, the boundaries of difference are continually repositioned in relation to different points of reference. Vis-à-vis the developed West, we are very much 'the same.' We belong to the marginal, the underdeveloped, the periphery, the 'Other' . . .
>
> At the same time, we do not stand in the same relation of 'otherness' to the metropolitan centres. Each has negotiated its economic, political, and cultural dependency differently. And this 'difference,' whether we like it or not, is already inscribed in our cultural identities. In turn, it is this negotiation of identity which makes us, vis-à-vis other Latin American people, with very similar history [transportation, slavery, colonialism], different – Caribbeans, *les Antilliennes* ('islanders' to their mainland). And yet, vis-à-vis one another, Jamaican, Haitian, Cuban, Guadeloupean, Barbadian, etc. . . . (Hall, 1990: 227–8)

For Hall, then, it is the convergence of the vectors of similarity and difference, of connection and disconnection within cultural identity, that inspires an uncanny doubling of vision. As in any self–other relations, the movement of similarity and difference – or what Homi Bhaba has identified as the perpetually reversible current of ambivalence – is potentially endless since, according to the dynamic of *différance*, the absolute self-presenting of the one or the other is clearly impossible. It is the positional 'cut', at once arbitrary and political, that enables the obligatory and temporary illusion of cognitive congealment: hence the movement, as captured in Hall's prose, of recognition (common experience of historical slavery) followed by misrecognition (different forms of postcolonial dependency). Discussing the 'cut' in terms of Alfred Schuetz's concept of mutual idealisation, Slavoj Žižek asserts that 'the subject cuts the impasse of an endless probing into the question "do we mean the same thing by the term 'bird'?" by simply presupposing and acting as if we do mean the same thing. There is no language without this "leap of faith"' (Žižek, 2004: 126). Since, however, the positional cut (in Hall's version) is arbitrary and can only occur in terms of the play of difference (spatial) as well as the supplementary play of detour and deferment (temporal), it is held that at 'different places, times, in relation to different questions, the boundaries [of identity] are resited' (Hall, 1990: 228). So boundaries do exist around the question of identity but these boundaries are constantly reconfigured through the play of *différance*. Having established this notion of shifting boundaries or sites, and with a sardonic eye on Derrida, Hall nominates three compositional 'presences' – *Présence Africaine, Présence Européenne* and *Présence Américaine* – that persevere within Caribbean cultural identity. The first is associated with trauma and repression, the second with power-knowledge while the third is a spatial category or territory. Although subject to repression and forgetting as a result of slavery, *Présence Africaine*, according to Hall, symptomatically permeates all facets of Caribbean life:

> Africa was, in fact, present everywhere: in the everyday life and customs of the slave quarters, in the languages and patois of the plantations, in the names and words, often disconnected from their taxonomies, in the secret syntactical structures through which other languages were spoken, in the stories and tales told to children, in religious practices and beliefs in the spiritual life, the arts, crafts, musics, and rhythms of slave and post-emancipation society. (Hall, 1990: 230)

But Africa, as he goes on to clarify, is not in any sense the *origin* of Caribbean identities. It is, rather, the holdall of cultural practices transformed by four hundred years of traumatic displacement, it is what these practices have *become* in their multiple contexts of dislocation; bereft of origins, Africa represents a trace in Derrida's sense of a leftover or residue without origin. Africa is no pristine psycho-territory that may be recovered or rediscovered; rather, it acts as a constantly deferred metaphor. Hall cites some compelling evidence in support of this view of deference and delay. One relates to Tony Sewell's photo-documentary project entitled 'Garvey's Children: The Legacy of Marcus

Garvey' which, in its attempts to reforge links to Africa and African identity, detours through London and the United States and ' "ends" not in Ethiopia, but with Garvey's statue in front of the St. Ann Parish Library in Jamaica: not with a traditional tribal chant but with the music of Burning Spear and Bob Marley's "Redemption Song" ' (Hall, 1990: 232). This is perhaps the clearest instance of the ingenious manner in which Hall deploys difference (between multiple psycho-territories) as well as deference (lateral detours) in formulating an internally split notion of cultural identity delinked from unitary understandings of homeland and hostland. *Présence Européenne* and *Présence Américaine* are complex additions to this mode of *schizoanalysis* – a neologism coined by Deleuze and Guattari to describe a critical performance based on acentred modes of argumentation (Deleuze and Guattari, 1987: 18). The internal subjective split within Caribbean cultural identity is negotiated in relation to the shifting boundaries of multiple compositional unities, and it is the positional cut that dictates the stance taken at any given point within the dynamic. Since *Présence Européenne* introduces the whole problem of internal hegemony of one presence (Europe) over another (Caribbean), for it is 'endlessly speaking *us*' (Hall, 1990: 232), the urgent question is how to stage a 'dialogue so that, finally, we can place it, without violence or terror, rather than being forever placed by it' (Hall, 1990: 233). *Présence Américaine* or the New World, on the other hand, is not power or repression but 'the juncture-point where many cultural tributaries meet, the "empty" land (the European colonisers emptied it) where strangers from every part of the globe collided'; it is 'the space where the creolisations and assimilations and syncretisms were renegotiated'; it 'stands for the endless ways in which Caribbean people have been destined to "migrate"; the signifier of migration itself – of travelling, voyaging, and return as fate, as destiny'; and as 'Terra Incognita' it represents 'the beginning of diaspora, of diversity, of hybridity and difference, what makes Afro-Caribbean people already people of a diaspora' (Hall, 1990: 234–5). For Hall, the three compositional unities or *Présences* are already fractured by a myriad heterogeneities, tensions and contiguities; similarly the higher unity of a Caribbean cultural identity alters as the trinity negotiate and renegotiate their sliding boundaries. If the psycho-territory is primordially a convergence point of diverse peoples and cultures, then there can be no simple correlation between an ethno nationality and the homeland. To be certain, *Présence Américaine* is neither hostland nor homeland but the scene of a diasporic assemblage or bricolage where the multidirectional lines of different cultures and histories intersect in a hybridity that knows no end:

> The diaspora experience as I intend it here is defined, not by essence or purity, but by the recognition of a necessary heterogeneity and diversity; by a conception of 'identity' which lives with and through, not despite,

> difference; by *hybridity*. Diaspora identities are those which are constantly producing and reproducing themselves anew, through transformation and difference. (Hall, 1990: 235)

Still, we do remain stuck in the bog of cultural consciousness with the difference that it is no longer grasped in terms of ethno-national exclusivity and circumscription but conceived, rather, in terms of eclectic incorporations, strategic positional cuts and perpetual transformations. One may understand, and even vociferously defend, this manoeuvre as a necessary rejoinder to colonial discourse that sought (and failed according to Bhabha's logic of ambivalence) to categorise the other's consciousness in terms of *absolute* difference – a difference, it is instructive to remember, that was simultaneously construed as being spatial (since the other was forever infantilised by topography and climate), biological (due to the lamentable consequence of inferior genotypes), ethical (as a result of sexual excess, lax morality and irrational behaviour), governmental (since the other's polity is always a polity of despots and slaves) and temporal (as a direct consequence of the other's evolutionary and techno-historical backwardness). Even so, the trouble with such rejoinders is that they are doomed to participate in the phenomenology of consciousness, already a privileged colonialist category, in order to pursue alternatives. To be pulled into the orbit of consciousness, that is to say consciousness as an object of scientific analysis, is to concede in the first instance the overwhelming relevance of such categories and frames of reference. It allows the opponent to prescribe the terms of the debate. Having thus yielded at the outset, it is easy to get caught up in the internal circuitry of subject constitution, agency and identity politics at the expense of extroverted forms of materialist analysis.

Crisscrossing the Atlantic

Even as the British-based diasporists, led by Hall, Gilroy and Mercer, were cutting adrift from the dual territorial framework, a similar trend was beginning to emerge across the Atlantic. In their editorial remarks to an issue of *Public Culture* that appeared in Autumn 1989, Arjun Appadurai and Carol Breckenridge make it clear that even 'to speak of diasporas – if by diasporas we mean phenomena involving stable points of origin, clear and final destinations and coherent group identities – seems already part of a sociology we have lost.' Apart from being a thinly veiled critique of the triadic relations theory, this statement suggests that the usual disciplinary terms are no longer adequate for thinking of the social trajectories of hyper capital:

> . . . [T]here has been a major change in diasporas over the last, post-industrial century. Previous diasporas involved large-scale population

> movements across human landscapes (and political boundaries) otherwise characterised by a sense of stability. Today's diasporas seem somehow normative, creating a pattern of human movement and instability, against which geographical and territorial certainties seem increasingly fragile. (Appadurai and Breckenridge, 1989: i)

It is possible that the temporal distinction between stable pre-industrial and unstable post-industrial diasporas are derived from wistful invocations of an organic past and its famously integrated communities. More crucially, however, by placing stress on the poststructural errantry of present-day flows, Appadurai and Breckenridge are drawing our attention to the anachronism of structuralist frameworks for analysing population movements. Since contemporary forms of dispersion are no longer characterised by a sense of relative stability (as was the case, for instance, in the nineteenth century), the analytical apparatus has to be overhauled to address the new situation. Be that as it may, Appadurai and Breckenridge forget to address a vital question. What precisely would be the *normative measure* for calibrating dispersals, distances and bounded communities according to patterns of stability and instability? In *The Satanic Verses*, Rushdie's narrator observes that the 'distance between cities is always small; a villager, travelling a hundred miles to town, traverses emptier, darker, more terrifying space' (Rushdie, 1988: 41). Is normative measure, then, inseparable from context and perspective? Still, the new disorder entails 'a revitalised cultural sociology of diaspora' that 'must centrally revolve around *lags* and *disjunctures*' (Appadurai and Breckenridge, 1989: ii). The lags include 'lags in memory' as '[m]ore and more diasporic groups have memories whose archaeology is fractured', while the disjunctures subsume everything from generation gaps (revolving around issues of adaptability in new contexts) and gender-power reversals – where women 'become brokers of new domestic cultures and of new kinds of sexual politics' (Appadurai and Breckenridge, 1989: ii) – to the non-synchronous relations between nation-states, capital flows, media effects and human movements. This, in turn, leads to the suggestion that 'the new sociology of diaspora will have to focus on . . . bricolage' or the assemblage of disparate elements by which 'the everyday miracle of reproduction is achieved'. Diasporas, it is felt, 'piece together housing and language, electricity and ethnicity, clothing styles and state entitlements with remarkable energy, in ways tailored to the idiosyncracies of their new locations' (Appadurai and Breckenridge, 1989: iii). The precise links (or discontinuities) between mnemonic lags on the plane of consciousness, the various non-synchronous migratory and technological flows and the activity of bricolage, remains, however, murky.[9] In general there is an emphasis on disjunctures at the level of consciousness (memory), of material reproduction (bricolage) and of techo-economic and demographic movements. Contributing to the same issue of *Public Culture*, Amitav Ghosh also has (territorial) disjuncture in mind when he asserts that the Indian diaspora bears with it an infinitely and differently reproducible 'symbolic spatial structure' which 'since it does not refer to actual places . . . cannot be left behind' (Ghosh, 1989: 76–7).

Appearing alongside Safran's article in the inaugural instalment of *Diaspora* (1991), Roger Rouse's study of the complexities of Aguilillan dispersal takes up the call for a new methodology made by the editors of *Public Culture*. Highlighting the inadequacy of the principal 'socio-spatial images [that] have dominated the modern discourse of the social sciences concerning the people of rural Mexico' (Rouse, 1991: 9), namely 'community' and 'centre-periphery',[10] Rouse contends that these socio-spatial tropes, based on stable correlates (community equals bounded territory, marked commonalities, shared structures and so on) or hierarchical dyads (first and third worlds, rural and urban divides, provincial and metropolitan contexts), are highly unsuitable when discussing the 'transnational migrant circuit' of dispersed Aguilillans (Rouse, 1991: 14). Focusing on the spatially disaggregated cultures of Aguilillans in Mexico as well as the United States, Rouse asserts that the kinship and friendship networks within these mobile micro-sites facilitate 'the continuous circulation of people, money and goods, and information', thereby rendering any static links between this multi-locale community and a centred nation-state largely untenable. Aguilillan migration, he maintains, cannot be thought of in terms of 'a movement between distinct environments'; indeed, 'it is the circuit as a whole rather than any one locale that constitutes the principal setting in relation to which Aguilillans orchestrate their lives' (Rouse, 1991: 13–14). After debunking the older community-oriented framework, Rouse realigns centre–periphery relations along poststructuralist trajectories by insisting on the centre's infiltration of the margin and the margin's of the centre, thereby disrupting both categories around a certain understanding of the border. He claims that foreign finances and cultures are becoming increasingly visible in Mexico; that the Mexican bourgeoisie are operating more easily outside the nation-state and 'within a transnational framework'; that global investments are reshaping the United States' economy hitherto reliant on domestic capital; and that all the customary symptoms of the third world may now be found in the first:

> Extreme poverty, residential overcrowding and homelessness, underground economies, new forms of domestic service, and sweatshops exist side by side with yuppie affluence, futuristic blocks, and all the other accoutrements of high-tech post-industrialism. (Rouse, 1991: 16)

If the third world is present in the first and vice versa, then the border (neither one nor the other) is internal to both and Aguilillans, it seems, perfectly illustrate this sort of split habitation in their circuitous operations. Compellingly, Rouse argues that this circuitous habitation should not be construed to indicate 'an inexorable move towards a new form of sociocultural order' for it does not lead to 'homogenisation or synthesis' or, we might add, to the transformative hybrid schema espoused by the British diasporists: 'Rather, they reflect the fact the Aguilillans see their current lives and future possibilities as involving simultaneous engagements in places associated with markedly different forms of experience' (Rouse, 1991: 14). It is implied that Aguilillans exist in a disjunctive or schizophrenic relationship to the spatial points of their simultaneous engagements. In spite of the ingeniousness of his argument, one is of the mind that Rouse displays too much haste in adopting poststructuralist theoretical approaches to explain the dynamics of Aguilillan society. To put it bluntly: does his theoretical framework critically mediate a new trend in dispersed social relations or fabricate one in line with scholarly fashion?

In their 1993 article, 'Diaspora: Generation and the Ground of Jewish Identity', Daniel and Jonathan Boyarin supply one answer to this question. In an attempt to disrupt the two stable but apparently opposed orders of group identity – one based on genealogical filiations and the other on geographical origins – the Boyarins undertake close recuperative readings of the Letters of Paul and assorted rabbinic Jewish texts while locking metaphysical horns with such poststructuralist thinkers as Jean-François Lyotard and Jean-Luc Nancy. The essay's argument depends on a complex series of moves. First, the Boyarins trace the pros and cons of Pauline and rabbinic Jewish positions; the former position, they maintain, is characterised by the institution of a rift between devalued flesh and exalted spirit. The flesh-world is the site of difference and often an object of disgust while the spirit-world is the realm of redemptive commonality. All human beings, without exception, are extended salvation in the spirit of Christ. However, this doctrine of spiritual sameness and universalism has its dark side in that it has fomented proselytising violence and imperial coercion. The *different* body of the other is subject to punishment so the soul may be admitted into sameness. Rabbinic discourses project a converse scenario in that they favour corporeal self-reflexivity and embodied practices. In the rabbinic scheme, the self is fused indissolubly to the body and related to a single founding ancestor, Abraham, thereby encouraging a kinship-based particularistic identity that takes *positive* difference as its starting point. Rabbinic discourses, however, also betray a dark side. Hitler's assault on German idealism, an idealism based on the Pauline (and Platonic) split between matter and spirit and indicative of the divergent points of spiritual (sublime, eternal) and bodily (vulgar, transient) habitation, may be actually bolstered by the rabbinic position. The Boyarins imply that the Nazi assault on German idealism led to the fierce equating of genealogy (corpus) with territory (terra), culminating in the industrial extermination of Gypsies and Jews. Or, as they put it, 'race and space together form a deadly discourse' (Boyarin and Boyarin, 1993: 714). In its fundamental logic, the Nazi position, drawing as it does on the 'myth of autochthony' (Boyarin and Boyarin, 1993: 699), is not unlike that espoused by Zionists in their summary treatment of the Palestinians. In what marks the second move, the Boyarins proceed to rehabilitate rabbinic Jewish theories of the diaspora, conflating selective aspects of Pauline philosophy on disembodied sameness with Judaic thinking on embodied difference. Exercising exemplary care, they detach kinship from territorial determinism and biological essentialism (since through the mechanism of conversion anybody may nominate Abraham as an ancestor) while placing stress on the rabbinic dissociation of Land (as sacred terrain) from bounded physical territory and the concomitant myths of loyalty and autochthony that sustain it. Citing W. D. Davies, the Boyarins remark that Jews transferred 'loyalty from place to memory of place not only to transcend the loss of Land but to enable the loss of the Land' (Boyarin and Boyarin, 1993: 719). Endorsing this positive view of diasporic dispossession, they recommend disaggregated identities as a solution to post-Enlightenment nationalist frameworks and their multifarious pathological offshoots (Nazism, Zionism and so on). The historical separation of genealogy from territory makes it possible for the Boyarins to think of 'Jewish identity not as a proud resting place (hence not as a form of integrism or nativism) but as a perpetual, creative, diasporic tension'; it follows that the recuperation of genealogical elements such as 'family, history, memory, and practice' occurs in terms other than territory, autochthony and hegemony. In their quest for non-nationalist patterns of differential identity, the Boyarins disconnect kinship from biology, genealogy from territory and autochthony from hegemony. Jewish identity-in-deracination, they insist, points to crossovers rather than natural correspondences since it is founded on non-racial kinship patterns forged in a variety of host territories. That such a situation existed historically for a particular set of Jews cannot be doubted (Jews of pre-1492 Moorish Andalusia are a case in point); the argument becomes less persuasive the moment the Boyarins attempt to turn this fetching idea of diaspora into an edificatory paradigm:

> What we wish to struggle for, theoretically, is a notion of identity in which there are only slaves but no masters, that is, an alternative to the model of self-determination, which is, after all, in itself a western, imperialist imposition on the rest of the world. We propose Diaspora as a theoretical and historical model to replace national self-determination. (Boyarin and Boyarin, 1993: 711)

The trouble with this recommendation is that it seeks to universalise the diaspora condition with the broader aim of bringing to an end all hegemonic forms of social relations and political organisation. While a certain structure of utopianism or a certain politics of transfiguration[11] must always serve as a premonitory ethical indicator (otherwise there is little point to the conscious life-drive as we know it), the above assertion appears to be based on a careless relinquishing of power mechanisms through which communities are imagined and formed. For surely a diaspora articulates its radical potentiality in relation to someone's conception of genealogy-as-territory or with reference to someone's fables of autochthony; power does not disappear simply because we, in our infinite wisdom, seek to will it away. Even if all links between territory, kinship and human groups were to be recast in ideal supra-nationalist or diasporic terms, power and hegemony would continue to infiltrate the nooks and crannies of social, economic and political relations. A subsequent statement concedes precisely this point:

> Diaspora can teach us that it is possible for a people to maintain its distinctive culture, its difference, without controlling land, a fortiori without controlling other people or developing a need to dispossess them of their lands. (Boyarin and Boyarin, 1993: 723)

Diasporas, it seems, must work against certain homogenising tendencies if they are to exercise some sort of ethical privilege over 'other people' of the land. For if sound ethicality demands that these others not be dispossessed of *their lands*, then clearly *they* must be adhering to some variant on the myth of autochthony or to some form of bound seriality. Whether imaginatively or in the context of actual political praxis, any supra-nationalist theory of diaspora will have to learn to figure out how different economies of power, privilege, agency, interpellation and hegemony may be negotiated in the new dispensation. It is certainly not about adopting liquid theories of power-knowledge where perpetually unstable and reversible tides prevent all talk of inequity and oppression or, indeed, about evading or devaluing the complex rhizomes of negotiation that take place in any given polity. As minority groups know only too well, forces of inequity and oppression need no nationalist framework for them to be felt within a diaspora and between diasporas.

Gilroy's *The Black Atlantic: Modernity and Double Consciousness* is, in many ways, an anti-amnesiac account of the complex dimensions of power-knowledge that shaped what is commonly, and indeed erroneously, understood as western modernity. On a fundamental level the work is an eloquent, ambitious and erudite elaboration of Gilroy's scathing critique of the absolutist symmetries of race, nation and culture as advanced in *'There Ain't No Black in the Union Jack'*. Gilroy is profoundly disturbed by lopsided conceptions informing any practice or formation, whether discursive (philosophical, political) or embodied (musical, cultural), since they rely obstinately on the maintenance of a deleterious blindness – often in the face of the obvious – to the constitutive role played by manifold others. Whereas in the earlier book Gilroy focused on disrupting the auto-affective links between Britain and whiteness (and all that that entailed in terms of Anglo-Saxon authenticity, nationalist hegemony, racial genealogy and so on), his preoccupations in *The Black Atlantic* are much more radically transnational or what he himself calls 'outer-national' (Gilroy, 1993: 16).[12] In this second book, Gilroy concentrates on the non-linear commerce of ideas, bodies and cultures that break up absolutist continuities and certainties (of race, nation, morality and culture) by mapping routes connecting the various points of the black Atlantic dispersal. These points include Britain, Europe, the Caribbean, Africa and America. Gilroy's revisionist ploy involves taking an invisible diaspora of blacks (during and after plantation slavery) and evaluating their peripatetic participation in the conceptual and brutally material enterprise known as western modernity. Drawing aside the dusty cobwebs of archival forgetting, he demonstrates how the outer-national is very much part of the inner-national and that, once activated, this memory helps us rethink Habermas's unfinished project of modernity in less hermetic terms. Aided and abetted by chaos physicists, Stuart Hall and Deleuze and Guattari, Gilroy turns away sharply from bounded territories and ethnically defined units in favour of the 'rhizomorphic, fractal structure of the transcultural, international formation' known as the black Atlantic (Gilroy, 1993: 4).

Before arriving at this perspective, he first debunks Eurocentric and Afrocentric viewpoints since, in his opinion, both are anchored to racially polarised yet conceptually congruent understandings of ethnic, cultural and national entities. Gilroy's real gripe is with settled and pure modes of ideological alignment based on *politicised* structures of forgetting. His project is to undertake a recovery of 'the cross catalytic or transverse dynamics' of cultural and political formations (Gilroy, 1993: 4). In Gilroy's mind there can be no real distinction between *suppressio falsi* ('misrepresentation committed') and *suppressio veri* ('representation omitted') so integral to the tradition of modernist historiography because an omitted representation of the other's role in *western* modernity could only be made possible through a distorted portrait of the self's role in the same historical event.[13] And this holds equally for Eurocentrism's *persistently positive* overvaluation of its contributions to modernity and Afrocentrism's dexterous side-stepping of hybrid encounters in its wistful (and post-traumatic) idealisation of pre-Middle Passage Africa. Citing mostly English examples drawn from sundry ideological and historical camps (Edmund Burke, John Ruskin, Thomas Carlyle, Raymond Williams, Edward Thompson, Eric Hobsbawn and so on), Gilroy contends that these thinkers, not barring the obvious disagreements and dissensions among them, draw on a system of referential interiority whereby concepts such as nationalism, nation-state, culture and race are routinely dovetailed *and* silently unhooked from external referents. 'England', he notes dryly, 'ceaselessly gives birth to itself, seemingly from Britannia's head' (Gilroy, 1993: 14). The overt ethno-nationalism of the English right and the quiet crypto-nationalism of the English left are merely symptoms of the broader problem with Enlightenment claims which banish from view those constitutive elements and contradictory others actually propping up congratulatory discourses of rationality, progress, ethics, democracy, liberal humanism, freedom and so on. To underscore the inherent contradictions within the Enlightenment position, Gilroy cites a number of disregarded factors expediting the universal march of reason and modernity. These include an atavistic and barbaric economic system (slave-holding plantation capitalism), the complicity of racial terror and reason in the murder, dispersal, thraldom and dehumanisation of millions of blacks and, somewhat less bleakly, the physical (manual labour) and intellectual contributions – more often than not transmitted in musical, political and aesthetic forms – of blacks to rationalist discourses of freedom, progress and rights.[14] In opposition to Eurocentricism, Gilroy argues for the constitutive internality of blacks banished to the hinterlands of modernity. By implication, he also argues for the referential externality of those seemingly autonomous categories of English and European. Or, as Whisky Sisodia would have it, 'The trouble with the Engenglish is that their hiss hiss history happened overseas, so they dodo don't know what it means' (Rushdie, 1988: 343). By hitching their wagon to an immutable African tradition sundered from modernity, Afrocentricists such as Shahrazad Ali and Molefi Kete Asante merely inhabit the other side of the intellectual divide. They advance a mirror possibility formed in reaction to Eurocentric assumptions. Consequently, they refuse to own up to the structure of 'antagonistic indebtedness' (Gilroy, 1993: 191) underpinning the encounter of blacks with the forces, ideas and institutions of modernity:

> The discourse of tradition is . . . frequently articulated within the critiques of modernity produced by blacks in the West. It is certainly audible inside the racialised countercultures to which modernity gave birth. However, the idea of tradition is often also the culmination, or centre-piece, of a rhetorical gesture that asserts the legitimacy of a black political culture locked in defensive posture against the unjust powers of white supremacy. This gesture sets tradition and modernity against each other as simple polar alternatives as starkly differentiated and oppositional as the signs black and white. In these conditions, where obsessions with origins and myth can rule contemporary political concerns and the fine

> grain of history, the idea of tradition can constitute a refuge . . . Slavery is the site of black victimage and thus of tradition's intended erasure. When the emphasis shifts towards the elements of invariant tradition that heroically survive slavery, any desire to remember slavery itself becomes something of an obstacle. It seems as if the complexity of slavery and its location within modernity has to be actively forgotten if a clear orientation to tradition and thus to the present circumstances of blacks is to be acquired . . . The history of plantations and sugar mills supposedly offers little that is valuable when compared to the ornate conceptions of African antiquity against which they are unfavourably compared. Blacks are urged, if not to forget the slave experience which appears as an aberration from the story of greatness told in African history, then to replace it at the centre of our thinking with a mystical and ruthlessly positive notion of Africa that is indifferent to intraracial variation and is frozen at the point where blacks boarded the ships that would carry them into the woes and horrors of the middle passage. (Gilroy, 1993: 188–9)

Rather than reject the notion of tradition outright, Gilroy seeks to redeploy it in the context of the black Atlantic world – his felicitous epithet for the non-linear, non-absolutist, impure, crisscrossing, non-teleological processes that characterise the black diaspora's[15] contributions to the material, political and philosophical values and ventures of modernity. The middle passage represents the contact zone – or the interstitial and mediating ground – that mongrelises centres and centrisms and spawns supplementary modes (and supplements never travel as the crow flies) that exceed all received polarities:

> The term 'tradition' is now being used neither to identify a lost past nor to name a culture of compensation that would restore access to it. It does not stand in opposition to modernity, nor should it conjure up wholesome images of Africa that can be contrasted with the corrosive, aphasic power of the post-slave history of the Americas and the extended Caribbean. We have already seen . . . that the circulation and mutation of music across the black Atlantic explodes the dualistic structure which puts Africa, authenticity, purity, and origin in crude opposition to the Americas, hybridity, creolisation, and rootlessness . . . We could shift here from the chronotope of the road to the chronotope of the crossroads . . . (Gilroy, 1993: 198–9)

And it is the chronotope (space-time image) of the ship that he fixes on most tenaciously to convey the spatial dynamics of deterritorialisation and reterritorialisation (or the simultaneous occurrence of movements and moorings, routes and roots) at the heart of his magisterial argument.[16] Around the maritime image of the ship, which he calls 'a living, micro-cultural, micro-political system in motion' (Gilroy, 1993: 4), Gilroy draws a nautical cartography that seeks to transversally interweave the various geopolitical terrains of the black Atlantic formation. He asserts that by means of this chronotope 'ideas and activists as well as . . . key cultural and political artefacts' such as 'tracts, books, gramophone records, and choirs' were moved, transmitted and circulated with little regard for discrete categories. He follows up this notion with a discussion of some influential practitioners of the black Atlantic phenomenon, including Martin Robinson Delany, Frederick Douglas, W. E. B. Du Bois, Richard Wright and the Fisk Jubilee Singers. Around these travelling figures he builds his theory of the lateral traffic of bodies, songs, objects, stories and ideas uniting the multiple points washed and webbed by the Atlantic. (By sheer coincidence the Tongan anthropologist, Epeli Hau'ofa, writing in the same year, proposed a similar recuperation of diasporic perspective by declaring that Oceanic islands, cultures, economies and peoples are joined by traditional sea routes and channels rather than forming disjointed 'little' dots in the sea – a belittling perception he attributed to post-contact developmentalism based on identifying and ranking nation-states in rigid economic terms.)[17] Delany's novel *Blake* is analysed, by Gilroy, for its projection of a 'metacultural identity' built on 'alliances above and beyond petty issues like language, religion, skin colour, and to a lesser extent gender' and 'signifies the utopian move beyond ethnicity and the establishment of a new basis for community, mutuality and reciprocity' (Gilroy, 1993: 28); Douglas, whose activism took him to England and Scotland, is hailed as the proponent of a purged ethics of Enlightenment because of his pugnacious critique of reason's complicity with slavery and racial terror; the travelling choir known as the Fisk Jubilee Singers, which drew liberally on the memory of slavery in public performances at multiple European venues, is singled out as an early example of 'distinctive patterns of cross-cultural circulation' that marked the tumultuous but remarkable 'passage of African-American folk forms into the emergent popular-cultural industries of the overdeveloped world' (Gilroy, 1993: 88); and Richard Wright is rescued from his detractors and lauded for his complex and instructive ambivalence towards the legacy of modernity. Above all, however, Gilroy settles on Du Bois' notion of double consciousness for the theoretical hardware with which to convert the spatial dispersal of objects, bodies, cultures and ideas into a diasporic phenomenology. Embodying the subjective split between black and white *and* their inevitable twinning, the concept of double consciousness permits Gilroy to juxtapose spatial-historical disseminations with the dispersed onto psychology of Atlantic blacks who employ tactical detours to avoid the totalising ethno-national statement. Writing about the double subjectivity of postcolonial feminists, Trinh T. Minh-ha perfectly captures the movement Gilroy perceives in Du Bois:

> The moment the insider steps out from the inside she's no longer a mere insider. She necessarily looks in from the outside while also looking out from the inside. Not quite the same, not quite the other, she stands in that undetermined threshold place where she constantly drifts in and out. Undercutting the inside/outside opposition, her intervention is necessarily that of both not quite an insider and not quite an outsider. She is, in other words, this inappropriate other or same who moves about with always at least two gestures: that of affirming 'I am like you' while persisting in her difference and that of reminding 'I am different' while unsettling every definition of otherness arrived at. (Minh-ha, 1990: 374–5)

Notwithstanding the strain of poststructuralist utopianism inherent in such conceptions of identity, it may be possible to envisage how selected groups – black Atlantic thinkers, musicians, postcolonial writers and feminists – *wittingly* dwell in the threshold place where the self never coincides with the same or its other. It is far more difficult, however, to attribute this form of positive hyper-consciousness of the psychic substrata to the hoi polloi, diasporic or otherwise. For, despite all scholarly professions to the contrary, diasporic agents may mobilise against – even while living it – the very processes of hybridity, threshold occupancy and fruitful ambivalence recommended by supra-nationalists of all descriptions. Benedict Anderson's article on long-distance nationalism (Anderson, 1994: 314–27), Vijay Prashad's work on 'Yankee Hindutva' (Prashad, 2000: 134–56); Steven Vertovec's treatment of South Asian religions (Vertovec, 1997: 277–95), Vinay Lal's investigation of the Hindu right's seizure of historiography on the Internet (Lal, 1999: 137–72) and Amit Rai's analysis of Hindu identity construction on electronic bulletin boards (Rai, 1995: 31–57) all testify to diaspora as the smithy where menacing forms of ethno-nationalisms are ritually hammered out. Such reactionary positions, if not openly then covertly, rely on the political disavowal of an ethical future based on recognising the asymmetry of race, ethnicity, nation and culture. Seeking a way out of the manifold crises generated by absolute nationalist categories, Gilroy delivers a warmly upbeat account of the black Atlantic network and suggests that it may serve as a heuristic model for thinking in transversal terms. While his utopian ethicality is necessary, alluring and even praiseworthy (especially as it is built on a non-retributive understanding of the damage, death and suffering engendered by binary forms of instrumental reason), it dangerously underrates the power and currency of the *negative* 'positional cut' against the grain of doubling, syncretism, ambivalence and hybridity. Even a subject alert to the doubling of their consciousness may not chose to live out its complex ethical promise; they may, for a whole plethora of reasons, embrace one or another absolutist option in the face of such ambivalence. An additional problem with the double consciousness paradigm is that it hinges too emphatically on the macro synergy of black and white (though always anti-essentialist) at the expense of internal heterogeneities. Gilroy is aware of the heterogeneous multiplicities that make up the black/white dichotomy, but prefers, barring the rare occasion, to treat them as nominal networks that subsist below the surface of the macro interactions. His own excellent example of the participation of Gandhi and Du Bois at the Universal Races Congress in London (1911) and their different bequests to Martin Luther King and, later, to Nelson Mandela points to a multiplicity of pistons at work in the engine rooms of modernity. To posit Gandhi (and the influence of philosophical Hinduism on his political thought) as just another heterogeneous order in the category of black is to undervalue the intensity of exchanges and influences among non-white cultures. As Avtar Brah writes, 'border crossings do not occur only across the dominant/dominated dichotomy, but . . . equally, there is traffic within cultural formations of the subordinated groups, and . . . these journeys are not *always* mediated through the dominant culture(s)' (Brah, 1996: 209). By which routes, in other words, did Hindu ideas travel from Gandhi to Du Bois to Luther King and then to Nelson Mandela? To what extent were these ideas already modified by Gandhi's training as a lawyer in the liberal tradition? We know Gandhi influenced Du Bois (since the latter actually wrote an article for *Crisis* in 1922 entitled 'Gandhi and India' in support of *satyagraha*), but what was Du Bois' contribution to Gandhi's philosophy?[18] In what measure was Gandhi's radicalism based on his concern for the well-being of indentured workers in South Africa and Fiji? To what degree did this concern enable him to identify with the plight of post-slaves in America and elsewhere? One could reconfigure this set of questions, of course, but it suffices to generate a vision of modernity where the heterogeneities are no longer secondary to the black/white dialectic. The *double* need not be privileged at the expense of the *multiple* in the story of modernity's consciousness. It is this history, Gilroy admits, that is in urgent need of recovery (Gilroy, 1993: 144).

In the opening chapter of *The Black Atlantic*, Gilroy acknowledges a debt to James Clifford's ethnographic work on travelling cultures which advances an 'outer-national transcultural' framework for assessing forms of dissemination and dwelling (Gilroy, 1993: 17). To be sure, it is Clifford who first suggested the use of travelling chronotopes – hotels, ships, buses, airports – to better interpret the hypermobility and hybrid intersection of modern cultural systems:

> In tipping the balance toward travelling as I am doing here, the 'chronotope' of culture (a setting or scene organising time and space in

> representable whole form) comes to resemble as much a site of travel encounters as of residence, less a tent in a village or a controlled laboratory or a site of initiation and inhabitation, and more like a hotel lobby, ship, or bus. If we rethink culture and its science, anthropology, in terms of travel, then the organic, naturalising bias of the term culture – seen as a rooted body that grows, lives, dies, etc. – is questioned. Constructed and disputed historicities, sites of displacement, interferences, and interaction, come more sharply into view. (Clifford, 1992: 101)

Or, as he remarks elsewhere with a certain epigrammatic force, ' "Cultures" do not hold still for their portraits' (Clifford, 1986: 10). In a wide-ranging article published in *Cultural Anthropology* in 1994, Clifford resuscitated and reshaped his ideas on travelling theory within the context of diaspora criticism. Entitled 'Diasporas', the paper proved to be influential because it afforded an intelligent overview of the emergent critical practice. A significant part of Clifford's argument is given over to nutshell summaries of the main theoretical positions and players and there is really no need to revisit them here; it is worth dwelling, however, on his critical asides and the overall picture he paints of the internal debates within diaspora criticism. Clifford does not speak in terms of scenes of exemplification or genres, but he is the first diasporist to properly distinguish between the divergent schools of dual territoriality (Sheffer, Safran and others) and situational laterality (Hall, Gilroy, Rouse and others); he is also one of the earliest critics to point out how various statements from related theoretical paradigms – border, travel, creolisation, migration, transculturation and hybridity – congregate at the scene of the new genre. Right from the outset, Clifford shows resistance to the territorial certitudes informing Safran's conception of the social-psychological attributes that define diasporic identity and consciousness. Declaring that 'there is little room in . . . [Safran's] definition for the principled *ambivalence* about physical return and attachment to land which has characterised much Jewish diasporic experience', he asserts that 'multi-locale diasporas are not necessarily defined by a specific geopolitical boundary' (Clifford, 1994: 304–5). Arguing against teleologies of origin and return and normative models (Jewish and Armenian), he refers to Gilroy's formulation of an Afro-Caribbean-British-American or black Atlantic network where continental Africa is no longer the primary referent. He also cites S. D. Gotein's account of the medieval *geniza* world (linking the Mediterranean countries, North Africa, Arabia and coastal India) in which commerce, travel, familial, cultural and communication networks were determined by the 'lateral axes' of dissemination rather than by diametrical concepts of origin and return, symbolic or otherwise (Clifford, 1994: 315–27). Although Clifford does not express it in such terms, his remarks on the *geniza* world end up describing the extensive 'affiliational structures' (Shapiro, 2000: 80) that governed ancient concepts of citizenship. In any case, his central argument seems to be that, as border communities, diasporas are not necessarily attached to or detached from the macrocosmic nodes of homeland and hostland; they may, in the manner of the *geniza* networks, create microcosmic alliances by attending to 'cultural forms, kinship relations [and] business circuits' or by attaching themselves to religious institutions and cities (Clifford, 1994: 305).

There is much merit in Clifford's resistance to Safran's emphasis on solid and symbolic territorial binaries and his encouragement of the border (decentred, lateral) dimensions to the diaspora experience (though one could justifiably argue that the border itself is a centring motif in his approach); even so, his framework departs only marginally from Safran's in its dogged focus on identity formations, identifications, defining features and distinctive consciousness. Dispersed forms of subjectivity and agency or 'dwelling-in-displacement' (Clifford, 1994: 310) are perceived to be at loggerheads with the assimilationist ideologies of the modern nation-state as well as with ethno-national unities of the autochthonous variety. (It is never made clear why and how the two lines of diasporic subjectivity and national politics intersect in the first place). Clifford adverts more than once to 'transregional identities' when discussing Rouse's observations about spatially disaggregated Aguilillans who maintain filiations through 'telephone circuits'; he talks at length about 'diaspora consciousness' as it is negatively and positively constituted – negatively, he asserts, 'through discrimination and exclusion' and 'positively through identifications with world historical cultural/political forces such as "Africa" or "China"' (Clifford, 1994: 311–12). One suspects that Clifford's understanding of 'world historical cultural/political forces' is not altogether different from Safran's notion of symbolic homelands which are politically and culturally constituted mythic points of reference. Clifford remarks that identifications when hitched to 'a negative experience of racial and economic marginalisation can . . . lead to new coalitions: one thinks of Maghrebi diasporic consciousness uniting Algerians, Moroccans, and Tunisians living in France, where a common history of colonial and neocolonial exploitation contributes to new solidarities' (Clifford, 1994: 312). Such coalitional solidarity based on short-term identifications may – to afford another example of this type of empathetic transference – periodically unite the Australia-based descendants of Indo-Fijian 'coolies' with the progeny of blackbirded 'kanaks' shipped to the sugar cane plantations of Queensland in the nineteenth century. In essence, however, Clifford does not depart significantly from the practice of analysing the group subjectivities of diasporas, albeit he does make a notable intervention by breaking away from ethno territorial models. Instead of thinking in terms of sending and receiving territories, he commends the anti-teleological 'history of displacement, suffering, adaptation, or resistance' (Clifford, 1994: 306) as the target *topos* for the inscription of definitional possibilities about dispersed peoples. What this means in practice is that the geo-psychical entities of homeland and hostland fade as referential points in the analysis of diasporic groups. In short, the conceptual framework need not extend beyond the dynamic situational narratives of dispersal itself. So it turns out that a history of timeless roots predicated on purist cartographies of the homeland is jettisoned in favour of a history of routes *plus* roots, predicated on itineraries of travel, hybrid exchanges and shifting localities. However, as has been noted by Susanne Schwalgin, the stress placed on roots (sedentary existence) in this formulation is largely secondary if not nominal (Schwalgin, 2004: 75). At any rate, the danger here is that the border paradigm starts to resemble a postmodern hyphen adrift from its prefix and its suffix. Yet, despite this drawback, the border approach has the virtue of galvanising debate on the unstable relationship between the classically autocentred and ideologically homogenised nation-state and communities whose affiliations and allegiances may be territorially as well as culturally disaggregated.

Although largely in sympathy with the scene of situational laterality, Clifford is not averse to pointing out the shortcomings of diaspora criticism. He queries celebratory anti-nationalist readings of diaspora cultures and admits that 'some of the most violent articulations of purity and racial exclusivism come from [within] diaspora populations'. However, it is his opinion that these are 'weapons of the (relatively) weak' and fuelled by 'nationalist critical longing and nostalgia or eschatological visions' rather than any ground-level participation in 'nation building – with the help of armies, schools, police, and mass media' (Clifford, 1994: 307). Clifford appears to forget that some diasporas actually encourage and finance hegemonic excesses in their homeland states, as is the case of Hindutva ideologues in North America who lobby actively for Hindu dominance in India. During the tenure of the BJP government (terminated in the elections of 2004), the support of such ideologues had a direct bearing on the utilisation of the repressive arms of the state against minority groups, and against Muslim Indians in particular. Vijay Prashad has shown how cash from the India Development and Relief Fund (IDRF), extracted predominantly from a non-partisan Indian minority in North America, was channelled by Hindutva sympathisers to the Rashtriya Swayamsewak Sangh (RSS) in support of a variety of Hindutva causes (Prashad, 2002: 1).[19] This is not the weapon of the weak, but of the strong against soft minorities in the homeland. In the light of such power differentials, the following caveat by Avtar Brah makes perfect sense:

> The concept of diaspora that I wish to propose . . . is embedded within a multi-axial understanding of power: one that problematises the notion

> of 'minority/majority.' A multi-axial performative conception of power highlights the ways in which a group constituted as a 'minority' along one dimension of differentiation may be constructed as a 'majority' along another. (Brah, 1996: 189)

The trend of inter-diaspora coalitions against minority religious entities in so-called homelands are an additional source of concern. One example is the virtual alliance forged between Hindu and Jewish extremists in North America against the political demands of Palestinians and Kashmiri Muslims.

Clifford's critique is on far better ground when it comes to exposing the dubious hypermobility of *taikongren* or 'astronaut' professionals galvanised by patterns of flexible capital accumulation:

> What is the political significance of this particular crossing-up of national identities by a traveller in the circuits of Pacific Rim capitalism? In light of bloody nationalist struggles throughout the world, the investor's transnational diasporism may appear progressive. Seen in connection with exploitative, 'flexible' labour regimes in the new Asian and Pacific economies, his mobility may provoke a less positive response. The political and critical valance of diasporic subversions is never guaranteed. Much more could be said about class differences among diasporic populations. In distinguishing, for example, affluent Asian business families living in North America from creative writers, academic theorists, and destitute 'boat people' or Khmers fleeing genocide, it will be apparent that degrees of diasporic alienation, the mix of coercion and freedom in cultural (dis)identifications, and the pain of loss and displacement are highly relative. (Clifford, 1994: 312–13)

If class, professional and power differences have to be held in careful tension when considering diasporic forms of travel and settlement (for the boat person travels very differently from the high-flying businessman or academic), then gender and sexual non-equivalences have to be taken into account as well. Clifford makes this point with salutary force in a provocative analysis of the Boyarins' 'Diaspora: Generation and the Ground of Jewish Identity'. He reproaches the authors for verging on 'a [dangerous] level of generality at which the specificities and tensions of diasporist, racialist, class, sex, and gender determinations are erased' (Clifford, 1994: 324). While at it, he also takes the opportunity to remonstrate with Gilroy over his masculinist 'skewing' of 'black Britain in the direction of an Atlantic world with the Afro-Caribbean at its center', 'for focusing on practices of travel and cultural production that have . . . not been open to women' and, perhaps thinking of Mercer's work on queer alliances, 'for not giving sufficient attention to crosscutting sexualities in constituting diasporic consciousness' (Clifford, 1994: 319–20). Most trenchantly, however, Gilroy is taken to task for the normative African American slant in his work:

> *The Black Atlantic* decentres, to a degree, a sometimes normative African *American* history . . . The specific experiences of plantation slavery, emancipation, South–North mobility, urbanisation, and race-ethnic relations have a regional, and indeed a 'national', focus that cannot be subsumed by an Atlanticist map/history of crossings. While the roots and routes of African *American* cultures clearly intersect with the Caribbean, they have been historically shaped into distinct patterns of struggle and marks of authenticity. They are not transnational or diasporic in the same way or to the same degree. Important comparative questions emerge around different histories of travelling and dwelling – specifically by region (for example, 'the South' as a site of diasporic longing), by (neo)colonial history, by national entanglement, by class, and by gender. It is important to specify, too, that black South America and the hybrid Hispanic/black cultures of the Caribbean and Latin America are not, for the moment, included in Gilroy's projections. He writes from a North Atlantic/European location. (Clifford, 1994: 320)

Clifford's critique of a black Atlantic cartography that pays only cursory attention to non-intersections and disjunctions as well as to regional and national differences has to be treated seriously in the light of such studies as Pierre L. Van Den Berghe's 'The African Diaspora in Mexico, Brazil, and the United States' (1976). For all his dated preoccupation with racial typologies, Van Den Berghe is alert to the differences among post-slave black diasporas residing in separate national polities.[20] One could go even further and claim that Van Den Berghe's approach prefigures the standpoint adopted by a number of third scene diasporists (such as Mishra, Gabaccia, Manalansan and Edwards) who caution against an obsessive pursuit of transhistorical and transnational continuities. At any rate, by 1994, the non-teleological, rhizomatic, fractal approach to diaspora criticism had clearly become the ascendant framework. Poststructuralist views of the groundless ground of diasporic subjectivity are standard fare by this time:

> Many appear reluctant to accept the unmappability of liminal spaces, spaces that can be pointed to but not occupied, these spaces of home, travel, and diaspora that are not fully known. As I cannot valorise place, I likewise cannot valorise placelessness. If it is thus that I am suspended between the two, then I cannot retreat to either side or transcend all boundaries. The pain of giving up home is intense, but as home is

> configured against not-home and vice-versa, home is neither absent nor present. Rather, the absence of presence and the presence of absence render home as a potential narrative of incommensurability, a narrative against order. (Puar, 1994: 104)

The trick, it seems, is to occupy the hyphen between a rock and a hard place.

The Third Time-Space: Enter the Border accompanied by the Hyphen

A number of significant studies were put out in 1996, which year turned out to be a fertile one for diaspora criticism. They included R. Radhakrishnan's *Diasporic Meditations*, Avtar Brah's *Cartographies of Diaspora*, Vijay Mishra's 'The Diasporic Imaginary' and '(B)ordering Naipaul: Indenture History and Diasporic Poetics', Gayatri Chakravorty Spivak's 'Diasporas Old and New: Women in the Transnational World', Roland Tolentino's 'Bodies, Letters, Catalogs: Filipinas in Transnational Space', Alan Sinfield's 'Diaspora and Hybridity' and *Displacement, Diaspora and Geographies of Identity* edited by Smadar Lavie and Ted Swedenburg. Although different in their various outlooks and concerns, all these studies are perfectly alert to the lateral 'turn' within diaspora studies. The influence of Clifford's border paradigm (via Gloria Anzaldúa and Roger Rouse) is, for instance, clearly evident in Brah's work. (This is not altogether unexpected as Brah was, at one point, part of a diaspora workshop organised by Clifford in Santa Cruz.) In fact, as I shall undertake to show, by 1996 the dual territorial pillars supporting the ethno-national architrave had collapsed, leaving behind an ungrounded milieu or mid-point. Drawing on Gregory Bateson's work on Balinese culture, Deleuze and Guattari talk of the mid-point as 'a plateau' or 'a continuous, self-vibrating region of intensities whose development avoids any orientation toward a culmination point or external end' (Deleuze and Guattari, 1987: 21–2). This focus on the mid-point gave rise to theories of the hyphen and border. Brah labels the space of the border/hyphen *the* 'diasporic space' (Brah, 1996: 181), which she understands to be a paradoxical non-space or, if you like, a spectral third space (Bhabha, 1990: 207–37). The argument runs as follows. In marking the joint/rupture between one space and another (or several others), the border is clearly devoid of its own space and yet indispensable to spatial categories. It is the function of the border/hyphen to break up structured unities and pre-given stabilities while positing them on every side. Inhabiting the hyphen, one is neither absolutely one thing nor another but constituted multiply in the line of fracture which, as logic would have it, is also the line of suture. From the vantage point of the hyphen/border, one is never solely one thing or another, but altogether something else – a veritable third. This third may be a void as well as a surplus or overdetermination. It is a void in that the border eviscerates all defined spaces (nationalist, cultural, class, gender or otherwise) and a surplus because all spaces jostle for definition at the border. It is because of the capacity of the border to hold such contradictory aspects in tension, yet always deferring them at the point of epiphany, that diasporists have found it, together with the hyphen, a handy metaphor for their theoretical excursions. Consider the following statements by Brah:

> The concept of diaspora signals processes of multi-locality across geographical, cultural and psychic boundaries.
>
> Diasporic identities are at once local and global. They are networks of transnational identifications encompassing 'imagined' and 'encountered' communities.
>
> The concept of diaspora places the discourse of 'home' and 'dispersion' in creative tension, inscribing a homing desire while simultaneously critiquing discourses of fixed origins.
>
> What is at stake is the infinite experientiality, the myriad processes of cultural fissure and fusion that underwrite contemporary forms of transcultural identities.
>
> . . . [T]he concept of diaspora space (as opposed to diaspora) includes the entanglements, the intertwining of the genealogies of dispersion with those of 'staying put'. (Brah, 1996: 193–209)

In their infinite contradictoriness these statements occupy a border or hyphen space which generates the condition for their articulation. Brah presents us with a camouflaged version of *différance* where the pursuit of presence, of the self or its other, of location or dislocation, of fissure or fusion, of national or transnational subjects, is constantly interrupted by the supplement. The drawback is that, unlike Hall, she has no clear sense of the positional cut that interrupts the tidal flow of supplementarity. She does take the disequilibrium of power relations into account but even this is emptied of its ideological content in the deconstructionist spirit of free play. Consider this version of the excerpt I had previously cited with approval:

> A multi-axial performative conception of power highlights the ways in which a group constituted as a 'minority' along one dimension of differentiation may be constructed as a 'majority' along another. And since all these markers of 'difference' represent articulating and performative facets of power, the 'fixing' of collectivities along any singular axis is called seriously into question. (Brah, 1996: 189)

The second part of the excerpt not only negates the perspicacity of the first, but also makes the implementation of any material, ethical or legislative policies on behalf of marginalised subjects wholly contingent on the distribution of power in contextually performed scenes. Since, in all likelihood, the context of such performances may alter from minute to minute, thereby changing the power status of the various participants, there is little point in drawing up policies and plans with regard to any cluster of subjects or with reference to any community. Advantages and disadvantages are endlessly won and lost in the above diagram. In all such extreme celebrations of non-fixity, the *congealed* macro and micro aspects of any given temporality or context are habitually overlooked.

Drawing on Bhabha's concept of the third-time space, Lavie and Swedenburg also employ the border/hyphen image in their ambition to break away from the structuralism of the dual territorial framework. First, however, they take care to sound this warning against any premature 'postmodern celebration of fragmentation . . . in which identity becomes an infinite interplay of possibilities and flavours of the month':

> In this version, culture becomes a multicolored, free-floating mosaic, its pieces constantly in flux, its boundaries infinitely porous. This postmodernist reading of new, emergent time-spaces and the dizzying array of fragments did deconstruct the spatially and temporally conceived hierarchical dualities of center/margin, but at the same time it ignored power relations, the continued hegemony of the center over the margins. Everyone became equally 'different,' despite specific histories of oppressing or being oppressed. (Lavie and Swedenberg, 1996: 3)

It is for this reason that dissident theorists have insisted that 'positions and temporalities of the margins were not only multiple and constantly shifting, but also historically anchored to specific locations that allowed for politicised interventions' (Lavie and Swedenberg, 1996: 4). Such a view appears to make room for Hall's positional cut, but Lavie and Swedenburg quickly dispense with this insight in a subsequent paragraph:

> We wish to stake out a terrain that calls for, yet paradoxically refuses, boundaries, a borderzone between identity-as-essence and identity-as-conjuncture, whose practices challenge the ludic play with essence and conjuncture as yet another set of postmodernist binarisms. This terrain is old in experience and memory but new in theory: a third time-space . . . In this terrain opposition is not only reactive but also creative and affirmative. It involves a guerrilla warfare of the interstices, where minorities rupture categories of race, gender, sexuality, class, nation, and

> empire in the center as well as on the margins. The third time-space goes beyond the old model of culture without establishing another fixity. Yet while the third time-space designates phenomena too heterogeneous, mobile, and discontinuous for fixity, it remains anchored in the politics of history/location. (Lavie and Swedenberg, 1996: 13–14)

Something very odd is happening here. In the above picture the singular subject is split up into univalent (immutably singular) and polyvalent (conjoint with others) forms of subjectivity. The split itself is dynamic in that it fosters the movement from one subjective mode to another and back. Within the dynamism of the split, identified as the border or hyphen, there are provisional and short-lived *moments of settlement* inasmuch as the subject opts for one form of identity or another. This self-identification sometimes favours an essential and sometimes a composite self. The drawback is that these moments of settlement are viewed in predominantly sanguine and even utopian terms. No matter what the positional cut in identity, the subject always has an ethical upperhand vis-à-vis others. In the identity-as-conjuncture scenario the diasporic subject, in its multiple identifications, is assumed to promote a revolutionary alternative to the stabilities of ethnic and nationalist identity formations. In the reverse scenario of identity-as-essence, the same subject draws on strategic essentialisms (not unlike indigenous minorities the world over) to upset hegemonic discourses – hence an implied ethics of essentialism. The trouble with this account is that it fails to entertain the possibility that the negative positional cut may occur over a longer duration. What if we were to think of the movement between one identity and another in terms of the *longue durée*, which is Fernand Braudel's conception of staggered duration or what he calls 'the slow pace of change and transfer' (Braudel, 1975: 773), carefully differentiated from clock time and calendars? What happens to ethics, in other words, when the diaspora espouses identity-as-essence over a protracted period in order to wrest territory and hegemony from other groups? Is it not true that identity-as-essence nurtured continuously over a significant duration encouraged the bloody fulfilment of the Zionist dream of Israel and the violent dislodgment of Palestinians? Lavie and Swedenberg are not completely oblivious to this idealising of the third time-space, for at one point they concede that 'we are really speaking of some utopian space whose future outlines we can only vaguely begin to make out' (Lavie and Swedenberg, 1996: 17).

One of the persistent dilemmas confronting diaspora criticism is how to configure dispersed subjectivity as hybrid, liminal, border and hyphenated without recourse to the strategy of consigning non-diasporic groups to imaginary domains of non-liminality, non-hybridity, non-heterogeneity and so on. Then again, if non-diasporic subjects are capable of the above type of diasporisation, then where does this leave the diasporic subject or, for that matter, the whole enterprise of diaspora criticism? By ascribing to the diaspora a third time-space, that is 'the borderzone between identity-as-essence and identity-as-conjuncture' (Lavie and Swedenburg, 1996: 17), diasporists withhold from non-diasporic subjects the experience of similar on-the-verge critical subjectivities obtained in contextually driven moments of epiphany. If we were to take the threshold of diasporic enclave spaces (restaurants, video outlets, cinemas, meeting halls, grocery stores, religious institutions and so forth) within the bourgeois nation-state as inscribing the hyphenated third time-space, then *any* subject inhabiting that zone would be susceptible to the experience of the border flux that constitutes identity-as-essence on the one hand and identity-as-conjuncture on the other. My point is that the threshold marks two differently coded spaces, one micro-cultural and the other macro-national, and interpellation will depend on how one subjectively negotiates the values within these spaces. Many diasporists, to their credit, are aware that while the border promotes democratic porosity and fusion, it also facilitates reactionary identity formations, identifications, dangerous disavowals of otherness (the anti-hybrid values of the Muslim patriarch married to an English woman, as depicted in the film *East Is East*, comes to mind) and nostalgias for racially pure domains.[21] Drawing on Amit S. Rai's research on the virtual web, Mishra points to six site 'postings [that] indicate a desire to construct India in purist [Hindu] terms' (Mishra, 1996: 424). Thinking along the same lines, Vertovec asserts that 'right-wing religious organisations in the homeland are known to gain much support from overseas populations: most notably Hindus, through the Vishwa Hindu Parishad (and, by extension, the Bharatiya Janata Party or BJP) in India, and Muslims, through Jamaat-i-Islami, a prominent Islamicist political party in Pakistan' (Vertovec, 1997: 280). Media accounts (never to be taken without the proverbial pinch of salt) regularly claim that the shadowy cells of Al Qa'ida are dispersed in several overdeveloped nation-states and made up of *jihadis* recruited from various Muslim diasporas. A recent column in a right-wing Australian newspaper cites Bruce Hoffman of the Rand Corporation telling his audience that 'al-Qaida has become something akin to a networked transnational constituency rather than a monolithic terrorist organisation' (*The Australian*, 15 September 2005). Whatever their individual merit, these examples alert us to the danger of ignoring the principle of *cognitive* congealment in identity-talk whereby the subject or collectivity may get off at the identity-as-essence station before the hybrid train can chug along to identity-as-conjuncture.[22]

Contemplating the nexus-cum-rupture paradox that informs the relationship between 'incompletely nationalised' diasporas (Appadurai, cit. Chuh, 1996: 93) and bourgeois nation-states, Mishra evolves a theory of diasporic subjectivity by attending to what he calls 'the semantics of the hyphen' (Mishra, 1996: 433). Sensibly restricting his analysis to the citizen-subject type, he builds his argument on the premise that the subject's unresolved position in relation to the homeland and the hostland creates a severed/sutured identity not dissimilar to the third time-space:

> Within a nation-state citizens are always unhyphenated, that is, if we are to believe what our passports say about us. In actual practice the pure, unhyphenated generic category is only applicable to those citizens whose bodies signify an unproblematic identity of selves with nations. For those of us who are outside of this identity politics, whose corporealities fissure the logic of unproblematic identification, plural/multicultural societies have constructed the impure genre of the hyphenated subject. (Mishra, 1996: 433)

Mishra cites Žižek to justify his remark about the 'unproblematic identification' of citizens who require 'no particular verification of this "Thing" called "Nation." For this group the "nation" simply *is* (beyond any kind of symbolisation)' (Mishra, 1996: 423). This Lacanian loss of selfhood through absorption into the imaginary realm of the nation is a condition available only to those citizens that view themselves as belonging to the foundational community ruled by the 'idea of "homogeneous, empty time"' (Anderson, 1991: 24) and not to those groups that bear in body (clothing, speech, culinary habits and so on) and in mind (corporeally 'here' but neurologically 'elsewhere') the markers of difference, creating the symbolic fracture. A theoretical difficulty arises from the above argument. How is it possible for the foundational citizen to achieve an imaginary identification with the nation thing in the space of the diasporic other without experiencing a rupture from the homogeneous, empty time of the imaginary? To put it differently: if the other is here in the same 'imaginary' space that I inhabit, then where am I? Does not the act of posing this question signal a loss of the imaginary order? Am I then outside the imaginary space and so in the space of the heterogeneous, brimming time of the symbolic? Surely this is the abiding contradiction of any nationalistic avowal of racial homogeneity – that it must be predicated on its loss. Stumbling upon the Patels at their dinner in the family-run motel, the narrator of Bharati Mukherjee's 'Loose Ends', a hitman yearning for a mythically pure America, maliciously admits to the loss of this imaginary order: 'They look at me. A bunch of aliens and they stare like I'm the freak' (Mukherjee, 1988: 52).

One of the most incisive and trenchant rejoinders to the third time-space and its depoliticised projection of liminal subject positions is tendered by R. Radhakrishnan in *Diasporic Meditations: Between Home and Location*. Claiming that 'the diaspora does not constitute a pure heterotopia informed by a radical countermemory', Radhakrishnan cautions against 'the temptation to read the diaspora as a convenient metaphorical/tropological code for the unpacking of certain elitist intellectual agendas' (Radhakrishnan, 1996: 173). In this, at least, he is recalling Rey Chow's perceptive critique of the 'masked hegemony' (Chow, 1993: 118) of diaspora intellectuals domiciled in the first world:

> The space of 'third world' intellectuals in diaspora is a space that is removed from the 'ground' of earlier struggles that were still tied to the 'native land'. Physical alienation, however, can mean precisely the intensification and aestheticisation of the values of 'minority' positions that had developed in the earlier struggles and that now, in 'third world' intellectuals' actual circumstances in the West, become defunct. The unself-reflexive sponsorship of 'third world' culture, including 'third world women's culture,' becomes a mask that conceals the hegemony of these intellectuals over those who are stuck at home. (Chow, 1993: 118)

According to Chow, speaking as the other on behalf of an *elsewhere* other (who fails to equate spatially, historically or materially with the self) poses a special problem that diasporic intellectuals have to address or accept complicity in the very processes of hegemony they are seeking to upset. Radhakrishnan has Chow's caveat in mind, but goes much further in his critique:

> The diaspora . . . offers exciting possibilities for the intellectual who has always dreamed of pure spaces of thought disjunct from ideological interpellations and identity regimes. The diaspora as the radical non-name of a non-place empowers the intellectual to seek transcendence through exile and an epiphanic escape from the pressures of history. As such, the diaspora holds possibilities of a 'virtual theoretical consciousness' sundered from the realities of a historical consciousness . . . Thus, given the alienated spatiality of the diaspora, one can both belong and not belong to either one of the two worlds at the same time. To the diasporic sensibility, it is easy to practice a perennial politics of transgression in radical postponement of the politics of constituency. To put it differently, travelling or peripatetic transgressions in and by themselves begin to constitute a politics of difference or postrepresentation. Belonging nowhere and everywhere at the same time, the diasporic subject may well attempt to proclaim a heterogeneous 'elsewhere' as its actual epistemological home. (Radhakrishnan, 1996: 173)

Under assault here is not only the understanding of home as a non-territorial abstraction (rendered variously in Hall's idea of belonging to several and yet no one home in particular, in Puar's notion of placeless place and in Brah's homing desire without an object), but the very conception of the third time-space as a 'perennial moment of crisis' (Radhakrishnan, 1996: 174). A crisis-oriented view of the subject deprives it of a grounded politics of interpellation and constituency. The material or everyday realities of deracination are, for Radhakrishnan, always stubbornly ethno-political. Noting that the 'liminal, phantasmal, borderline phenomenology' slips too easily and vacantly into discourses of post-representation, he urges the adoption of 'multidirectional, heterogeneous modes of representation' to counter fanciful diagrams of 'unsituated anarchism' (Radhakrishnan, 1996: 175) and subjective indeterminacy:

> Whereas the term 'diaspora' indicates a desire to historicise the moment of departure as a moment of pure rupture both from 'the natural home' and 'the place of residence,' the ethnic mandate is to live 'within the hyphen' and yet be able to speak. (Radhakrishnan, 1996: 175–6)

An acknowledgement of the subject's capacity to speak the hyphen, then, returns the political element to diaspora criticism. But there is more:

> The repoliticisation of the diaspora has to be accomplished in two directions simultaneously. First of all . . . diasporic communities need to make a difference within their places/nations, cultures of residence. This cannot be achieved unless and until the metropolitan location is understood as problematic and, in some sense, quite hostile to 'ethnicity.' The use of location by diasporic/ethnic . . . communities has to be 'oppositional.' If 'ethnicity' is to be realised both as an 'itself' and as a powerful factor in the negotiation of the putative mainstream identity, it must necessarily be rooted in more than one history: that of its present location and its past. I am not suggesting for a moment that the ethnic self indulge in uncritical nostalgia or valorise a mythic past at the expense of the all-too-real-present, but rather that it engage in the critical task of reciprocal invention. Particularly, in the American context, it is of the utmost importance that a variety of emerging postcolonial-diasporic ethnicities (Asian-American, Latina, Chinese-American, Chicano, and so forth) establish themselves 'relationally' with the twin purpose of affirming themselves and de-mystifying the so-called mainstream . . . These 'emerging relational ethnicities' may be said to be interpellated in more than one direction: there is (1) the affirmation of 'identity politics' inherent in each historically discrete ethnicity; (2) the relational cultivation of each ethnicity in response to other coeval ethnicities; (3) achieving common (and not identical) cause with those deconstructive metropolitan identity productions that stem from within dominant histories; and (4) opposing perennially dominant historiographies that resist change and ethnopolitical persuasion. (Radhakrishnan, 1996: 176)

Radhakrishnan may be vulnerable to the accusation that he is reverting to a dual territorial typology on the basis of the above recommendation. After all, he freely adverts to present and past territories, to discrete ethnicities and, in principle if not by default, assumes the autonomy of the classical bourgeois nation-state. As such he skirts around one of the more radical strands holding together the exemplars of the second scene, that is, to their dogged resistance to the containment of subjectivity and citizenship within bounded geopolitical terrains. His call for a politics of solidarity among the various diasporas in the hostland also puts an exceedingly high premium on the ethnic factor (as distinct from such factors as gender, sexuality, class, religion, language and profession) while charting a programme that is perhaps too ingenuously cheerful in its motivations. Hoped-for solidarities are all very well, but what about the persistent realities and bitter politics of antagonisms within diasporas? To take a case in point: Serbs and Croats in Australia express hostility, even acrimony, towards each other because of Balkan politics while showing little opposition to mainstream positions and perspectives in their hostland. Moreover, since ethno-national categories are a part of the essentialising discursive regimes of North America, as Radhakrishnan openly acknowledges, why settle for the ground-rules of the mainstream in the first instance?[23] Despite these reservations, it is conceivable that the concept of 'reciprocal invention' (which affords scope for imaginary projections) along the juxtaposed axes of past and present histories, together with the call for inter-diaspora coalitions, holds out the promise of an American nation-state not hijacked by dominant values and mainstream agendas.

Summing up his argument, Radhakrishnan suggests that dispersed ethnopolitical cultures, bearing the burden and memory of several histories, would do well to cultivate alliances with other similar deterritorialised and deracinated cultures so as to remould the contours of mainstream American. With typical pluck, Radhakrishnan is recommending no less than the activation of what Lisa Lowe describes as 'the unrepresentable histories of situated embodiment that contradict the abstract form of citizenship' (Lowe, 1996: 2). Lowe notes that culture is usually experienced in two incommensurable ways. It is lived in the present as an imagined communion with the national collective and its values, and in the past, which haunts the embodied subject with its flashes and narratives of indissoluble difference (Lowe, 1996: 2–3). For Radhakrishnan, this unrepresented ethnic past has to find representation in a reimagined communion with the national collective and its values, so as to facilitate material changes in the latter. If in theory this sounds acceptable, it is less so in practice. What if the ethnic past contained ethically regressive practices, such as a *panchayat*-style jurisprudence that condemned a woman to gang-rape because of her brother's transgressions with a high-caste woman?

I refer, of course, to the notorious case in Pakistan where a woman, Muktar Mai, 'was gang-raped in 2002 on the orders of village elders as punishment for her brother's alleged affair with a high-caste woman' (*The Age*, 17 September 2005). No doubt this is an extreme example, but it does invite us to keep in mind the impasse wherein no encounter is possible because of absolutely incommensurable positions, cultures and practices. Lyotard calls this sort of impasse the *différend*; he observes that '[a] case of *différend* between two parties takes place when the "regulation" of the conflict which opposes them is done in the idiom of one of the parties while the injustice suffered by the other is not signified in that idiom' (Lyotard, 1984: 5). There is, in other words, no scope for transportability between idioms. Finally, however, even though he rejects apolitical liminality of the postmodern variety and the subject-in-perpetual-crisis thesis, Radhakrishnan prefers to think in terms of crabwise alliances rather than discrete bipolar interactions.

Of the three scenes of exemplification that make up the genre, the key concepts of the scene of situational laterality have found most favour with latter-day diasporists. This scene's suspicion of stabilities, aggregations and commensurabilities, both at the level of the subject as well as the nation-state, has won over a whole generation of scholars trained in poststructuralist modes of analysis. With a nod in the direction of Appadurai, Michael Shapiro, for example, asserts that the 'increasing movements of bodies, a growing global diaspora – of refugees, exiles, aliens, migrant workers and intellectuals – has encouraged post-national, non-territorial forms of affiliation and solidarity' whereby 'populations affiliate themselves translocally – in other places and times' (Shapiro, 2000: 83). Brian Keith Axel, too, is unflinchingly anti-territorial when he moots the idea of the '*diasporic imaginary*'[24] to replace the 'analytic model of place' – the obligatory straw target for aspiring diasporists by this stage. Writing some ten years after the publication of *The Black Atlantic*, Axel claims, rather post-maturely, that his framework would 'account for the creation of the diaspora, not through a definitive relation to place, but through formations of temporality, affect, and corporeality'; that is to say, the 'diasporic imaginary . . . does not act as a new kind of place of origin but indicates a process of identification generative of diasporic subjects' (Axel, 2002: 412). In a discerning essay called 'Interrogating Diaspora: Wang Gungwu's *Pulse*', Philip Holden conveys a similar anti-territorial sentiment but with greater lucidity and persuasion:

> The production of national culture may . . . cauterise and seal off cultural flows which existed before the nation, and which continue to exert powerful forces: the use of a national culture as an explanatory framework, especially in the context of a past marked by the disruption of

> colonialism, may result in a neglect of the importance of migrant or regional cultural forms. Thus if the creation of specifically national cultural traditions now holds less appeal, diaspora seems to answer a ready need – it looks beyond the nation in a world that we perceive as increasingly globalised. (Holden, 2002: 106)

Thinking along the same lines, but targeting the Portuguese diaspora in Australia and Canada, Edite Niovo sets her sight on boundary-breaching transnational flows as expressed through language systems and affects. Citing David Morley's *Home Territories: Media, Mobility and Identity*, she comments that 'a homeland need not necessarily be a physical place. It can just as well be a rhetorical territory, mediated through language and sentiment.' She goes on to state that '[s]uch alternative conceptualisations of "home" find a strong resonance in the Portuguese diaspora' (Niovo, 2002: 257). Taking as his theme 'German-Language Diasporas', Dirk Hoerder also has laterality in mind when he declares that the 'concept of dispersed, diasporic settlement across vast social spaces, with its emphasis on networking and on relational approaches, challenges earlier conceptions of enclosed groups and settler colonies . . .' (Hoerder, 2002: 9). All in all, then, the lateral axes argument, where the emphasis is fundamentally on longitudinal weavings rather than on national autonomy or cultural insularity, prevails among diasporists schooled in post-structuralist modes of analysis.

Of these latter-day diasporists, Stanley Tambiah looms large in the picture because of his attempt to cobble together a methodology that includes elements from the first *and* the second scenes of exemplification. In an article that appeared in *Daedalus* entitled 'Transnational Movements, Diaspora, and Multiple Modernities', Tambiah notes that diasporas evince 'three forms of consciousness regarding their existential circumstances' (Tambiah, 2000: 170). One is the result of vertical networks and two of lateral ones:

> Vertical networks concern the relations and negotiations through which immigrants attempt to secure their existence in host societies. There are two orders of lateral networks: one is concerned with maintaining, reinforcing, and extending relationships with immigrants' communities of origin ('home communities'); the other maps the networking that transcends the borders of both the countries and states of origin and resettlement that I label it the transnational global network. (Tambiah, 2000: 170)

The vertical networks proposition has been developed by several diasporists, and perhaps most evocatively by Radhakrishan. It seeks to examine the shifting attitudinal ground of ethnic diasporas in their places of translocation, and the way these shifts impinge variously on their exclusivist practices, on inter-diaspora coalitions, on strategic alliances with the empowered and on nation-state politics in general. Verticality, then, refers to the multitudinous ways in which ethnic diasporas seek to negotiate subjectivity and ideology within a bounded territory. Tambiah believes that diasporists pay little heed to the empirical aspects of these intra-national networks:

> We need to know better than we do today how diaspora communities placed in different host environments voluntarily form, or are constrained to form, spatial and social enclave communities; how they coalesce to resist discrimination and prejudice when they face it; how they develop their economic niches and specialise in the businesses and services in which they are competitive; and how in time they become effective voting banks when they become eligible to participate in local, state, and national politics and generate their own politicians, mediators, and political bosses.
>
> In studying these dynamics, it is pertinent to note that, for any diasporic community, the host society in question is not a single homogeneous entity but is itself segmented and stratified according to social class and other criteria; it also contains other immigrant communities that are involved in the politics of finding and negotiating their niches in the vertical framework. This vertical frame thus deals with the exchanges and exclusions between these various segments, consisting of resistance and rejections as well as cooperation and incorporation, fights against discrimination, and eagerness to take advantage of opportunities. (Tambiah, 2000: 170–1)

All this is very well, but what about the absence of coalescence within diasporas? Some diasporic gays and lesbians, it is possible to contend, may find an ethnically based heteropatriarchal order more acutely discriminatory and disempowering than inter-ethnic homosexual networks and alliances. Aside from the usual segmentations and stratifications within the diaspora (according to gender and other social categories), it is also essential to consider – as has been duly pointed out by a number of third scene participants – historical divisions within systems of dissemination as well as discrepancies within cultural forms evolving at spatially dispersed points. Just as nineteenth-century indentured coolies are unlike the professional Indian migrants of today, including those labelled 'cyber coolies' (or contracted information technology sojourners), so the cultural practices of Trinidadian Indians may not exactly resemble those of their counterparts in Fiji or Mauritius.

The first of Tambiah's lateral networks concerns the diaspora's relationship with its host and home countries and, therefore, presents nothing less than a dual territorial framework for discussing such interactions. It is his view that the connection with the home country takes place through cultures of remittance and investment, returning home to marry, undertaking special pilgrimages, helping in the upkeep of ancestral sites or even financing local festivals. The host country, conversely, becomes the site for hosting 'cultural groups, musical and dramatic ensembles and troupes', not to mention 'charismatic holy men and women' who come to reinforce the diaspora's pride in their ethnic identity and unparalleled civilisation (Tambiah, 2000: 171). Tambiah, it goes without saying, has the professional Indian diaspora in mind, but treats its experience as representative of diasporas in general. His understanding of hostland interaction is also somewhat perturbing. As a rule, hostland interaction would refer to the diaspora's relationship with hegemonic subjects, cultures and politics at the site of its dispersal. Cultural incursions from the home territory would, I imagine, constitute homeland interactions. That said, how would one describe lateral networks in this first instance? According to the spatial cartography drawn by, among others, Gilroy, Rouse and Clifford, lateral networks are strictly at odds with the dual territorial framework which renders diasporic exchanges in linear, oppositional and dichotomous terms rather than in terms of spatial detours and peripatetic itinerancy. It is Tambiah's second lateral networks framework or the 'lateral transnational global networks' that actually accords with Gilroy's concept of transversal movements across spatially dispersed points:

> The actors in this arena, be they individuals, families, groups, or business enterprises, for whole national and state boundaries as such are irrelevant or secondary for certain purposes, constitute crisscrossing and intersecting networks that Ulf Hannerz has dubbed 'the global ecuneme.' This, the ability and incentive to circulate between these sites, to exchange money, goods, and information, and to conclude marriage contracts and exchanges pose for anthropologists the task of mapping this extended, sprawling, and yet connected social world. Thus, transnational connections linking diasporas need not be articulated primarily through a real or symbolic homeland. Decentred, lateral connections may be as important as those formed around the teleology of return. (Tambiah, 2000: 172)

A few pages later, Tambiah draws on Anita Khandelwal's work on virtual nationalism to demonstrate 'how each of the vertical and lateral networks . . . is simultaneously used to promote and enact 'different kinds of nationalism'' (Tambiah, 2000: 175), but fails to tackle the more urgent issue of the perceived incompatibility of the three frameworks. How is it possible to marry a vertical framework, which assumes a certain intactness and insularity of the host nation-state in spite of inner dissensions, fissures, disgruntlements and debates, with a lateral framework fundamentally opposed to the idea of linear routes as well as bounded territories, cultures and subjects? Likewise, what is the precise impact of complex hostland engagements recorded in the vertical axis upon the home territory and its politics? Is the home country here an emotional domain or an intact nation-state with its own vertical networks? If the former, then what are the links between affective categories and long-distance nationalism? (Or is the affect sundered from actual participation in the material or political affairs of the home country?) If the latter, then how is the diaspora situated between the two vertical networks? Does it use the advantages (financial, political, psychological and so on) gained in one nation-state to interfere, for better or for worse, in the affairs of the other? Further, how is it possible to talk in territorial terms (where the ethno-national diaspora is wedged between two intact nation-states) *and* in terms of peripatetic mobility where no political territory has a prior or constitutive presence for the diaspora? If it is true that some diasporas establish relationships in terms other than the national or ethnic, what sort of actual or utopian promise does this hold for the post-national future? Paradoxes and aporias are by no means alien to diaspora criticism, but the success of any methodology, it has to be said, finally depends on the dexterity with which one is able to sift through such anomalies.

In his 1994 essay, Clifford briefly mentions the distinction Mishra draws between diasporas of the border and diasporas of exclusivism in his analysis of dispersed Indians. At this point in the genre's development the lateral or post-structuralist approach, based on non-territorial alliances, micro filiations and hybrid identities, had clearly gained the upper hand over the structuralism of the dual territorial framework. Even as the stars of the second scene shone brightly, some diasporists started to express alarm at the overall lack of any serious archival interrogation of specific diasporas. Apart from the usual suspects of class, race, gender and sexuality, it was felt that historical discontinuities within specific diasporas were routinely overlooked in favour of ahistorical alliances and spatially dispersed coalitions. It was no longer simply a matter of 'denying the possibility of common themes, motives and practices within diaspora history' (Gilroy, 1987: 158), but of paying heed to those histories, narratives and practices that told a different story. It was also suggested that the comparative approach, with its preference for analogies and juxtapositions, left little room for historically informed studies of single diasporas. Consequently, there was an urgent need to attend to the specific archives of dispersion and relocation. It is this intimate focus on discontinuities in the narrative of specific diasporas that engendered the third scene of exemplification. This scene, which I have dubbed the scene of archival specificity, is the subject of my next chapter.

Notes

1. Although the present 'mention' does have the effect of turning it into a proto-generic instance.
2. The 'identity of passions' idea was first mooted by Ralph Ellison in *Shadow and Act*: 'It is not culture which binds the peoples who are of partially African origin now scattered throughout the world, but an identity of passions. We share a hatred for the alienation forced upon us by Europeans during the process of colonisation and empire and we are bound by our common suffering more than by our pigmentation. But even this identification is shared by most non-white peoples, and while it has political value of great potency, its cultural value is almost nil' (Ellison, 1967: 263–4).
3. Hall and others deal with the question of bricolage, the seemingly random assemblage of social forms, and homology, the suggestive fit between values, styles and practices, in *Resistance through Rituals:Youth Subcultures in Post-war Britain* (Hall and Jefferson, 1976).
4. Derrida observes that 'the trace is not only the disappearance of an origin . . . it means that the origin did not even disappear, that it was never constituted except reciprocally by a nonorigin, the trace, which thus becomes the origin of the origin. From then on, to wrench the concept of the trace from the classical scheme, which would derive it from a presence or from an originary nontrace and which would make of it an empirical mark, one must indeed speak of an originary trace or arche-trace. Yet we know that that concept destroys its name and that, if all begins with the trace, there is above all no originary trace' (Derrida, 1976: 61).
5. In *Discipline and Punish:The Birth of the Prison*, Foucault observes that the soul serves as a 'reality-reference' on which 'various concepts have been constructed and domains of analysis carved out: psyche, subjectivity, personality, consciousness, etc.; on it have been built scientific techniques and discourses, and the moral claims of humanism' (Foucault, 1991b: 29–30).
6. Edward Said's concept of Orientalism both designates and critiques the western project of representing others – Orientals – supposedly incapable of representing themselves. (See Said, 1978.)
7. Explaining his use of the phrase 'imagined community', Anderson remarks: 'It is imagined because the members of even the smallest nation will never know most of their fellow-members, meet them, or even hear of them, yet in the minds of each lives the image of their communion' (Anderson, 1991: 6)
8. This is Bakhtin's phrase for fundamental categories such as '[a]uthorial speech, the speeches of narrators, inserted genres, the speech of characters . . . with whose help heteroglossia [*raznorečie*] can enter the novel' (Bakhtin, 1981: 263). The overall suggestion is that certain conceptual unities have to be posited in order to speak of destabilising multiplicities.
9. Appadurai addresses this issue more fully in 'Disjuncture and Difference in the Modern Cultural Economy' (1990). I discuss this article at some length in the fifth chapter.

10. The first, 'community', is an 'abstract expression of an idealised nation-state' and 'has been used concretely at numerous levels, from the peasant village to the nation itself'. It is predicated on 'a discriminable population with a single, bounded space – a territory or place' which exhibits a 'multiplicity of similar actions' and shares an 'internally consistent set of rules, values, or beliefs'. Consequently, 'the heterogeneities and complexities of the worlds we actually encounter' are 'either superficial interactions between distinct communities or transitional moments in the movement from one form of integrity and order to another'. The centre–periphery image, on the other hand, 'suggests that differences are organised concentrically around a dominant core'; that 'the centre exercises a privileged capacity to shape outcomes, whether it is extending its influence to the margins or moulding people from the periphery who enter its terrain'; and that 'fields ordered in this way are autonomous: each peripheral site is oriented to a single centre and each centre is independent of all others at the same level' (Rouse, 1991: 9–10).
11. I have borrowed the phrase from Gilroy who, in turn, borrows it from Seyla Benhabib. The politics of transfiguration invokes 'utopian references' to indicate 'the emergence of qualitatively new desires, social relations, and modes of association within the racial community of interpretation and resistance *and* between that group and its erstwhile oppressors' (Gilroy, 1993: 37).
12. Gilroy employs 'outer-national' in two specific senses. The first relates to the unbounded practices of black Atlantic thinkers, writers and musicians, while the second refers to critical projects that seek to go beyond nation-based or bounded accounts of ideas, politics and cultures.
13. Perry Anderson attends to the distinction between *suppressio falsi* and *suppressio veri* in a powerful essay on Andreas Hillgruber in *A Zone of Engagement* (Anderson, 1992: 180).
14. Gilroy notes that 'interest in the social and political subordination of blacks and other non-European peoples does not generally feature in contemporary debates around the philosophical, ideological, or cultural content and consequences of modernity. Instead, an innocent modernity emerges from the apparently happy social relations that graced post-Enlightenment life in Paris, Berlin, and London. These European locations are readily purged of any traces of the people without history whose degraded lives might raise awkward questions about the limits of bourgeois humanism' (Gilroy, 1993: 44).
15. Like Homi Bhaba, Gilroy understands 'black' as an ambivalent not absolute category.
16. 'How could movements of deterritorialisation and processes of reterritorialisation not be relative, always connected, caught up in one another? The orchid deterritorialises by forming an image, a tracing of a wasp; but the wasp reterritorialises on that image. The wasp is nevertheless deterritorialised, becoming a piece in the orchid's reproductive apparatus. But it reterritorialises the orchid by transporting its pollen. Wasp and orchid, as heterogeneous elements, form a rhizome. It could be said that the orchid imitates the wasp, reproducing its image in a signifying fashion (mimesis, mimicry, lure, etc.). But this is true only on the level of the

strata – a parallelism between the two strata such that a plant organisation on one imitates an animal organisation on the other. At the same time, something else entirely is going on: not imitation at all but the capture of code, surplus value of code, an increase in valence, a veritable becoming, a becoming-wasp of the orchid and a becoming-orchid of the wasp. Each of these becomings brings about the deterritorialisation of one term and the reterritorialisation of the other; the two becomings interlink and form relays in a circulation of intensities pushing the deterritorialisation even further' (Deleuze and Guattari, 1987: 10).

17. Epeli Hau'ofa, 'Our Sea of Islands', in Hau'ofa et al. (1993).
18. Bill V. Mullen traces the Gandhi–Du Bois connection in a fine article entitled 'Du Bois, *Dark Princess*, and the Afro-Asian International' (Mullen, 2003: 218–39).
19. Since I have cited the electronic version of the article, the page number is likely to be different in the hard version. For the electronic version, see: http://www.hinduonnet.com/fline/fl1925/stories/20021220005302800.htm.
20. Van Den Berghe observes: 'The contrasting experience of Afro-Americans in various parts of the western Hemisphere has been a concern of scholars for several decades. Tannenbaum . . . stressed the difference between the status of slaves in the Latin American colonies and the English ones, attributing the divergence to contrasting legal traditions in the concept of slavery, to differences in past history of contact with darker groups, and to religious distinctions between Protestantism and Catholicism. Wagley and Harris presented a typology of intergroup relations in the Americas, suggesting that the criterion of group membership differs in various countries. In Anglo-America, the criterion of ancestry is paramount: a "black" North American is defined as such if he has any African ancestry at all. Luso-America, by contrast, stresses physical appearance rather than ancestry, giving rise to a multiplicity of phenotypes rather than a sharp dichotomy. Finally, Hispano-America adopts almost purely sociocultural (and especially linguistic) tests of group membership' (Van Den Berghe, 1976: 531).
21. Mishra, for instance, claims that '[u]nder a gaze that threatens their already precarious sense of the "familiar temporariness," diasporas lose their enlightened ethos and retreat into discourses of ethnic purity that are always the "imaginary" underside of their own constructions of the homeland' (Mishra, 1996a: 426).
22. For an extended analysis of the cognitive difficulties of hybridity as theorised by Homi Bhabha, see Sudesh Mishra (1996).
23. In a superb analysis of the symbiosis between census and ethnic categorisations, Anderson notes that '[t]he powerful interlocking effects of census categorisation and enrirlement politics can be seen from the political emergence of such recent American imaginings as the Hispanic vote and the Asian American constituency, perhaps even in the electoral elision of race into ethnicity in the case of "Blacks"' (Anderson, 1998: 130).
24. Keith Axel appears unaware of Mishra's paper, entitled 'The Diasporic Imaginary', which appeared in *Textual Practice* in 1996.

4

The Scene of Archival Specificity

It would be unjust to profess that second scene participants are simply blind to the issue of historical discontinuities within diasporas. Such is plainly not the case. It would be less contentious, however, to assert that diasporists of the second scene are, for most part, attracted to intra-diaspora and inter-diaspora networks, alliances and coalitions. While seldom evading the complexities of border identities, supra-territorial forms of attachment and reactionary as well as radical politics, this bias encourages the impression that the historical continuum and the ethnic continuum (as distinct from gender, class, sexuality and other continuums) are somehow one and the same. Gilroy, for instance, erects his theory of the black Atlantic on the *longue durée* of an unfinished modernity. Consequently, he understates or even underrates the significance of historical and generational breaks within narratives of dispersal and translocation. By mapping routes across the Atlantic Ocean, he builds a macro web of filiations and affiliations whereby blacks, hailing from different historical, cultural, linguistic and territorial points of dispersal and relocation, form an epidermal-cum-historical continuum under the aegis of modernity. It is this surreptitious linking of the ethnic (via the epidermal) and historical continuums that worries the third scene participants.

Vijay Mishra

Some eight years after James Clifford's reference to his work on the Indian diaspora, Vijay Mishra published a cutting-edge monograph on Bombay Talkies entitled *Bollywood Cinema: Temples of Desire*. This study, which contains a probing chapter assessing the reception of Indian films by its multi-locale diasporas, sets itself openly against the lures of an idealist approach to diaspora criticism:

> Against the idealist theory of diasporas (practiced by the Boyarin brothers, Radhakrishnan, Bhabha, Safran, Clifford), which reads diasporas as the exemplary condition of late modernity and as an incipient critique of homogeneous definitions of the nation-state, a realist turn would take us back to the complex and at times strained life-worlds of the people of the diaspora. (Mishra, 2002: 236)

The realist turn entails, for Mishra, a sustained archaeology of the *uneven* sediments to be found in the archives of particular diasporas. My understanding (and doubtless Mishra's) of the two terms, archaeology and archive, coincides with Foucault's here. The first is to be grasped as an analytic procedure that 'questions the already-said at the level of existence', whereas the second refers to 'systems that establish statements as events' while differentiating them in their multiple existence and situating them in their unique duration (Foucault, 1992: 128–31). Whereas the comparative framework relies on weighing one ethno-national cluster against another with an eye on a holdall typology (heuristic or otherwise), Mishra recommends a particularist approach that duly observes historical and archival principles. This approach, focusing *nominally* on a single diaspora but taking on board the anomalies and divergences that break up the rubric along diachronic and economic lines, affords an overdue corrective to the generalist paradigm:

> A corrective to the generalist theories of the Indian diaspora must be immediately made at this point: the Indian diaspora has grown out of two distinct moments in the history of capital. The first moment (of classic capitalism) produced the movement of indentured labour to the colonies (South Africa, Fiji, Trinidad, Guyana, etc.) for the production of sugar, rubber, and tin for the growing British and European markets. I have called this the old Indian diaspora of plantation labour . . . The second moment (of late modern capital) is largely a post-1960s phenomenon distinguished by the movement of economic migrants (but also refugees) into the metropolitan centres of the former empire as well as the New World and Australia . . . This Indian diaspora . . . is very different from the traditional nineteenth- and early-twentieth-century diaspora of classic capital, which was primarily working class and connected to plantation culture . . . The old diaspora broke off contact with India which, subsequently, existed for it as a pure imaginary space of epic plenitude . . . The new is the complex and often internally fissured communities of Indians primarily in the United States, Canada, Britain, and

> Australia who have had unbroken contact with the homeland . . . While in the old diaspora of racialised communities (the terms of reference in them are always 'multiracial' and not 'multicultural'), race was a pre-given category of ethnic classification to be politically sorted out (the demand for racialised constituencies against a common roll in Fiji for instance), in the new diaspora race and ethnicity are linked to questions of justice, self-empowerment, representation, equal opportunity, and definitions of citizenry. The differences between V. S. Naipaul's West Indian novels (where the diasporas are relatively exclusive social formations) and the novels and films of Hanif Kureishi, Gurinder Chada, and Srinivas Krishna (where the diaspora is keyed into the social imaginary of the larger nation) may be explained with reference to the politics and history of the old and new Indian diasporas. (Mishra, 2002: 235–6)

The above framework, while clearly distinguishing between plantation and post-colonial diasporas, omits a phase of Indian dispersion with a much older history. Arthur Helweg has identified it with the simple tag of the 'ancient Indian diaspora' (Helweg, 1986: 103–5). One explanation for the omission may be that the archival records essential for any thorough investigation of the early dispersion are too thin on the ground or no longer extant. It may also be the case that, as Helweg puts it, 'in spite of the strong influence Indian culture had on the East [Cambodia, Vietnam, Thailand, Indonesia and Malaysia], a distinctive overseas Indian population did not develop there . . . [as] the emigrants married local women and soon became indistinguishable from the indigenous people' (Helweg, 1986: 104). That said, Mishra's categories of the old and new Indian diasporas serve to reinforce a decision, made in 1996, 'to return to historical specificities' by adopting an approach that takes as its focus the 'archaeological and [the] genealogical and not [the] transcendental' (Mishra, 1996b: 190). It is the extensive documentation available on subject peoples in the aftermath of (bureaucratic) colonialism that clearly persuaded Mishra to limit his archaeology of the Indian diaspora to the post-Enlightenment era. Contemplating the old diaspora, he notes that the process of colonial subjectification effectively transformed a 'motley crowd' into proper historical subjects. Wrenched from an '"ahistorical" continuum', peasant labourers entered 'for the first time the regulative history of the Empire' (Mishra, 1996a: 429). It is also this turbulent epoch, inaugurated by the techno-industrial revolution and the onset of bourgeois modernity (which had the incendiary effect of turning, as Marx famously quipped, all solid and fixed things to ether), that set in motion the migratory trends we continue to witness, albeit at a vastly accelerated rate, to this day.

Along the historical continuum of modernity (subsequently broken up into two temporal segments), Mishra charts the internal disjoints within the greater

Indian diaspora. Although he develops his framework over the course of several studies, it is 'The Diasporic Imaginary: Theorising the Indian Diaspora', which appeared in *Textual Practice* in 1996, that presents perhaps the most comprehensive version. It is in this essay that Mishra first speaks of a 'radical break' (Mishra, 1996a: 421) between the old/exclusivist and the new/border diasporas. In a move that is reminiscent of Frederic Jameson's division of capitalist development into the three orders of classical, monopoly and advanced, Mishra justifies his own twofold division on materialist grounds by declaring that the Indian diaspora of the classical or industrial phase (and the plantation system has been called industrial agriculture) was markedly different from that of the advanced or post-industrial phase. In short, modernity's first and second phases encouraged centred and decentred modes, means and relations of production. The old and new diasporas, while sharing the rubric 'Indian', are creatures of different temporal and economic periods, and this difference is symptomatically present in their divergent life-worlds and practices. At any rate, since it is largely[1] made up of descendants of illiterate peasant workers shipped to far-flung plantation colonies (Fiji, Trinidad, Natal, Guyana, Surinam, Mauritius, Malaysia and so on) mostly in the nineteenth century when modes of travel and communication were relatively antiquated, the old diaspora is characterised by an enduring dissociation from its territorial homeland. Mishra observes that the shared experience of recruitment and documentation, the gruelling journey aboard sailing and (later) steam ships, the caste-violating cohabitation and commensality, the collective drama of the passage itself, the repetitive nature of quarantine and disembarkation, the treatment at the hands of overseers and the intensely regulated conditions of plantation life led to the creation of self-contained or exclusivist communities. In effect, then, the motley crowd composed of tribal Dhangars, landless Ahirs, proud Rajputs and Oudhi Brahmins were changed by the rigours of indenture into a self-referential enclave. In the case of Fiji, this enclave was enriched by the shipment of labourers drawn from the Madras Presidency (Tamil Nadu, Kerala as well as parts of Karnataka). Traumatic severance from the homeland was, it seems, followed by cultural reconstitution. While the icons of Indian culture were an integral part of this reconstitution (Mishra restricts his illustrative examples to Hindus),[2] these forms were spatially reproduced without India as their material referent. Or, as he puts it, 'In the old Indian diaspora this absence had become a true fantasy because India had no real, tangible existence in the socio-political consciousness of the people' (Mishra, 1996a: 442). Elsewhere, I have called such deterritorialised cultural markers 'milieu effects' (Mishra, 2002b: 27). Milieu effects have the virtue of transforming any alienating territory into hospitable terrain, or *habitus*. They generate commonalities and may consist of anything from a shared language or collective memories to culinary habits and culture-specific acts of domesticity. Having dislodged it from the homeland territory, Mishra claims that the exclusive practices of the old diaspora arose out of the apocalyptic experience of indenture. He discusses the bonds 'created through the *jahaji bhai* ("ship-brotherhood") confraternity' and points to the spatial alliances forged by the uniform nature of the rationed diet: 'Since food rations on the sugar plantations were identical for all indentured Indian labourers throughout the colonies, food linked the old Indian diaspora from Surinam to Mauritius to Fiji' (Mishra, 1996a: 429–30). He also underscores the familiarising impact of transplanted fauna and flora – mango, bulbul, mynah, jackfruit and so on – and the communal cohesion achieved through an almost monotheistic concern with a single sacred text, Tulsidas's *Ramayana*. For those shipped to Fiji, language, too, could be considered a unifying factor as all recruits, even those from the Madras Presidency, ended up speaking Fiji *bhasa* or *baat*, a localised version of Hindi. Cobbling together a culture from the ruins of the indenture experience, the old diaspora cultivated a form of racialised self-referentiality. That is the gist of the argument. If it is simply a matter of *relative* emphasis based on the juxtaposition of the old and the new, then there is little to fault here. When treated in isolation from the comparative framework, however, the old diaspora may not be entirely as self-centred or exclusivist as claimed. Indians in Fiji, for example, may be insular to the degree that members of the diaspora seldom marry outside the racial-ethnic enclave (and there is a *discourse* and a *history* to this as well), but this should not be taken to intimate a form of *cultural* isolationism. Actually, the reverse holds true. Fiji *bhasa*, for instance, continues to draw liberally on English and Fijian language systems; kava consumption, a cherished indigenous custom, is an indispensable part of diasporic sociality; *dalo* (taro), *kokoda* (raw fish in coconut milk) and *palusami* (smoked taro leaves in coconut milk) regularly feature in the Indian diet as does *tarcari* (curry) in the diet of the *taukei* (ethnic Fijian). Mishra is not oblivious to such crossovers and fusions (as revealed by his witty aside on the Caribbean *dhal puri* as Bust Up Shut); however, within the historically divided framework of shared nomination, the old diasporas represent – and V. S. Naipaul's *oeuvre* is a worrying source for much of this representation – largely 'self-enclosed' or internally 'continuous' societies (Mishra, 1996a: 441).

Since he is working with something akin to dialectical categories, it follows that the new diaspora exhibits border traits in line with the decentralised trends of late capital:

> The cultural logic of the new Indian diaspora has to be located in the idea of the hyphen itself, in what may be called the epistemology of borders. (Mishra, 1996a: 432)

The law of the hyphen concerns intermediate states and impure exchanges that trouble the *pure* genre of the nationalised citizen. Mishra draws a distinction between the juridical citizen, rendered as an abstract entity capable in theory of accommodating all nationalised subjects, and the embodied citizen embroiled in the helter-skelter of daily life within the nation-state where '*access to citizenship is always segmented along different social fault lines*' (Itzigsohn, 2001: 293). The embodied citizen comes in two categories. The bodies of the first, being largely unmarked, 'signify an unproblematic identity of selves with nations' (Australian equals Anglo and so on), thus ratifying the promise of the abstract juridical citizen, whereas those of the second, being densely marked, 'fissure the logic of unproblematic identification' with the nation-state. This second category, made up of *visible* minorities and diasporas, punctures the all-encompassing fantasy of the abstract citizen. In a bid to domesticate these marked bodies within some sort of taxonomical grid, 'plural/multicultural societies have constructed the impure genre of the hyphenated subject' (Mishra, 1996a: 433). The process of hyphenated interpellation is, for Mishra, fairly intricate. If the hyphen implies a political imposition conceding the presence of an imperfect citizen, it also signifies a subject that actively internalises this condition. One consequence is that the subject resists the effacing injunctions of assimilation and struggles for ownership of the hyphen. In the 'race to occupy the space of the hyphen – Indo-Americans, Indian-Americans, Hindu-Americans, Muslim-Britons' (Mishra, 1996a: 433) – diasporic subjects live lives of selected discontinuities. Attributed to Salman Rushdie, this insight permits Mishra to summon up an enormous archive of cultural material to back up his claim about the border features of the new Indian diaspora. He builds his case for the border paradigm by referring to the fusion of bhangra, reggae, soul and hip-hop in discs cut by Bally Sagoo and Apache Indian; he points to Nusrat Fateh Ali Khan's hybrid synthesis of the classical Sufi *qawali* with jazz and other non-Eastern genres; he adverts to Bharati Mukherjee's novels in which diasporic characters form 'part of a global odyssey as they renegotiate new topographies through the travails of travel' (Mishra, 1996a: 435); and he performs politically shrewd readings of films made in the diaspora and about diasporic existentiality by Gurinder Chada and Hanif Kureishi. In their scorching critique of Britain under Thatcher, Kureishi's films open up a cinematic space that simultaneously depicts and upsets the reactionary hegemony of nationalist discourses. Kureishi, writes Mishra, 'uses the (diasporic) body as the border zone where transgressions occur'; by depicting 'from the establishment's perspective, extreme aberrations: black and white homosexuality; black and white heterosexuality; black upon white upon black heterosexuality' (Mishra, 1996a: 439), Kureishi not only highlights the libidinal economy of the border in a specific corporeal sense but restores to Britain the repressed history composed of the hybrid narratives of its colonial adventure. Mishra is perfectly alert to the obnoxious and virulent forms of long-distance nationalism espoused by some members of the new Indian diaspora, but for him these are exceptions that run against the inexorable law of the hyphen. Finally, however, the cultural forms and practices of the old diaspora, being independently continuous, betray signs of self-referentiality (exclusive practices) whereas those of the new, being hybrid and selectively discontinuous, are characterised by a radical other-referentiality (border practices). Anticipating Pheng Cheah's charge that diasporists had turned ethnicity into an ahistorical trope (Cheah, cit. Lee, 2005: 26), Mishra's essay delivers a timely blow to the transhistorical lumping together of dispersed and deracinated peoples. Still, he institutes this historical 'turn' without relinquishing the practice of designating diasporas in ethno-national terms. While orthodox materialists may baulk at this compromise, it may be argued that Mishra's ethnonym – Indian – is already ruptured in class terms according to historical principles. For, as he notes, the nineteenth century coolie labourers were all illiterate and impoverished peasants, whereas the postwar Indian migrants hail from various classes, especially the middle, but seldom from the peasantry. With Hall's insight in mind, it may also be possible to argue that ethnicity, like race, is one of the several modalities in which class is lived. Still, how one modality rubs up against another – class against race against gender against sexuality – only begins to make sense in the light of historical analysis. The historical approach, in turn, cannot be detached from the question of generational shifts across specific geopolitical terrains. The following example will serve to illustrate the point. Descendants of Fiji's coolie labourers have for some time belonged to a thriving professional middle class based in Fiji's urban centres, namely Suva, Nadi and Lautoka. In the wake of the coups of 1987 and 2000, some 80,000 persons from this class fled to various metropolitan havens in Australia, North America, New Zealand and Canada. In these centres they rub shoulders with members of the new diaspora in video outlets, spice shops, cinema houses, cultural festivals and religious institutions. This invites at least three questions. What happens to the historical categories of exclusivism and border, founded on an arbitrary generational division, during such encounters? Does the old merge into the new or vice versa?[3] Why not use the much sounder synchronic principle of comparing contemporaries?

Donna R. Gabaccia

In *Italy's Many Diasporas*, Donna R. Gabaccia follows Mishra's lead (albeit with the fastidiousness of a trained historian) in recommending adherence to strict historical principles in the assessment of diasporas. Unlike the latter, however, she sets herself firmly against the transhistorical overvaluation of the ethno-national designation (or ethnonym) by rejecting the holdall description – Italian – as the departure point for her project. Observing that there 'was no Italian nation or Italian people before 1861' (Gabaccia, 2000: 1), she explains:

> The modern diasporas of Italy were webs of social connections and channels of communication between the wider world and a particular paese (village) or patria (hometown). They rested on migrants' close identification with the face-to-face communities of family, neighbourhood, and native town. This combination of loyalties left but little space for a nationalism that put identity with a nation or with a national state above all others. It is no accident that the modern Italian word for country is the same as its word for village (paese). Nor is it accidental that modern Italian words for citizenship (cittadinanza) and citizen (cittadino) originally defined loyalty to a city, not to a nation (nazione or nazionalità), people (popolo), or race (stripe or razza). (Gabaccia, 2000: 3)

Seen through the long lens of history, the nation-state of Italy and its ethnonym (Italian) are recent constructions. In fact:

> . . . [M]igration rarely created a national or united *Italian* diaspora. But it did create many temporary, and changing, diasporas of peoples with identities and loyalties poorly summed up by the national term, Italian. There have been diasporas of people from Sambuca (in Sicily) and the Biellese area (in Piedmont, in Italy's northwest). There have been diasporas of merchants, chimneysweeps, and hurdy-gurdy men from specific Italian towns. And there have been diasporas of Italian-speaking anarchists and Mussolini-inspired fascists. Only in the last few decades . . . can one speak of migrants from Italy united by a national identity, seeking and sustaining firm connections to a national government at home, or with a shared sense of identity around the world. (Gabaccia, 2000: 6)

It is this understanding of Italian nationalism as a recent discursive formation that allows Gabaccia to discredit the ethno-nationalist framework whereby the terms Italy and Italian operate in hindsight as self-evident categories. Her remarks also bear out Michael Mann's claim that transnational flows were an important feature in early industrial forms of European capitalism 'with virtually free mobility of capital and labour . . . in border or cross-border areas, like the Low Countries, Bohemia and Catalonia' (Mann, 1993: 119). Gabbacia herself makes the point that far from being 'an invention of the late twentieth century . . . transnationalism appears as a recurring dimension of life in every world system, and an "ethno-scape" of ancient origins' (Gabaccia, 2000: 11). She concedes that there is a present-day nationalist position that is hardwired to an overarching rubric (Italy or Italian), but notes that this is really a belated and fraught achievement. A perdurable Italian nationalism collapses under the weight of historical detail. While most diasporists regard transnational alliances as a radical or utopian alternative to the bounded expectations of the modern nation-state and its nationalising discourses, Gabaccia notes that trans-territorial networks (which is precisely what she has in mind) may be found in Italy's diasporas prior to the birth of an Italian nationality. If these pre-nationalised diasporas had a homeland referent at all, it was usually a village or a locality, a city or a family, but never the politically managed macro territory captured by the idea of the nation-state. Since the nationalism of bourgeois elites is finally bound up with the project of nation-centred capital accumulation, does this mean that Italy failed to construct, at least until recently, 'core industrial systems as national autocentred systems' (Amin, 1997: 1)? Gabaccia neither poses nor answers this question.

The Italian political state may have been founded in 1861, but it was a far cry from the imagined community that constitutes a nation. Gabaccia argues that a significant time lag was experienced between the institution of the state and the emergence of a corresponding national consciousness. Even as her account approaches the second millennium, Gabaccia remains doubtful whether the age-long transmission of *civilità italiana*, as expressed in cultural practices, bears any relation to nationalist discourses in the strictest sense (Gabaccia, 2000: 191). This picture is arrestingly at odds with the customary view of the modern nation-state as the holy grail of popular or mass nationalisms. The late flowering of Italian nationalism opens up the possibility of discusing Italy's diasporas outside the terms of the nation-state and with close reference to minute trans-territorial webs and linkages. For her framework, Gabaccia relies on two moves. The first seeks to highlight the ruptures (never total) between the political state, its 'elite' nationalist activists working towards an imagined community and the scattered pre-nationalised networks of migrants. The second endeavours to investigate these ruptures, as well as the abortive attempts at forging an overarching nationalism, in diachronic – sometimes overlapping – segments. Gabaccia shuns the phenomenology of identity politics and presents an argument that is beautifully nuanced, refreshingly orthodox and endorsed by statistics that hark back to the thirteenth century. Diachronic segments are divided roughly as follows: pre-Enlightenment period (before 1790); the Garibaldi-led Risorgimento years after the French Revolution (1790–1893); the time leading up to the Great War (1870–1914), the epoch dominated by Mussolini and fascist politics (1915–43); and, finally, the postwar era (after 1945) of economic miracle and renewed emigration. It is almost impossible to do justice to the detailed analysis of migratory trends and motivations, gender and class ratios, sending and receiving milieus, ideological and vocational diversity (from anarcho-syndicalist to organ-grinder) or the manifold political and economic determinants catalogued in each of the historical segments. Despite the richness of her analysis, Gabaccia's definitional ambiguity and resistance to the term diaspora does have a drawback. One is at times left wondering exactly when her migrants or sojourners turn into diasporas (even if pre-nationalised) and the reverse. The trouble may not be with Gabaccia's analysis per se, but with the available statistics that point to the high frequency of counter-migration even among the children of Italy's diasporas.

Still, as she traverses the various diachronic segments, Gabaccia paints a portrait of migratory Italians that is at once scrupulously historical and attentive to the political and economic shifts experienced in Europe and the New World. Never neglectful of the various cause-effect relations that underwrite migratory trends or nation-state formations, Gabaccia betrays an uncanny talent for highlighting anomalous cases that do not quite fit the bill. For instance, she observes that the non-existence of an Italian nation in the eighteenth century contrasts sharply with the long-established imagined communities of neighbouring Spain, Portugal and France (Gabaccia, 2000: 15). Her diachronic segments assist her in specifying a horizon where synchronic or spatial differences among diasporas – gender and class affiliations, left and right politics, departure and destination points, etc. – may be mapped alongside the differences instituted by the chronological breaks. This scheme allows her to point to the epistemic breaks between the pre-Enlightenment era, characterised by the mobility of merchants, artists, colonisers and clerics, and the period after the French Revolution when the migrants were represented by small independent bands of elites (artists, scholars, doctors, etc.), Risorgimento exiles (such as Mazzini and Garibaldi) and bigger companies of peasants and plebeian workers (nearly 550,000 between 1789 and 1871). A further epistemic 'turn' witnessed the emergence of proletarian diasporas – national and international – in the interval between the Risorgimento and the Great War. Between the two world wars, Mussolini discouraged emigration because it enfeebled the *stirpe* (race or tribe) while, paradoxically and for insidious demographic motives, attempting to redirect traffic to the Italian colonies of Libya and Ethiopia. Although his policies had no perceptible impact on migration patterns, except in the way of departing dissidents, the anti-immigrant policies and restrictive 'guest' conditions of some receiving nations, especially after the Great Depression, led directly to a decline in labour migration from Italy. After the Second World War, significant waves of workers (some seven million inside thirty years), now regulated by the *padrone* state rather than an individual *padrone* (recruiting patron), left for America, Australia, Brazil, Argentina and Canada, but the numbers dwindled once the Italian economic miracle gained momentum. Thereafter the trend was for localised migration, guest working and sojourning (South to North as well as within Europe) as the Italian state, with a reluctance verging on hypocrisy, started to play host to a variety of incoming diasporas.

Gabaccia's synchronic approach to temporal segments works rather well. It keeps in view the historical and material factors that catalysed the dispersal and formation of Italy's many diasporas while attending to the welter of spatial differences (such as status, class, gender, vocation, habit, region and ideology) that distinguished them from each other. It is the particularist concept of *natio*, designating 'a specific occupational group with specific origins in one patria' and not 'every migrant from anywhere in Italy' (Gabaccia, 2000: 29), that inspires Gabaccia's search for relative discontinuities and lends to her study a robustness, nuance and authority lacking in some transnational models that merely seek to plot alliances and continuities. The discontinuities exist on several fronts. There is discontinuity, for instance, between urban elites espousing *civiltà italiana* and peasant satellites identifying with an actual *paese* (Garibaldi's nationalist army of labour migrants is an exception and not the rule); another relates to the gender disproportion within the labour migrants (men were always numerically superior although less so in the twentieth century); while a third concerns the different experiences of diaspora women in Buenos Aires and New York. Gabaccia observes that women in the former city were 'more willing to leave home to work [either] because they found employment in small-scale shops owned by fellow migrants . . . or because more were from Italy's North', whereas 'Southern women in New York . . . had to move well beyond family circles to work for wages in garment manufacturing owned by Jewish, German, or American employees' (Gabaccia, 2000: 101). The implication is that Northern women in Buenos Aires were doubly advantaged as they worked for Italian employers and were not hamstrung by the patriarchal mores of Italy's South. By comparing the two major settlement cities of Italy's diasporas, Gabaccia makes a compelling case for the discontinuity framework. Since they constituted a significant part of its population, Italians in Buenos Aires were obliged to interact with the city's other denizens. In New York, it was exactly the reverse:

> In New York, the self-segregation of migrants – a relatively much smaller group in this multi-ethnic city – was far more noticeable. In Lower Manhattan, some blocks housed Sicilians and others Neapolitans. The Sicilian village of Cinisi had its own colony farther up the East Side . . . Kinship, friendship, and neighbourliness rooted in the village remained important sources of social and financial security for migrants living in insecure incomes far from home. (Gabaccia, 2000: 104)

Such situational particularities gave rise to 'other Italies' segmented along very different lines:

> In Tampa, Florida . . . labour activists successfully defined the Italian community as a bastion of labour internationalism and anti-clericalism.

> In Argentina, liberal, republican, and middle-class migrants dominated as leaders, producing a pluralist diaspora nationalism that embraced, rather than foundered on, class differences among migrants. In New York, battles between internationalist exiles and nationalist prominenti enamoured of civiltà italiana continued until World War I. Paese-based diasporas and the continuation of regionalism prevented even the illusion of a unified community there. (Gabaccia, 2000: 120–1)

In her concluding remarks, Gabaccia notes that Italy's non-returning diasporas were eventually transformed or nationalised into Argentines, Brazilians, Americans and Australians. Even so, the pre-nationalised, *paese*-oriented forms of trans-territorialism practised by Italy's diverse proletarian diasporas provides 'an important alternative to modern nationalisms, even those of Italy' (Gabaccia, 2000: 191).

Brent Hayes Edwards

In *The Practice of Diaspora*, Brent Hayes Edwards also thinks of diasporic difference in the context of metropolitan milieus (Paris and New York, and to a lesser extent London) but with specific reference to the dispersed figures of black internationalism. Despite his tactical disclaimer, Edwards' project is really a sustained retort to Gilroy's notion of the black Atlantic as the 'changing same' or what Edwards describes as the 'principle of continuity' based on an 'oceanic frame' (Edwards, 2003: 12). Instead of a theory of linking chronotopes (ships, hotels, buses, etc.), Edwards moots the idea of *décalage* where the emphasis is on the 'changing core of difference' (Edwards, 2003: 14). While concurring with Gilroy's fundamental premise that black internationalism mounts an antagonistic response to modernity and is therefore constitutive of it, Edwards does not countenance the view that this response is characterised by consensual politics on the part of black international cultures and actors. On the contrary, these 'cultures are equally "adversarial" to themselves, highlighting differences and disagreements among black populations on a number of registers' (Edwards, 2003: 7). By focusing on disjoints in the conversations taking place between Francophone *noirs* and their Anglophone counterparts in the first fifty years of the twentieth century, Edwards reveals Gilroy's partiality to a male-dominated Anglocentric archive. Not only does he complicate the epidermal issue by pointing to the differences obtained through other forms of interpellation, but his anti-abstractionist approach to diaspora (where every political and cultural linkage is haunted by the *practice* of difference) also shows greater appreciation of the role of specific historical events (such as Mussolini's invasion of Ethiopia in 1935) in mobilising black internationalists. Any theory of dialogic alliances within black international cultures has to, in his opinion, take stock of the practice of linguistic, ideological, cultural and spatio-temporal differences. Edwards' diachronic segment consists of the first fifty years of the twentieth century and lends to his account a specificity it might have otherwise lacked. This diachronic segment comprises an archive understood not as a repository of traces, but rather as a 'generative system' (Edwards, 2003: 7) that governs the possibilities of an utterance.

Edwards employs *décalage* in tandem with other difference-generating concepts such as articulation, translation, reciprocity and detour. Reworking Léopold Senghor's original idea, he remarks that *décalage* expresses 'either a difference in time (advancing or delaying a schedule) or in space (shifting or displacing an object)' and proposes combining the two concepts (so as to include disjunctions in time *and* in space within the same unit) into an innovative framework for appraising 'the structure of . . . unevenness in the African diaspora' (Edwards, 2003: 13). Stuart Hall's notion of articulation, which refers to a system of difference-in-unity structured in relations of dominance as well as resistance, affords another version of disjointedness or *décalage*. This is also the case with Edwards' take on translation. As a relation forged on the brink of incommensurability and misalliance, translation testifies to the possibilities of dialogue occurring across rifts and chasms. It demands reciprocity, which is 'not just mutual attention, mutual translation, but also mutual answerability' (Edwards, 2003: 116). Translation, however, also induces misunderstandings, silences and disputes that draw attention to the impossible work of conversion. In this second sense, translation weaves no magic and testifies to the impossibility of holding the *same* conversation across cultures, languages, times and spaces. Edwards supplements this double notion of translation (in fact, all his variant terms for *décalage* are precisely that – supplements) by rehabilitating Edouard Glissant's idea of the detour to refer to the 'elsewhere' of the *point d'intrication* or the point of entanglement. This 'elsewhere' is the constitutive other of roots, fixed cultures and natal country. In Edwards' reformulation, the detour leads to an elsewhere that forms the site of entanglement (or articulation, *décalage* and translation) for the detouring agents. This elsewhere is resolutely material and not abstract. Exactly because of the French involvement in the scramble for Africa and the Caribbean, one such *point d'intrication* is the teeming metropolis of Paris:

> . . . Paris represents a different detour for African Americans (whether soldiers, musicians, artists, or the New Negro intelligentsia), for Antilleans, and for Africans. Travelling to Paris is obviously a detour for the African American, a voyage considered an escape (even if partial, even if temporary) from the outrages and frustrations of racism in the

> United States. But it must be considered another sort of detour even for the Franchophone citizen or subject travelling from colony to metropole – if only because the move allows certain unpredictable kinds of boundary crossings and encounters. There is multiple detour, in other words, in the way that, arguably more than anywhere in the world, Paris functions as a space of interaction among populations of African descent. (Edwards, 2003: 24–5)

Each statement or subject, if I may express this sort of entanglement in terms of genre theory, comprises a unique event that takes a different detour to the *point d'intrication* without completely yielding up its unique standpoint even in the likelihood of an understanding being reached. On a theoretical level, and notwithstanding the heady proliferation of substitutes for *décalage*, Edwards performs a simple fillip on Gilroy's transversal approach which places emphasis on the cultural continuities of the black Atlantic. He does not reject the strategic continuities of black internationalism outright, but draws attention to the site-specific practices that inflect these continuities differently. In Gilroy's work, cultural continuities tend to override differences for complex ethical, political and survivalist reasons; for Edwards, continuities are always differently addressed, translated, measured, received, weighted and represented among the black internationalists. The idea of an abstract continuity, and thus of an abstract communality, holds little water in the metropole of entanglement entered through the laneways of detour and difference. The practice of communality among the black internationalists is shot through with difference. Heterogeneity and dissent shine through even in the most intense moments of collaboration. Subtly reworking Anderson's point about a national community of simultaneous readers forged by serial print culture, Edwards observes that black international networks, caught up in the act of translating speeches, books, anthologies, newspapers and periodicals, introduce the problem of irreducible difference to the conception of simultaneity. *Décalage* intrudes in the experience of shared simultaneity for black internationalists because 'translations so regularly highlight the specificity and irreducibility of difference: particular examples of "black" people elsewhere doing different things, or the same things in different ways' (Edwards, 2003: 115).

Once he has established *décalage* (time-space lag and discrepancy) at the heart of all engagements with the *point d'intrication* (and this *point* may be territorial or textual, public or private), Edwards provides a host of compelling examples to back up his assertions. In a move that counters Gilroy's coalitional understanding of the appellation 'black', he delivers his exposition of diasporic difference by attending to the acoustic, semantic, cultural and territorial shifts suggested by the term's many variants: *négre*, Negro, *noir*, nigger, Afro-Latin,

Africo-American and so on. While he never intends to draw a summary correlation, it would not be far wrong to suggest that Edwards sees these variant etymological forms as furnishing symptoms of the disjoints that haunt the cultural and ideological practices of black internationalism. One such instance of *décalage* is to be found in an exchange between the award-winning Martinican writer, René Maran, and Marcus Garvey, the black American intellectual and activist from Harlem. Speaking before an audience of around 1,500 people at the Club du Faubourg in Paris in 1928, Garvey infuriated many black Parisians by delivering a talk based on selective historical memory. His lavish praise of France's extension of legal equality and citizenship rights to blacks (in brazen contrast to North America) drew the following acerbic retort from the Antillean: 'Is it out of love for France that American Negroes [*noirs*] came to fight on her soil, or were they convinced by the promises of liberation they'd be given?' And: 'In America, aren't there clubs for light-skinned Negroes [*noirs peu colorés*] that deny entry to dogs and to full Negroes [*noirs intégraux*]?' (Edwards, 2003: 104). Maran also castigated Alain Leroy Locke, another black American intellectual who was inclined to favour 'Latin justice and tolerance' over 'the racism and segregation of the U.S.' (Edwards, 2003: 106). In an open letter to Locke, he observed that '[t]he benevolence of France toward subject races . . . is a matter of theory and official pretence. It is little more than a subterfuge' (Edwards, 2003: 106). The detours of an Antillean *noir* and two black Americans intersect at the *point d'intrication* (Paris) only to beget a discordant discourse about freedom, equality, citizenship, justice and rights. But if the absence of consensus between squabbling *male* transatlantic blacks presents one type of *décalage*, the competing perceptions of the gendered pool of black intellectuals in Paris affords another. In a revelatory chapter on emergent black feminism, Edwards cites an essay[4] that attributes the rejection of the patronising policy of national assimilation, and the subsequent international reorientation of *noir* Francophone cultures, to women students from the Antilles. The author of the essay was one Paulette Nardal, a member of the editorial collective of *La Revue du monde noir* (*The Review of the Black World*):

> . . . [T]he aspirations which were to be crystallised around 'The Review of the Black World' asserted themselves among a group of Antillean women students in Paris. Until the Colonial Exposition, the coloured women living alone in the metropolis have certainly been less favoured than coloured men who are content with a certain easy success. Long before the latter, they have felt the need of a racial solidarity that would not be merely material. They were thus aroused to race consciousness. The feeling of uprooting which they experienced . . . was the starting point of their evolution. (Edwards, 2003: 124–5)

Edwards reads Nardal's comments as putting forward a dissenting view about the provenance of Négritude – a movement almost exclusively associated with the towering male figures of Léopold Senghor and Aimé Césaire. It is also to Nardal that Edwards turns for his examples of *décalage* in black dance and music practices. Nardal, he writes, 'sketches the differences between the "two genres of music" then confronting one another in Paris: Antillean music such as the beguine, which she describes as "essentially choreographic," and U.S. black music such as jazz and the spirituals' (Edwards, 2003: 176).

Scrutinising the lives of black internationalists, Edwards finds evidence of *décalage* everywhere. He finds it in the American Countee Cullen's sense of a loss of common ground as he fronts up to the defamiliarising force of Creole language and beguine on the dance floor of the Bal Negré in 1928 (Edwards, 2003: 175); he discovers it in the 'discursive frame' of anthologies, such as James Weldon Johnson's *The Book of American Negro Poetry* (1922) which, by including poets from the West Indies, Haiti, Brazil and Cuba, admits to 'the instability – even the impossibility – of framing [blackness]within national bounds (Edwards, 2003: 44–9); and he detects it in the quarrel, as reported by Jessie Faucet in the *Crisis*, that broke out at the Second Pan-African Congress in 1921 'between the U.S. delegates led by Du Bois and the Francophone constituency led by Senegalese *député* Blaise Diagne' and sparked by the latter's collusion with the Belgian representatives on the sensitive topic of their presence in the Congo (Edwards, 2003: 136).

Far and away, however, it is Claude McKay's narrative of black vagabondage that provides the most elaborate instance of *décalage*. The black drifters of the novel *Banjo*, according to Edwards, may be read as living labour that evades the capitalist expropriation of surplus value by opting out of the social relations of production.[5] They are the motley crowd that resist interpellation into some predetermined proletarian register prescribed by capital. Hence their persistent criminalisation by the coercive apparatuses of the bourgeois state. Wandering around the Vieux Port area of Marseilles (which is their arena of entanglement), these wayward dissenters perform odd jobs but refuse incorporation into systemic wage labour. Consequently, they cannot be said to constitute an emergent proletariat. This, coupled with their blackness, sets them at loggerheads with organised white unions, creating another violent disjoint. Black vagabondage becomes a mode of dissent and survival outside the racialised work ethic of petit bourgeois civilisation, and presents a view of life that is insolently anti-organisational and anti-nationalist. There is, however, a further discrepancy. The community of black drifters is not united by any easy sense of racial consciousness and solidarity; indeed, by emphasising their diverse backgrounds and verbal skirmishes over 'race' matters and definitions, McKay produces 'a transnational black novel

. . . [that] is paradoxically also a radical critique of black internationalism' (Edwards, 2003: 210):

> More than any other interwar work, *Banjo* relentlessly underlines the inescapable, nearly mundane, gaps in comprehension: the impossibility of translating a racial consciousness through some foolproof system. We are left with the vertigo of intradiasporic communication, the small and crucial work of carrying words over, one by one, often only to have them thrown back or misconstrued. (Edwards, 2003: 212)

Gaps, lags and ruptures haunt the grand order of proletarian internationalism as well as the little company of black vagabonds. Even when certain social and historical forces, such as bourgeois capitalism and plantation slavery, create a common ground for exchanges to take place across cultures, languages and borders, these interactions are perpetually haunted by non-equivalences. Differences of context, culture, language, hurt and struggle keep postponing the utopian moment of mutual recognition.

Mishra, Gabaccia and Edwards approach the issue of historicising diasporas in three divergent ways. The first institutes a neat diachronic break between exclusivist (old) and border (new) Indian diasporas. Inspired by two different phases of capital, one where the modes, means and relations of production are centred (industrial) and the other decentred (post-industrial), Mishra juxtaposes the two historical types without attending to the problem of comparing non-synchronous clusters. His mapping of disjoints *within* each of the territorially dispersed clusters that make up the old and the new diasporas is also largely embryonic. Nevertheless, he is the first diasporist to insist on tracking historical differences within the single dispersed ethno-national formation and has to be given credit for inaugurating the third scene of exemplification. Gabaccia, too, opts for a system of diachronic breaks in her account of the history of Italian migration, counter-migration, sojourning and settlement in the aftermath of the Renaissance. But she is also alert to the many differences that persist at the synchronic or vertical plane of each diachronic or horizontal segment. These differences of village, region, status, class, gender, vocation and political orientation, and the overall absence of a national consciousness in the migrants, renders it difficult for her to talk of an overarching ethnonym that binds together Italy's many diasporas. While Mishra is largely comfortable with an ethno-historicist form of inquiry, Gabaccia's account is full of ambiguity about the precise value of such forms of ethno-history.[6] Edwards' strategy is somewhat different. By concentrating on the black diaspora in the interwar period, he provides a close-up view of a single diachronic segment. Within this segment, he captures the occurrences of *décalage* (or spatial, temporal, linguistic and cultural gaps and disjoints) that

– in practice and *as praxis* – break up the abstract unity of the black internationalist formation.

KHALID KOSER, MARTIN BAUMANN AND KANISHKA GOONEWARDENA

The trend away from inter-diasporic to intra-diasporic analysis where the stress falls on the specific archives that attest to historical and other differences within particular diasporas has won over many converts to the third scene. In his preface to *New African Diasporas* edited by Khalid Koser, Donald Carter expresses his dissatisfaction with the ahistorical commonality sustaining the usual pan-African approach to dispersed African communities:

> Explorations of pan-African diasporic consciousness must . . . be disambiguated from the essential markings of race, place and temporal anchoring . . . There is no trans-historical box large enough to contain such disparate and heterogeneous processes, rather linkages must be accounted for with greater care and specificity. (Carter, 2003: x–xi)

This view is echoed by the editor's introduction which sums up the historical approach taken by several contributors to the volume. Koser is of the opinion that the African diaspora has been described and theorised almost exclusively in relation to the dispersions engendered by the slave trade. Although a handful of scholars have dealt with 'earlier African diasporas comprising . . . Egyptian and Ethiopian seafarers, Moor traders and the Mandingo mariners', for most 'slavery has been the principal focus . . . and has been subjected to exhaustive analysis' (Koser, 2003: 1). Then, in a move that is reminiscent of Mishra's distinction between the old and new Indian diasporas, Koser recommends the use of a diachronic framework to account for the 'second "wave" of African migration' to metropolitan centres in the United Kingdom and Europe. (In one of the anthologised essays, Jayne O. Ifekwunigwe calls this the post-Columbian phase[7] of African dispersal.) Once he has instituted the diachronic break between the African diaspora of the transatlantic slave trade and the new post-industrial African migrants (refugees, workers, petty traders and so on), Koser observes that – on the synchronic or vertical level – dispersed African communities are often treated as comprising a single continental diaspora. This, he correctly observes, may be more an outcome of the emphasis placed on 'unifying characteristics' than the result of a failure on the part of commentators to note the differences (1) in the slaves' points of origin and destination, (2) in the discrepant social relations witnessed in the plantations of the United States, the Caribbean and South America, (3) in the gender-specific experiences of women slaves and (4) in that 'other' forgotten slave trade of the Indian Ocean.

Like Edwards, however, Koser finds an inverted paradigm – one based on targeting *décalage* and discontinuities – more helpful in examining the plural character of the second wave. Not only are the new African diasporas fractured along ethno-national lines – Congolese, Somalis, Senegalese (which, presumably, already contain multitudes) – but they are also divided in terms of their interpellation by receiving countries: students, illegal aliens, petty traders, asylum seekers and so forth (Koser, 2003: 2–3).

In his work on religious identity among Hindu Trinidadians, Martin Baumann too shows a preference for the diachronic framework. Concerned with the pre-eminence of ethnicity (which he calls an academically fabricated category) in conceptions of identity formation, he believes that religion has been fashionably neglected as an important variable by scholars who favour secularist principles of analysis. A sacraliser of belonging, religion may 'serve as a vital marker of . . . [a] group's identity' (Baumann, 2004: 170). Taking the Hindu diaspora in Trinidad as his case study, Baumann adopts a five 'phase model' that spans one hundred and fifty years of Indian settlement on the island. Each phase is subdivided into a general analytical statement supported by historical data. Characterised by acts of cultural reconstruction, phase one, beginning around the 1870s, corresponds to the historical transformation of indentured servants into freed labourers, smallholders and permanent dwellers. According to Baumann, the liberated labourers reintroduced the cultural practices of the homeland, formed villages in the cane belt and instituted a *panchayat* system of jurisprudence. Phase two is characterised by a loosening of bonds with territorial India and an attenuation of the myth of return. Material symptoms of the trend are found in newly erected temples, mosques and churches in the hostland and in the accelerated investment in social and educational institutions. This phase is closely linked to the presence of visiting *swamis* (priests) and *gurus* (teachers) from around 1910 and the consciousness-raising activities of Indian nationalists both in India and Trinidad. Paradoxically, the break from India reinforces Indian cultural forms and practices. In phase three, the diaspora becomes preoccupied with its place and position in the hostland. No longer hailed by India, it becomes upwardly mobile and seeks to improve its political and economic status. Desiring to participate in the national culture of the hostland, it is faced with the dilemma of retaining exclusivist practices or generating adaptive forms. In this phase, dating from the 1940s to the early 1960s, independent India's lack of interest in the welfare of its diaspora is met with disillusionment. There is a move towards self-reliance, self-assertion and increased activism in the hostland, resulting in the award of numerous rights and concessions, including political enfranchisement and the recognition of traditional marriage practices. There are internal conflicts between orthodox adherents and those wanting to align their practices to the new context, as well as between 'east Indians' of different religious persuasions: Muslims, Hindus and Christians. In this ambiguous atmosphere, some practices are modified to suit dominant trends. For instance, the rural schools established by the Sanatan Dharm Maha Sabha, a Hindu organisation formed in 1950 and led by Bhadase Sagan Maraj, commences to stress Hindu values but along lines that adhere to standardised patterns and principles (such as the seven-point declaration of faith and the prayer book) found in Christian practices. Architecturally, Hindu temples are built in the simple church-style and provide a regular Sunday service for the *bhaktas*. Phase four is governed by the dynamics of ambivalence which sees the diaspora adapting to or reacting against political and social circumstances in the host society. If the diaspora believes that it is being treated equitably and as fully-fledged citizens, then the process of adaptation, incorporation and innovation continues apace; if, however, it encounters impediments and runs up against inequities, perceived or otherwise, then there is a tendency to espouse exclusivist or conservative positions. The impact of Pentecostalism among rural Hindus in the 1950s testifies to a certain flexibility, whereas Hindu evangelism in the wake of the Black Power Movement suggests a reactive revivalism. In the aftermath of the oil boom of the 1970s and the creation of a vibrant middle class, Hindus are finally admitted into the imagined community of the nation-state. In this fifth and final phase, the diaspora actively identifies with the national polity and its symbols but without forsaking cultural specificities or religious practices. It remoulds the national imaginary to subsume difference and so manages to gain acceptance in the public domain. To back up this claim, Baumann points to the election of a Hindu prime minister in 1995, the recording of a Hindi version of the national anthem and the newfound popularity of the *diwali* festival among Trinidadians in general. This leads him to conclude that a clear sense of religious identity actually encourages participation in the nationalist imaginary (Baumann, 2004: 173–81). By drawing on historical archives to test the analytical statements supporting the five diachronic phases, Baumann develops a persuasive paradigm for his particular case study. It is doubtful, however, that his framework would hold up to scrutiny if seen in the light of other diasporas.

In a pungent critique of postcolonial studies and diaspora criticism, Kanishka Goonewardena contends that the idealised definition of diaspora (and she is thinking of the first scene participants here) 'says less than little about the *politics* of diasporas' (Goonewardena, 2004: 665). She argues that the ethno-cultural modes of analysis, popularised in English and Comparative Literature Departments, must be 'enriched with due reference to political, economic, spatial, sociological, and (more broadly) historical factors . . . that explain why people move the way they do, to and from cities, regions, and nation-states, and with what lived experiences and political consequences at places of departure as well as destination' (Goonewardena, 2004: 667). To achieve this type of enrichment, Goonewardena proposes the resurrection of a materialist framework that, profiting from Althusser's work, demonstrates how each diaspora 'evolves historically through overdetermined contradictions'. She continues:

> If diasporas, like much else, are conditioned by circumstances of global scope and happen to be internally contradictory . . . then they too need to be properly *historicised.* (Goonewardena, 2004: 668)

A political understanding of diasporas, one that attends to their lack of internal resolution, would have to seriously engage with the capitalist world system in an historically informed way. Unlike Appadurai (whose work is discussed at some length in the next chapter), Goonewardena insists on the old-fashioned usefulness of a coherent materialist framework for examining the forces of capital. Citing the work of Immanuel Wallerstein, Étienne Balibar and Fredric Jameson, she suggests that the inner contradictions within diasporic social relations, symptomatically detected in cultural practices, ideologies and effects, may be better understood against an evolving macro economic backdrop. These contradictions haunt diasporas in intricate ways:

> Just as there are differences between different diasporas that evolve in their own ways in relation to others under particular historical conditions, so there are distinctions to be made within them as well. These may be called 'good' and 'bad' from any given political standpoint, but we should also . . . attend to social differences within what Benedict Anderson calls the 'imagined community.' (Goonewardena, 2004: 668)

The political dimension appears in the social contradictions at the heart of migratory patterns driven by capital, inviting comment about the maintenance of ideological and class-based distinctions. For there is little in common

> between the world of Sri Lankan stock-brokers, surgeons, and lawyers living in the Upper West Side and that of gas-station attendants, casual labourers, and cashiers in the 'bookstores' of 42nd Street in New York City . . . or among Indians, between the dot.com fortunes amassed in the stock options of Silicon Valley enterprises by 'business-minded' engineers and the small change collected by others low on instant karma in the 7/11 stores and cheap motels, as featured, respectively, in Deepa Mehta's *Bollywood/Hollywood* and Mira Nair's *Mississippi Masala.* (Goonewardena, 2004: 669)

These contradictions inform the material realm of history (why, when and how diasporas are *divisively* formed), the collective body of the ethno-national cluster and the interior realm of the individual subject. Goonewardena observes that there are good and bad diasporas, progressive and regressive elements within the single diaspora and ambivalent diasporic subjects who shift mercurially from liberal to reactionary positions with every shift in their geopolitical point of reference. She situates these overtly ethical categories of good and bad in political terms and refuses to sever them from their specific historical circumstances. Long-distant nationalism, she argues, may indeed be of the disgustingly virulent sort when one considers the rise of Hindutva ideology among right-wing Hindus settled in North America, but it may be less unpalatable when seen in the light of the Filipino diaspora's contribution to the struggle against the dictatorship of Ferdinand Marcos in the 1980s. Goonewardena takes pains to analyse diaspora politics against the backdrop of the rifts, tensions and alliances she detects between diasporas, capitalist interests, nation-states and ideologies. Citing Vijay Prashad's work on the Hindu right in North America, she notes:

> In the wake of the anti-Muslim Gulf War, these desis found an avenue to make an alliance with the US state against what the United States called 'Muslim Fanaticism.' Some even used the conjecture to argue that India could be the Israel of Asia, a US fortress against Islam (Pakistan) and communism (China). (Goonewardena, 2004: 663–4)

The strength of Goonewardena's work clearly lies in her attempt to think through the internal contradictions within diasporas in historical-economic terms that keep in view the political aspects of their multiple engagements in the various contexts and territories.

Martin F. Manalansan IV

In his pioneering work on queer Filipinos in New York, Martin F. Manalansan IV affords a radically different slant on the historical approach to diaspora criticism. In an influential paper entitled 'In the Shadows of Stonewall: Examining Gay Transnational Politics and the Diasporic Dilemma', first published in 1997, he unpacks the proposition that the police raids on a gay bar in Manhattan in 1969, and the riots they triggered, marked the founding or originating moment of a *truly* international gay, lesbian and transgender movement.[8] For Manalansan this position has several drawbacks. First, it assumes a normative western queer subject and all queer subjects, regardless of cultural, religious and national differences, must adhere to this profoundly *political* norm. Second, it creates a dichotomy between an emancipated first-world metropolitan person and a yet-to-be-emancipated third-world one, thereby instituting a hierarchy where the western subject is the privileged norm. Third, it assigns a contemporaneous political value to western as against non-western queer practices and categories which are described, more or less, in anthropological terms. This, in turn, has the effect of instituting temporal differences between modern gay practices, inevitably western, metropolitan and individualistic, and the *anachronistic* same-sex practices found in non-western cultures. Manalansan makes the above point as follows:

> *Gay* [as a western category] . . . is meaningful within the context of the emergence of bourgeois civil society and the formation of the individual subject that really only occurs with capitalist and western expansion. Categories of same-sex phenomena are placed within a western-centred developmental teleology, with 'gay' as its culminating stage. Other 'non-gay' forms or categories are constructed metaleptically, rendered 'anterior,' and transformed into archaeological artefacts that need only to be reckoned with when excavating the roots of pan-cultural/pan-global homosexuality. In other words, the 'internationalising' transnational gay and lesbian movement does not as yet contain a critique of its own universalising categories; without an interrogation of its Eurocentric and bourgeois assumptions, this globalising discourse risks duplicating an imperial gaze in relation to non-western non-metropolitan sexual practices and collectivities. (Manalansan, 1997: 488)

Manalansan observes that Eurocentric assumptions are embedded in terms such as closet, homophobia, gay and lesbian, and frequently employed without any reference to the context of their 'specific national histories'. In the western paradigm, the gay subject is seen to graduate 'from the "immature" in the "concealment" of his or her sexuality to the "mature" visibility of political participation in the public sphere' and the 'lack of explicitly gay-identified people in the public arena signifies that a "homophobic" attitude is prevalent' in that society (Manalansan, 1997: 489–90). For Manalansan, this logic replicates a developmental discourse that consigns non-western queer practices, which may be based on culturally different conceptions of the public and the private, to a pre-liberated archaic order and temporality. Coming late to modernity, the queer other lags behind the western bourgeois norm. The privileging of western cultural systems in the temporal division of queer subjects is symptomatic of an inability, on the part of some scholars, to examine 'the imbrication of gender and sexuality within race and nationality' (Manalansan, 1997: 490). Disembedding queer practices from an evolutionary teleology, Manalansan suggests that we treat them as 'multiply determined by notions of culture, history, religion, class, and region, in and across various cultural and political locations and even within a single group' (Manalansan, 1997: 486).

To illustrate his point about multiple determinations in queer identity formations, Manalansan turns his attention to gay Filipinos domiciled in New York.[9] After assessing the life histories of his informants, he argues that their subjectivities are shaped by a number of factors. These include the historically uneven relationship between the United States and the Philippines; the discriminatory immigration policies of the United States that barred 'sexual deviants' from its territory until as recently as 1990;[10] the culture-specific Filipino understanding of the queer as *bakla*; the race- and class-based encounters and experiences of gay Filipinos in the queer circles of New York; the anxieties caused by their minority status, marginal citizenship and even illegality; the symbolic capital carried over from the Philippines and the social and financial obligations to family networks in the home territory;[11] and the tactical alliances forged with other gay minorities of Asians, Latinos and African Americans. In the 'Introduction' to *Queer Migrations: Sexuality, U.S. Citizenship, and Border Crossings*, Eithne Luibhéid summarises Manalansan's work as follows:

> Martin F. Manalansan IV has built on transnational, diasporic, and other models that reject strictly nation- and state-centred analyses in favour of analyses that highlight the salience of historical and ongoing links among different regions. In a 1997 essay, he highlights these linkages in order to underscore that while queer Filipino migrants may be searching for freedom from oppression, their oppression has been significantly shaped by the legacies of U.S. colonisation and by ongoing economic and political relationships between the United States and the Philippines. Under these circumstances, queer Filipinos' migration emerges not simply as a search for freedom in the United States, but also as a search for alternatives to circumstances in the Philippines in which the United States is centrally (though not sorely) implicated. Consequently, queer Filipino immigration cannot be read as a comfortable reiteration of dominant U.S. nationalist myths.

On the contrary:

> By stressing historical and ongoing connections between the United States and the Philippines, Manalansan makes clear that queers migrate not simply as sexual subjects, but also as racialised, classed, gendered subjects of particular regions and nations that exist in various historic relationships to U.S. hegemony. In this way, he echoes a crucial thread of sexuality scholarship that insists on treating queers not solely as sexual subjects, but in relation to multiple identities that directly affect them. At the same time, he revises that scholarship by transporting it to a global

> field structured by historic legacies and contemporary forms of inequality and exploitation between and among nations and regions. He also revises migration scholarship by centring sexuality as a critical structuring factor. (Luibhéid, 2005: xxv–xxvi)

What is particularly attractive about Manalansan's approach is his emphasis on individual life histories where different practices and identities are dialogically co-present.[12] Discussing how queer Filipinos deal with conceptions of *bakla* while engaging with western gay practices in the context of New York, he argues for the concurrence and simultaneity of western and non-western queer practices. These practices share the same time of modernity, but have divergent national and cultural histories. *Bakla*, he explains, is an overdetermined concept in Filipino culture:

> *Bakla* is a Tagalog term used for particular types of men who engage in practices that encompass effeminacy, transvestism, and homosexuality. The *bakla* is conceptualised in terms of epicene characteristics. On one hand, the *bakla* is stereotypically seen to exist in the vulgar public spaces of the carnival (*baklang karnabal*), the beauty parlour (*parlorista*), and the marketplace (*baklang palenge*). On the other, the *bakla* is also seen as the cross-dressing man with the female heart (*pusong babae*), searching for the real man and trying hard not to slip into vulgarity or dismal ugliness. These images form part of everyday discourse . . . (Manalansan, 1997: 491)

After reviewing the material supplied by his diasporic informants, Manalansan concludes that the 'coming out' syndrome was antithetical to their perception of self-dignity and decorum, and that public display, instead of being a marker of gay social liberation, represented the vulgar practices of a certain type of *bakla*:

> For some Filipino gay men, public spaces such as the 'streets' (as in the Stonewall slogan, 'Out of the bars and into the street') are not spaces of pride, but, on the contrary, are potential arenas of shame and degradation. These informants' views are not the result of homophobia, but are racialised and classed readings of the gay world. (Manalansan, 1997: 497)

Rejecting the drama and ostentation of a certain understanding of *bakla*, Manalansan's informants insist on the importance of restraint and propriety in their physical demeanour. This different take on *bakla* turns the negative notion of the western closet, suggesting fear of the heteropatriarchal norm, into a positive of sorts. For these diasporic informants, 'coming out' is linked to the extravagant display found among a certain vulgar subcategory of *bakla*; the absence of demonstrativeness, in their opinion, makes for a more subtle, dignified and streetwise politics. In the end, however, the question of reserve and flourish, closet and coming out is of secondary importance to these informants because other factors – class, race and citizenship – take precedence in shaping their agencies:

> For my immigrant informants who self-identify as gay, narratives of the 'closet' and 'coming out' fragment and are subordinated in relation to the more highly fraught arena of the law and citizenship. (Manalansan, 1997: 498)

Or, as tersely noted by one informant, 'When you are an illegal alien, you have other things to hide apart from being gay' (Manalansan, 1997: 498). Enumerating the variables that constitute diasporic Filipinos as different subjects within a western queer polity, Manalansan's emphasis falls squarely on individual biographies, everyday practices and transported cultural histories.

In a more recent article entitled 'Migrancy, Modernity, Mobility: Quotidian Struggles and Queer Diasporic Intimacy', Manalansan continues to delve into the everyday practices of the queer Filipino diaspora in the United States. Noting that 'most ideas about queer community and identity formations are based on organised public enactments of gayness and lesbianness', he declares that the 'focus on the everyday reveals not only the inadequacy of conventional narratives where self and community progressively unfold, it also points to the complexities of various intersections of race, gender, class, and sexuality in diasporic and immigrant groups' (Manalansan, 2005: 149). Essentially, then, he suggests an approach based on scrutinising the life histories of his subjects, thereby downplaying the magnified eventfulness of activities that take place in the public domain. Derived from Michel de Certeau's theoretical work on everyday practices, this approach provides an alternative form of historiography:

> Everyday life is a site for critically viewing and 'reading' modernity. Unlike traditional historiography, which depends on grand narrative of 'famous men' and great events, the narrative of everyday life reveals the rich intricacies of the commonplace. Everyday life intersects and engages with the intimate, the private, and the search for home in modern life. (Manalansan, 2005: 148)

In everyday practices the dimensions of the subjective (memories, affects) and the objective (spaces, effects) intersect in ways that are most revealing of the informant's personal approach to pressures exerted by the absent family, by various heteropatriarchal structures, by the juridical requirements of the state, by racially determined queer formations and by the competing cultural practices of the host and home societies. In their most private and banal acts, hidden from the public gaze, and often enacted in the domestic arena – or, rather, in that arena where an attempt is made at a type of domesticity – queer Filipinos generate intimate and entangled narratives that capture the diverse forces that impinge on their day-to-day lives in the diaspora. These narratives attest to 'diasporic intimacy . . . achieved either through counterpublic cultural productions or through more mundane routes that translate and transform "the habitual estrangements of life abroad"' (Manalansan, 2005: 148). Of the fifty or so informants he interviews, Manalansan affords a detailed overview of two life histories. The first concerns Alden – a middle-aged gay man occupying a rented apartment in Greenwich Village – while the second concentrates on the leisure and work-day activities of Roldan, an illegal immigrant in New York. Manalansan claims that Alden's apartment holds the key to the history of his life in the United States because it constitutes a private spatial archive, affording a valuable 'interior' narrative, that visually supplements the testimony provided by his informant. Melding oral and spatial testimonies, Manalansan outlines the moments of interpellation that attest to the complex and contradictory paths travelled by the gay Filipino in New York. Alden's remark about learning the 'different drama' (Manalansan, 2005: 150) of individual autonomy at a distance from the extended family is taken to indicate the persistence of Filipino queer slang (or swardspeak) in the renegotiation of cultural values in the host society. Manalansan describes Alden's apartment as being partitioned into two non-contiguous sections: one bedecked with the icons and effects of American popular culture (such as a poster of Herb Ritts) and the other adorned with solemn emblems of the Philippines: family photographs, devotional statuettes, and so on. If the apartment represents the different drama (or cultural difference articulated from one's own standpoint) of self-sufficiency in the overdeveloped world, its schizophrenic spatial arrangement narrates an equally intricate tale of partial translation, anxious coexistence and incomplete assimilation. Alden's apartment evinces an '"imperfect aesthetics of survival"' (Manalansan, 2005: 155) rather than triumphant stories of hybridity.

The second informant, Roldan, also discloses anxieties with regard to interpellation (racial, sexual as well as class-based) in his various statements and practices. At one point, reflecting on his work-day clothes, he wonders whether he might pass for a Wall Street executive but immediately counters this possibility with another that, he admits, is nearer the mark: '"People will take one look at me and say – immigrant – fresh off the boat"' (Manalansan, 2005: 152). There is a further shift in this self-assessment as Roldan contemplates the sexual and cultural reasons for the different treatment he receives at his workplace. He believes that it has to do with the behavioural modes of an Asian *biyuti*[13] as mediated by his fellow workers. Normal sartorial attire – such as the formal suit or the informal tee shirt – fails to induce the desired response from others in quotidian situations. When the same occurs in 'masculine' gay bars, thereby exacerbating his feelings of isolation, Roldan seeks solace in cross-dressing homosexual taverns. In these radically deviant spaces where the signs for gender and sexuality are cross-wired, he discovers affirmation in the eyes of the white other. But this, too, comes at a price. Instead of becoming the 'masculine' gay man of his ideal, Roldan is feminised in this other space. Fixed attitudes in the host society towards slight-bodied Asians, coupled with Roldan's psychological need for social and sexual affirmation, transforms him into a real *bakla* – 'a broad Tagalog rubric that encompasses cross-dressing, hermaphroditism, homosexuality, and effeminacy' (Manalansan, 2005: 153). Reacting to a racially loaded situation, the informant reclaims the *bakla* excesses he had once been so eager to shed. But there is a further complexity. Roldan is an undocumented migrant and cross-dressing in public has it own risks of visibility. Contemplating the possibility of arrest and deportation, the informant observes that this would have an adverse economic impact on his family in the Philippines since they relied on monthly remittances from New York. Gradually it becomes clear that Roldan is the financial benefactor and reluctant head of that far-off household. This bears out Peggy Levitt's observation, via Itzigsohn, that transnational networks lead to the rejuggling of authority within the far-flung units of the family (Itzigsohn, 2001: 285–6). To complicate an already complex picture, Manalansan notes that Roldan's 'weekends, apart from his jaunts to the cross-dressing bars, also included attendance at Sunday mass' (Manalansan, 2005: 154). Assessing the various phases in his informant's day-to-day living, Manalansan concludes:

> Roldan's astute observation of the forms of racialisation in America and their articulation with gender points to the power of his daily experiences and their impact on identity. Because of this situation, bakla as an identity becomes a possibility in the metropole. While bakla is seen to be rooted to the homeland, it becomes a tool to negotiate Roldan's cultural discomfort with mainstream gay public life. Immigration narratives are conventionally and popularly constructed as a linear movement from tradition to modernity, but Roldan's observations of being bakla in America rejects this particular teleology. At the same time, his condition is not a retreat from modernity; rather, it unwittingly destabilises a monolithic gay identity. (Manalansan, 2005: 156)

Playing 'straight' constitutes another such moment of destabilised gay identity. Of the several roles Roldan assumes in his everyday life, one concerns that of a patriarchal provider and decision-maker – a role that eludes his father in the economically deprived context of the Philippines.

Composed of micro events, Manalansan sees everyday practices as framing an alternative historical narrative to the one based on grand events. Evaluating the life histories of queer Filipinos, he discovers that his informants stage their identities differently, and even paradoxically, in response to a multitude of factors (race, gender, culture, sexuality, family) and with reference to several contexts: gay bars and apartments, offices and churches, home and host countries. These different *stagings* of identity comprise the extracted events that make up the narrative of the everyday. They are aspects in the diaspora's 'flexible performative repertoire' (Manalansan, 2005: 156). To extract an event (and this applies to the informant as well as the analyst) entails the institution of a 'positional cut' in the sense implied by Hall. Just as the positional cut arrests the unstable processes of identity formation, thereby making possible determinate actions and decisions, so certain events constitute nodal points in the life histories of queer diasporic Filipinos. These events may relate to other events within the narrative of the everyday, or they may not. But all such events inevitably form part of the flexible performative repertoire. Roldan's espousal of a *bakla* identity is conditioned by the lack of self-recognition in the racialised offices and gay bars of New York, but this event bears little relation to his role as the patriarchal provider of his Philippines-based family. On the other hand, Alden's sexual commerce with the Herb Rittses of American gay society impinges directly on his periodic retreats to the Filipino 'guilt corner' of his apartment, thereby attesting to his psychological need to atone for his transgressions. What we have, in each case, is an account of the various sutures and ruptures that make up the everyday histories of gay Filipinos. Indeed, the strength of Manalansan's approach lies in the hermeneutical value he puts on 'minor' incidents that make up the everyday practices of queer Filipinos in New York. He connects these seemingly negligible moments to a number of macro issues, including transnationality, globalisation, heteropatriarchal value-systems, remittance economies, modernity, neocolonialism, sexual-gender-race discrimination, religious economies, and so on.

Transnationalism, modernity and globalisation form the holy trinity of diaspora criticism. Used routinely by all manner of diasporists, they bear witness to the social, political and cultural repercussions, felt more or less across the planet, of purportedly a new economic regime. Since the regime and its effects remain largely untested, the next chapter sets out to assess the viability of what may be, without exaggeration, called the three pillars of diaspora criticism.

Notes

1. Mishra notes that a smattering of non-indentured Punjabis and Gujaratis were, historically speaking, part of the older migration but excludes them from his framework (Mishra, 1996a: 427).
2. A significant minority of indentured labourers in the colonial plantations were Muslims.

3. In his article 'Nation, Nostalgia and Bollywood', Manas Ray provides one answer to this question: 'The Fiji Indians, with a long tradition of attachment to *bhajan* and other devotional songs, have been influenced by the recent boom in devotional music market in India. Coming in contact with mainland Indians has not only meant digging up casteist and indenture memories; it has, more positively, opened new possibilities for creative expressions by exposing the community to the wider world of Indian music and dance. There are many more Indian dance and music (especially classical) schools in Sydney than was the case in Fiji. The result has been quick to materialise: from receiver of Indian cultural artefacts, the community has become a producer. In the field of devotional music, however, this exposure is impacting the community in a significant way. For more than a century, Fiji Indians were used to singing the Bhojpuri (from the district in Bihar called Bhojpur) style *bhajan* called *tambura bhajan*. Now this is giving way (at least for a section of the community) to the more classically oriented *bhajan* of Anup Jalota, Hari Om Sharan, Anuradha Paudwal and others through audiocassettes produced in India. The CDs of some of the *bhajan* singers of the Sydney community are clear proof of this trend' (Ray, 2003: 29).
4. Entitled 'Eveil de la conscience de race' or 'Awakening of Race Consciousness', the essay appeared in the last issue of *La Revue du monde noir* (Edwards, 2003: 122).
5. For this insight, Edwards draws on Peter Linebaugh's essay 'All the Atlantic Mountains Shook' (1982) and on Peter Linebaugh and Marcus Rediker's *The Many-Headed Hydra* (2000).
6. Ethno-histories are, by definition, bound up with the nationalist project. Anthony D. Smith observes: 'If "nationalism creates nations" in its own image, then its definition of the nation was a piece with its aspirations for collective autonomy, fraternal unity and distinctive identity. The identity and unity that was sought was of and for an existing historic culture-community, which nationalists thought they were reviving and returning to a "world of nations." It depended, therefore, in large measure on the rediscovery of the community's "ethno-history," its peculiar and distinctive cultural contribution to the worldwide fund of what Weber called "irreplaceable culture values"' (Smith, 2000: 242–3).
7. In the article 'Scattered Belongings: Reconfiguring the "African" in the English-African Diaspora', Ifekwunigwe institutes a diachronic break between pre-Columbian and post-Columbian (*locus classicus*) forms of African dispersal (Ifekwunigwe, 2003: 57–8).
8. In a later article, Manalansan notes that he uses '"gay" as a provisional term and intersperse[s] it with "queer" as a rubric . . . to signal the cultural dissonance queer immigrants experience with identity categories and cultural practices' (Manalansan, 2005: 146).
9. In 'Diaspora and Hybridity: Queer Identities and the Ethnicity Model', Alan Sinfield comments on the disadvantages of the ethnicity-and-rights framework: 'There are drawbacks with envisaging ourselves through a framework of ethnicity-and-rights. One is that it consolidates our constituency at the expense of limiting it. If you are lower-class, gay lobbying and lifestyle are less convenient and may

seem alien. If you are young, the call to declare a sexual identity imposes the anxiety that exploration of your gay potential may close options for ever. And if you are a person of colour, the prominence of a mainly white model makes it more difficult for you to negotiate ways of thinking about sexualities that will be compatible with your subcultures of family and neighbourhood. Also, fixing our constituency on the ethnicity-and-rights model lets sex-gender off the hook. It encourages the inference that an out-group needs concessions, rather than the mainstream needing correction; so lesbians and gay men, Herman observes, may be "granted legitimacy, not on the basis that there might be something problematic with gender roles and sexual hierarchies, but on the basis that they constitute a fixed group of 'others' who need and deserve protection" ' (Sinfield, 1996: 272–3).

10. Eithne Luibhéid remarks that 'some scholars date lesbian and gay exclusion from 1917, when people labelled as "constitutional psychopathic inferiors" were first barred from entering the United States. This category included "persons with abnormal sexual instincts" as well as "the moral imbeciles, the pathological liars and swindlers, the defective delinquents, [and] many of the vagrants and cranks." The 1952 McCarran-Walter Act recodified exclusion categories to include a ban on psychopathic personalities. There is no doubt that lesbians and gay men were targeted: a U.S. Senate report related that "the Public Health Service has advised that the provision for the exclusion of aliens afflicted with psychopathic personality or mental defect which appears in the instant bill is sufficiently broad to provide for the exclusion of homosexuals or sex perverts." Court cases from the 1950s and 1960s show that the Immigration and Naturalisation Service . . . used the ban on psychopathic personalities as grounds for excluding men and women whom they thought were, or might become, homosexual. In 1965, when immigration law underwent another sweeping revision, lesbian and gay exclusion was again recodified, this time under the ban on "sexual deviates" ' (Luibhéid, 2005: xii–xiii).
11. These obligations are most obvious in the remittance culture, which is both financial and *social*. Reviewing Peggy Levitt's work, *The Transnational Villagers*, José Itzigsohn points out that she uses the term 'social remittance' to describe ' "the ideas, behaviours, identities, and social capital that flow from host to sending-country communities." In other words, the concept of social remittances refers to the process of cultural transformation that takes place when migrants' cultural practices change as a result of their encounter with a new society and parts of their new cultural repertoires are then transmitted to their relatives and friends in the country of origin' (Itzigsohn, 2001: 284).
12. Manalansan does not refer to Mercer's work on queer diasporic alliances, but it is likely he is aware of it.
13. *Biyuti*, a derivative of beauty, is gay Filipino swardspeak that 'may . . . refer to aesthetic experiences and features, [but] also points to a particular notion of the self as highly mercurial and plastic' (Manalansan, 2005: 149).

5

The Three Pillars of Diaspora Criticism

It has been said that the total statement eludes the genre, any genre, but incites this or that generic statement from its place of hiding. These statements or propositions remain partial, incomplete, sustaining and sustained by the nomination. Since they uphold, interrupt or contravene each other in pursuit of the total statement, these secondary statements form a network of detours around the total statement. Each statement works as a substitute, that is to say, as a fragment that stands in for the whole without ever being equal to it. The total statement, in other words, propagates a series of surrogates for its semantic evasions. In their attempt to pin down an object called diaspora, a project in which the present writer is wryly implicated, diasporists deploy a plethora of surrogate concepts drawn especially from the fields of migration studies, social anthropology and economics. Of the many supplementary terms that swirl in the orbit of diaspora criticism (hybridity, *décalage*, discontinuity, multi-locality, nomadism, double consciousness and so on), the prominent ones are transnationalism, globalisation and modernity. This chapter investigates how these concepts, which form powerful discourses in their own right, contribute to the pursuit of the elusive law of diaspora criticism.

Transnationalism and Modernity

In his editor's preface to the inaugural issue of the journal *Diaspora*, Khachig Tölölyan comments that 'diasporas are the exemplary communities of the transnational moment' (Tölölyan, 1991: 5). Since the prefix *trans*, originally a Latin preposition, bears the sense of 'across', 'beyond', 'over' and 'outside of', *trans*national would denote that which lies outside the national. The national, in turn, derives from nation or *natio* ('breed', 'stock' or 'race'), suggesting an imagined polity (usually an ethno-cultural and linguistic commune) forged within a bounded territory and sustained by the notion of sovereignty. A deifying or hypostasising category, sovereignty guarantees political entities (such as states) the right of dominion over demarcated territories. Tölölyan observes that although cross-border networks and population dispersions are as old as the hills, the modern nation-state is essentially a product of the Enlightenment era. Dispersions and displacements occurring during and after the consolidation of the autocentred bourgeois nation-state have to, consequently, be seen in a different light:

> Crucially, these dispersions, while not altogether new in form, acquired a different meaning by the nineteenth century, in the context of the triumphant nation-state, which as a polity claims special political and emotional legitimacy, representing a homogeneous people, speaking one language, in a united territory, under the rule of one law, and, until recently, constituting one market. (Tölölyan, 1991: 4)

From this statement one may infer that the transnational moment, and any moment comprises a temporal or historical segment, presupposes the existence of a nation connected to an actual or imagined political territory. The coupling of nation to a geopolitical realm, and hence to a *bounded* imagined community, begets that hyphenated creature known as the modern nation-state.[1] It follows that the transnational moment is made up of those aspects that violate the circumscribed structures, polities and ideologies of nation-states. This paradox is at the heart of most conceptions of transnationality. Out of sync with the time of the nation-state, the transnational moment is yet somehow coeval with it. In keeping with this approach, Tölölyan views diasporas as exemplary communities that upset bounded categories in a number of senses: political, territorial, cultural and psychological:

> Diasporas are emblems of transnationalism because they embody the question of borders, which is at the heart of any adequate definition of the Others of the nation-state. The latter always imagines and represents itself as a land, a territory, a place that functions as the site of homogeneity, equilibrium, integration; this is the domestic tranquility that hegemony seeking national elites always desire and sometimes achieve. In such a territory, differences are assimilated, destroyed, or assigned to ghettoes, to enclaves demarcated by boundaries so sharp that they enable the nation to acknowledge the apparently singular and clearly fenced-off differences *within* itself, while simultaneously reaffirming the privileged homogeneity of the rest, as well as the differences *between* itself and what lies over its frontiers. (Tölölyan, 1991: 6)

Indeed, the question of the bourgeois nation-state[2] and its troubled relations with displaced groups and practices, frequently seen as symptomatic of transnational capital, has preoccupied many diasporists. The debate seems to focus on the *perceived* divergence between the ideology that permeates the nation-state and the ideology-disabusing – and this need not be, and seldom is, a deliberate act – presence and practices of various diasporas.[3] Michael Shapiro writes that '[t]he primary understanding of the modern "nation" segment of the nation-state is that a nation embodies a coherent culture, united on the basis of shared descent or, at least, incorporating a "people" with a historically stable coherence.' Since this is so transparently a myth, 'the symbolic maintenance of the nation-state requires a management of historical narratives as well as territorial space' (Shapiro, 2000: 81). It is this activity of symbolic maintenance (via, for instance, the mass media's construction of shared audiences) that renders the nation-state an 'imagined political community' (Anderson, 1991: 6) based on 'the paradox of constructed primordialism' (Appadurai, 1990: 2). Indeed citizen-subjects receive a 'double coding' in that 'citizenship is located both in a legal, territorial entity, which is associated with the privileges of sovereignty and the rights of individuals, and in a cultural community where it is associated with a history of shared ethnic and social characteristics' (Shapiro, 2000: 81). Diasporas are inserted schizophrenically into this scheme, by integrationist as well as pluralist nation-states. As citizens of a nation-state, diasporas may enjoy the abstract rights and privileges of citizenship manifested in a juridical or constitutional sense. Since, however, they may not share a common cultural ground with the hegemonic community whose particular values and goals are mediated by the nation-state, and subtly or openly incorporated into its laws, the right to culture-specific practices may be denied them. Even a pluralist nation-state will brook only those practices that do not directly collide with the universal rights abstracted from the particular belief systems, historical struggles, discursive practices and economic ambitions of the foundational community. If a British subject of Pakistani origin were to wed more than one wife as is permitted under *sharia*, his action, if it occurred inside the dominion, would contravene Britain's marriage laws based on the monogamous expectations of its 'mythic' foundational community. It would also be argued that the practice of polygamy constitutes an anachronism in the time of modernity and tramples on the basic rights of women. Generally speaking, then, diasporas are regarded as estranged and estranging sharers of the national life-world. Cut off from the dominant national forms of their host country, transmigrants find solace in self-familiarising practices. They cling to mother tongues and exotic sartorial habits, they run 'ethnic' outlets and form suburban enclaves, and they build culture-specific meeting halls and places of worship. These markers of difference, in turn, have the effect of estranging members of the hegemonic community from their (subconscious) assumptions about the isomorphism of national codes and territory. Appadurai is of the opinion that deterritorialised populations have turned the hyphen that connects the nation to state into a sign of rupture rather than a figure of continuity:

> One important new feature of global cultural politics . . . is that state and nation are at each other's throats, and the hyphen that links them is now less an icon of conjuncture than an index of disjuncture. This disjunctive relationship between nation and state has two levels: at the level of any given nation-state, it means that there is a battle of the imagination, with state and nation seeking to cannibalise each other. Here is the seed-bed of brutal separatisms, majoritarianisms that seem to have appeared from nowhere, and micro-identities that have become political projects within the nation-state. At another level, this disjunctive relationship is deeply entangled with the global disjunctures discussed throughout this essay: ideas of nationhood appear to be steadily increasing in scale and regularly crossing existing state boundaries; sometimes, as with Kurds, because previous identities stretched across vast national spaces, or, as with the Tamils in Sri Lanka, the dormant threads of a transnational diaspora have been activated to ignite the micro-politics of the nation-state. (Appadurai, 1990: 13–14)

Characterised as being constitutionally different from subjects rooted in the national territory, transmigrants do not adhere easily to the regime of some long-established geopolitical order. By failing to accede to the hegemony of enclosed structures, ideologies and filiations, at least in their attitude to the host country, they constitute one in a number of vital symptoms that epitomise the transnational moment:

> These include massive and instantaneous movements of capital; the introduction of previously 'alien' cultures through the practice of 'media imperialism;' issues of double allegiance of populations and the plural affiliations of transnational corporations. All these developments point to the need to interrogate the national context in which certain assumptions about collective identity once prevailed; they also raise questions about the global context. (Tölölyan, 1991: 5)

The suggestion here is that *current* trans-border transmissions in finance, goods, services, peoples, cultures, allegiances and media effects are at odds with nation-oriented and nationally organised practices associated with classical forms of surplus accumulation. The older patterns of accumulation were administered by the bourgeois national state and the modes and relations of production, not only of commodities but also of labour power, social relations, cultural forms and citizens, were mostly carried out within the borders of the nation-state. Led by free-spirited mercantile entrepreneurs in its early stage (such as the itinerant factors of the East India Company),[4] it is evident that even colonial forms of accumulation, both of capital and territory, gradually lost their trans-territorial character and became nation-centred.[5] The Industrial Revolution, and the technological innovations it inspired, was a crucial contributing factor in determining this shift. A combination of military coercion and parliamentary legislation ensured that colonised territories yielded to the interests of Europe's newly industrialised centres. These territories became economic outposts, supplying the centre with cheap raw material and opening up fresh markets for the sale of manufactured commodities. For the economist, Samir Amin, this older form of capital accumulation was distinguished by 'the crystallisation of core industrial systems as national autocentred systems which paralleled the construction of the national bourgeois states' (Amin, 1997: 1). It is his opinion that since about 1945 the processes of capital accumulation have become gradually *delinked* from core industrial systems overseen by bourgeois nation-states. This has instigated a crisis on a global scale because nationally based social and political institutions have not been able to adapt to this operational shift. What we see instead is the persistence of crisis management structures such as the World Bank, the International Monetary Fund and the International Trade Organisation. Like Amin, Tölölyan thinks of the transnational moment as being qualitatively in advance of but taking place at the same time as the national moment characterised by bounded regimes. Despite the sundering of economic regimes from bounded territories (which bears no relation to the fundamental issue of capital *redistribution* to less fortunate societies), the national moment still holds sway, and even obtains strength, by virtue of the political power it wields over one or another imagined community. Diasporas are sometimes seen as both harbingers and symptoms of this contradiction.

By thinking of the transnational moment in present-day terms, Tölölyan means to draw a distinction between the pre-modern or classical diasporas – old-world Jews, Greeks, Parsis and Armenians – and the large-scale dispersal of significant ethnic clusters, or 'ethnoscapes' (Appadurai, 1990: 7), witnessed in the time of late modernity. This periodising move is significant because it places diasporas within rather than outside the durational horizon of modernity. While murmurs of protest have been raised in various quarters concerning the appropriation of an ancient category,[6] diasporists have largely endorsed this annexation. Iain Chambers notes that the 'chronicles of diasporas – those of the black Atlantic, of metropolitan Jewry, of mass rural displacement – constitute the ground swell of modernity' (Chambers, 1994: 16), while Vijay Mishra writes of diaspora as 'the exemplary condition of late modernity'

(Mishra, 1996a: 426). For James Clifford, the exemplarity of this condition takes on a counter-normative aspect inasmuch as diasporas are bearers of 'discrepant temporalities . . . that trouble the linear, progressive narratives of the nation-state and global modernisation' (Clifford, 1994: 317). This assertion echoes Gilroy's original observation that transnational practices of the black diaspora have inspired the dissenting cultures of modernity, thereby begetting a structure of 'antagonistic indebtness' (Gilroy, 1993: 191). There is, then, a fundamental link between modern forms of dispersion, transnational practices and modernity. But what precisely is modernity? The concept appears to possess a horizontal as well as a vertical dimension. The horizontal dimension is historicist in that the term is suggestive of a definite chronological break between the past and the present instituted by the Industrial Revolution. The mercantilist phase of capital (1500–1790), consequently, falls outside the strictly modern. Étienne Balibar, for instance, sees the merchant phase as a crucial period of transition to industrialised forms of capital accumulation (Balibar, 1970: 271–308).[7] Depending on the analyst one consults, the long present of modernity consists of one single or two or three different episodes. Drawing on the work of Jürgen Habermas, Gilroy sees modernity as an unfolding historical continuum with its own contrapuntal narratives. It is this sense of an unfinished duration that allows him to plot continuities in black cultural practices during and beyond the age of slavery, and in the context of multiple terrains. Mishra departs from Gilroy in that he breaks up the time of modernity into the stages of plantation (monopolist) and advanced (transnational) capital. Plantation capital is linked to the colonial practices of technologically privileged European nation-states in the nineteen and early twentieth centuries, while advanced capital is seen in terms of the global instability of markets and nation-states. It is also characterised by non-peasant forms of deterritorialisation. The exclusivist practices of the agrarian migrants of the indenture period (1834–1920) are hitched to the logic of a modernity driven by colonial modes of industrial agriculture, whereas the border or hybrid practices of postwar migrants to the various urban centres are indicative of a transnational world. Mishra's model provides a modified version of Jameson's threefold division of historical modernity in his famous treatise on postmodernism. Following Ernest Mandel's system of historicising quantum leaps in technologies of production, Jameson argues that capital accumulation has occurred over three dialectical stages: market, imperial-monopolist and multinational (Jameson, 1991: 35–36). To the last of these techno-economic stages he assigns the decentred, dehistoricising and depthless effects of postmodern cultural practices. Although his periodising breaks are somewhat different, Amin too believes that 'modernity is . . . synonymous with capitalism' as it has emerged since the period of Enlightenment (Amin, 2001: 12). He subdivides it into the classical period (1800 onwards), the postwar period (1945–90) and the current period beginning around 1990 (Amin, 1997: 1–2). The classical period is distinguished by the overwhelming dominance of core industrial economies (Europe, North America), the middle period sees the industrialisation of selected peripheral societies in the scramble to 'catch up' (Asia, Latin America) and the increased marginalisation of others (sub-Saharan Africa), while the contemporary period is characterised by stagnation and a systemic crisis arising from the mulish persistence of older forms of social and political organisation in an era of unchecked capitalism. In a nutshell, the operational changes within the system of surplus accumulation have not been matched by the evolution of social and political institutions capable of administering this runaway system.

In the vertical approach to modernity, the temporal breaks are no longer strictly chronological; rather, temporal differences are viewed spatially. Since space is measured in the context of technological advancement and economic development, time becomes a matter of spatio technological apportionment and territorial position: North and South, East and West, Third and First, etc. The less developed the society, the weaker its claim to the time of the present. Here modernity functions as an instrument for calibrating time according to a techno-developmental yardstick. Some societies are characterised as woefully traditional backwaters (Africa), others as developing peripheries (Asia) and others still as dynamic contemporary cosmopolities (United States, Japan, western Europe). Social systems existing at the same time may not, consequently, dwell in the same temporality. Time takes on a spatial dimension, becomes spatially fragmented. Each of these fragments turn into ' "naturally" discontinuous spaces' made up of distinct societies, cultures and nations (Gupta and Ferguson, 1992: 6). This gives rise to the notion of the simultaneity of the non-simultaneous or the synchronicity of the non-synchronous. Some polities are in time, others sadly out of joint with it. Reflecting on temporal divisions within the time of the present, Dipesh Chakrabarty observes that although every culture is contemporary some are *markedly* less contemporary than others (Chakrabarty, 2000: 87). Less contemporary cultures exist in the present but remain outside the progressive time of modernity. Modernity, then, functions as sign of value. It is aligned to industrial development, scientific categories, division of church and state, separation of private and public domains, various rights discourses, nuclear families, metropolitan lifestyles, nation-state polities, liberal jurisprudence, consumerism, secular life-worlds and collective civic responsibility. Societies that lack some or most of these aspects are deemed, and doubtless doomed, to suffer from time lag. Constituting archaisms in the present, they are exhorted (by their own elites as well as by such bodies as the World Bank, the International Monetary Fund and the World Trade

Organisation) to evolve modern forms of capital accumulation. They are prevailed upon to catch up, compelled to modernise. Comprising the standard value in the assessment of time-as-development (not unlike the greenback in matters of currency exchange), modernity's historical stages are no longer simply an affair of chronology. The historical past is not a spectral memory but coexists materially alongside the present as well as the future. Different territories and cultures are simultaneously at different stages of modernity, and some are even outside its sphere of influence, as is the case with subsistence economies in sub-Saharan Africa or Papua New Guinea. The different geo-temporalities of modernity are caught up in a process that culminates in a grand teleological illusion whereby capitalist modes of accumulation (which know neither limit nor end) become inseparable from the quest for a utopia of universal development. The theory is that, at some point, all the heterogeneous temporalities will meet up in the homogenous, empty time of the overdeveloped. For the political left, this utopia is a cynical mirage because its attainment would put in jeopardy dominant forms of capital accumulation based on the relentless exploitation of impoverished peripheries. Indeed, it has been argued that there is no automatic link between capital accumulation and the development of productive forces and institutions (Amin, 1997: 17), or democracy for that matter.

The modern world systems theory of capital accumulation affords the best template for this vertical approach to modernity. The chief proponent of this approach, Immanuel Wallerstein, insists that capitalism constitutes a worldwide web that perpetuates a set of divisions and imbalances that are, more or less, intrinsic to the system and cannot be resolved without its termination. The historical dynamics of capital accumulation and economic expansion are, in other words, manifested in the cartography of spatial divisions. The world is cut up into core, semi-peripheral, peripheral and external areas. The core areas have evolved social and political structures, namely states and state machineries (industrial, communication, transport and military technologies), that put them at a distinct advantage over the rest. This advantage allows core states to dictate the terms of capital accumulation and to harvest the lion's share of the wealth. Wallerstein argues that the semi-peripheries (developing: suppliers of vital skills, etc.) and peripheries (underdeveloped: suppliers of raw material, etc.), service the core areas, the peripheries service the semi-peripheries, while the external areas are on the extremities of the system. But this geo-economic hierarchy is fluid rather than eternally fixed:

> World-economies . . . are divided into core-states and peripheral areas. . .There are also semi-peripheral areas which are in between the core and the periphery on a series of dimensions, such as the

> complexity of economic activities, strength of the state machinery, cultural integrity, etc. Some of these areas had been core areas of earlier versions of a given world-economy. Some had been peripheral areas that were later promoted, so to speak, as a result of the changing geopolitics of an expanding world-economy.
>
> Hence, the ongoing process of a world-economy tends to expand the economic and social gaps among its varying areas in the very process of its development. One factor that tends to mask this fact is that the process of development of a world-economy brings about technological advances which make it possible to expand the boundaries of a world-economy. In this case, particular regions of the world may change their structural role in the world-economy, to their advantage, even though the disparity of reward between different sectors of the world-economy as a whole may be simultaneously widening. It is in order to observe this crucial phenomenon clearly that we have insisted on the distinction between a peripheral area of a given world-economy and the external arena of the world-economy. The external arena of one century often becomes the periphery of the next – or its semi-periphery. But then too core-states can become semi-peripheral and semi-peripheral ones peripheral. (Wallerstein, 1974: 349–50)

Clearly, while the relations among the various spatial domains of the world system may be historically unstable in that semi-peripheries may turn into cores and cores into peripheries and so on, what remains constant is the disequilibrium within an ever-expanding capitalist system. So, for instance, the rise of peripheral China may potentially result in the decline of core Japan. The disequilibrium is, in turn, territorially circumscribed (even though economic factors are manifestly not) in the sense that the peripheries do not necessarily inhere in the cores nor the cores in the peripheries. Wallerstein's model depends on a double manoeuvre. On the one hand, the spatio-temporal differences among the various areas are patently unstable over the *longue durée* of history; on the other, the set of definitional properties that constitute the values of the core, semi-periphery and periphery are associated with discrete territorial entities. Sets of properties and territories shift about in relatively stable units. A designated territory may not, therefore, possess more than one set of properties. The properties defining the core states, the peripheries and the semi-peripheries belong exclusively to each of these categories and cannot feature simultaneously in a single enclosed territory. Core properties may not be found in the periphery and vice versa.

An overwhelming number of diasporists are concerned with an emergent world system that breaches such territorially bounded conceptions of socio-economic disequilibrium. Furthermore, it is insinuated that this breach, whereby core and peripheral properties habitually crisscross territorial borders, may be noticeable on several fronts: political, financial, demographic, informational, aesthetic and subjective. Transnationalism, late modernity, multinational capital, wildcat or disorganised capital, global capital and globalisation are some of the terms used to describe this emergent system. While there is little agreement about the number of periodising breaks that mark the time of modernity or the different diachronic categories that break up the time of diasporas (classical, plantation, modern and so on), there seems to be a general belief that the late twentieth century has undergone a transformation in the mode of capital accumulation. Rouse, for example, follows Jameson's lead and points out that 'the global shift from colonialism and classic forms of dependency to a new transnational capitalism' has opened up a 'social space' we are only just beginning to apprehend. 'Suddenly', he writes, 'the comforting modern imagery of nation-states and national languages, of coherent communities and consistent subjectivities, of dominant centres and distant margins no longer seems adequate' (Rouse, 1991: 8). It has become increasingly difficult, in short, to map transnational social and economic relations within the integrated framework of 'community' or in terms of the 'centre–periphery' dichotomy. Solidly anchored to stable correlates (community equals bounded territory, distinct commonalities, shared structures and so on) or to hierarchical dyads (first and third worlds, rural and urban divides, provincial and metropolitan contexts), such socio-spatial tropes, according to Rouse, fail to do justice to the intricate migratory circuits of disaggregated peoples such as the Aguilillans (Rouse, 1991: 14). Characterised by the circulatory transmission of people, money, goods and information across the core (United States) and peripheral (Mexico) arenas, Aguilillan practices are symptomatic of late modernity. According to Rouse, these practices suggest something of a crisis in forms of cognitive mapping since – notwithstanding his own efforts – they appear to be uncannily in advance of the idiom needed to describe them. The essential point is that aspects of the peripheries may now be found in the core and that of the core in the peripheries. Nations, spaces, cultures are no longer isomorphic. There is a new mobility of properties, labour, cultures, images, concepts and capital that tends to defy the old temporal divisions of North and South predicated on the fenced-off compounds of nation-states. These symptoms, it is supposed, testify to the new transnational or global character of capitalism.

Rouse is, of course, not alone in making this point. Writing on the Chinese diaspora, Aihwa Ong and Donald Nonini also hold to the opinion that transnationalism concerns 'migrations, dislocations, and cultural upheavals associated with the "hypermodernity" of late capitalism' and 'point to the necessity of reconceptualising the relationship between the study of Chinese identities and place-bound theorisations of preglobal social science, implied in such terms as *territory, region, nationality*, and *ethnicity*' (Ong and Nonini, 1997: 3–5). They accept that transnational practices existed prior to the late twentieth century, but maintain that, in its contemporary manifestation, transnationalism is the product of a flexible or footloose capital unshackled from the nation-state. This view appears to have wide currency among diasporists as well as globalists. Dwelling at length on the growing mobility of transnational firms and the removal of institutional barriers to capital expansion, Lavie and Swedenburg assert that the 'economic horizon of capitalist internationalisation' in the post-Fordist era 'remains crucial to any understanding of how sensibilities of identity are dislocated between cultures and territories' (Lavie and Swedenburg, 1996: 6). Sarah Lamb advances a similar point but with more precision: 'The term "transnational" refers broadly to social, cultural, political, and/or economic forces that "extend across or beyond" (*trans*) two or more nations' (Lamb, 2002: 303). Expressing a finicky regard for subcategories, Stanley Tambiah thinks in the context of three overlapping currents:

> Under the label 'transnational movements' I should ideally deal with three flows: the flow of people through transnational migrations; the flow of capital in our present time of multinational capitalism; and the flow of information over vast distances in the context of modern developments in communication. I should like to state at the outset that these phenomena are by no means new and that historically there have been large-scale occurrences of these flows, with momentous consequences. Nevertheless, I support the view that in recent decades the three flows of people, capital, and information, *dynamically related and interwoven*, together are generating some intensified effects that are said to be distinctive of our so-called postmodern world. *In combination* they test and breach the autonomy, sovereignty, and territorial boundaries of extant nation-states hitherto considered as the primary units of collective sociopolitical identity and existence. (Tambiah, 2000: 163–4, italics mine)

The common thread that binds all these pronouncements is the assumption that one type of transnational practice automatically involves or incorporates the others. Descriptions of interweavings, dynamic relations and embeddings (Ong, 1999: 4) clearly imply a process whereby the various dimensions of transnationalism are simultaneously present in any given practice. It follows that the transnationalism of capital subsumes the transnationalism of people which, in turn, subsumes the transnationalism of information, and so on. Not only does this assumption engender a vulgar mimetic model, but, perhaps more worryingly, it encourages the negation of the strands of contradiction that inform each dimension as well as the relationship between one dimension and another.[8]

The assumption shuts out the possibility that transnational capital may produce incongruent effects such as, for instance, the long-term immobilisation of low-skilled labour and an expanding base of unassimilable reserve labour in peripheral countries, or that some transmigrants may participate in long-distance nationalism or bolster nation-state formations through the remittance system, or that the global flow of information might actually generate reactionary ethno-cultural formations or, more positively, strategic localisms rather than the hybrid utopia of a shared global culture. Recently, to cite a specific case of reactionary ethno-culturalism, the SMS facility built into cell-phone systems (which are manufactured, distributed and consumed transnationally) was used with terrifying success to summon hordes of white supremacists to a Sydney beach where they proceeded to defend Anglo-Australian values (identified emblematically with beach culture and the surfing confraternity) against 'interlopers' with a 'Middle Eastern appearance'. (Significantly, *appearance* and *apparition* have the same etymological root.) It mattered little to the assailants that these interlopers were fellow citizens from suburbs without beaches or that the phenotype is an unreliable marker of ethnicity.[9]

A further drawback with the embedded approach is that the elements in question, whether economic, social, cultural or informational, end up surrendering their irreducible and concrete intensities, merging into each other like so many rings inside an eddy. Žižek has warned us against any logic of embedding that promotes a sense of social totality at the expense of the concrete intensities of integral concepts:

> The trap to be avoided . . . is the naïve idea that one should keep in view the social totality, of which democratic ideology, the exercise of power and the process of economic (re)production are merely parts. If one tries to keep all these views simultaneously, one ends up seeing nothing – their contours disappear. (Žižek, 2004: 129)

In a dynamically related structure, any one element may replace another in terms of the pressure it exerts in the transnational arena. This generates a system of false equivalences whereby one category may act *as if* it were another and so on until we attain the social totality. Hence diaspora culture may act *as if* it were transnational capital, thereby begetting the neoliberal category of cultural capital. Discussing ethno-racial identity formations among South Asians in the United States, Kamala Visweswaran makes this point bluntly:

> Without more attention . . . to how class determines the differential nature and experience of racial formations, there is a danger . . . that 'popular diaspora theory' of neoliberals like Joel Kotkin or conservatives like Thomas Sowell will substitute uncontested stories of culture for accounts

> of capital, contributing to the deployment of culturalist arguments against economic 'failures' of inner-city minorities. (Visweswaran, 1997: 5)

She proceeds to ask a most penetrating question: '. . . what does it mean when culture increasingly grounds the language of capital?' (Visweswaran, 1997: 11). The classical response from the left would be that instead of comprising a subsidiary element in the social relations of production, it means that culture takes on the role of principal agent. Rather than the arena where social contradictions get played out, either subversively or symptomatically (as in literary texts), culture becomes the key determinant in the success or failure of a given ethno-racial entity within a system of capital accumulation. Granted that culture is not bereft of agency (as Althusser reminds us in his famous statement on the relative autonomy of superstructures), but to treat it as somehow anterior to or detached from surplus accumulation yet capable of impinging on it negatively or positively, is to put the proverbial cart before the horse. Just as the weight of a cart impinges on the driving power of the horse, so a cultural system may impinge, for better or for worse, on systems of capital accumulation. It cannot, however, become the raw power that actually drives the process. Visweswaran remarks that popular diasporists explain 'the economic failures of inner-city blacks' as opposed to 'the success of particular Asian immigrant groups not by accounting for how Asians organise capital, but by positing the existence of essential cultural traits which blacks are seen to lack' (Visweswaran, 1997: 7). This practice of 'ethnicising . . . capital', she argues, conceals the fact that 'the globalisation of the bourgeoisie is increasingly being understood in cultural, racial, or ethnic, rather than class terms' (Visweswaran, 1997: 11). Visweswaran is very much on the mark here. Any approach that seeks to equalise the unequal intensities associated with such terms as culture, race, gender and class is bound to come up with highly dubious explanations for social and economic disparities. If gender, for instance, is one of the forms in which class is lived, and if gender and class are further inflected by the modality of race or culture, it is plainly not enough to say that they are mutually embedded categories. It pays to isolate the peculiar intensities of class, race, culture and gender as they function in a given context, each alongside or against the others, without equalising them in some sort of strange pseudo-egalitarian manoeuvre.

In her work on flexible citizenship practices in the Chinese diaspora, Aihwa Ong tends to lapse into this sort of error. Insisting on the 'embeddedness' of economic, cultural, social and political factors 'that stream across spaces', she offers an omnibus definition of transnationality:

> *Trans* denotes both moving through space or across lines, as well as changing the nature of something. Besides suggesting new relations between

> nation-states and capital, transnationality also alludes to the *trans*versal, the *trans*actional, the *trans*lational, and the *trans*gressive aspects of contemporary behavior and imagination that are incited, enabled, and regulated by the changing logics of states and capitalism . . . [W]hen I use the word *globalisation*, I am referring to the narrow sense of new corporate strategies, but analytically, I am concerned with transnationality – or the condition of cultural interconnectedness and mobility across space – which has been intensified under late capitalism. I use *transnationalism* to refer to the cultural specificities of the global processes, tracing the multiplicity of the uses and conceptions of 'culture.' (Ong, 1999: 4)

The end result is that the prefix 'trans' may be attached to any of the mutually embedded categories of culture, subjectivity, politics, imagination and economics to account for border-breaching movements. The various 'trans' regimes get articulated within a conjoined system where each category is just as revealing as any other of the processes of transnationalism. The embedded categories, to be sure, are subject to a single shared gravitational field. The disembedded approach, by contrast, gains in complexity precisely by treating each category as if it were emanating from and dwelling in its own gravitational field *within the same system*. In this latter approach influence is largely a matter of the disequilibria resulting from the relative proximity or distance of one category to the others. Profoundly shot through with contradictions, each category may betray points of continuity at certain levels and discontinuity at others. Instead of pursuing a mimetic strategy that equilibrates the various categories, the disembedded approach is open to the suggestion that the force field of one category may distort the force field of another, thereby procuring aberrant and antagonistic effects. Transnational capital, to take a case in point, might reinforce conservative rather than transgressive attitudes within certain communities. Many multinational outfits in the third world prefer to employ women workers because of their perceived docility to national patriarchal structures and suitability for regimented labour. Àtu Emberson-Bain has pointed out that the practice of targeting women, initially adopted 'by world market factories in regions like Asia and Central and South America' and then extended to the Pacific region (Emberson-Bain, 1994: 155–6), successfully draws on gender assumptions:

> The policy has its roots firmly planted in the economic benefits that derive from the so-called 'traditional' gender division of labour which encapsulates discriminatory values about 'women's work' and well-worn arguments about their 'natural' dexterity and precision (or 'nimble fingers'), patience, speed and efficiency, and thus their suitability for assembly line work. (Emberson-Bain, 1994: 156)

Similarly, as I shall presently show, the globally integrated financial markets that generate virtual surpluses may be greatly responsible for creating battalions of stranded reserve labour in the fourth world. There is also, as we saw previously, the case of transnational information networks (such as the world-wide electronic web) being used by long-distance jingoists to intervene in the political affairs of the home territory. Here transnational publics draw on transnational media networks in pursuit of a fiercely nationalist agenda. Ong is not totally oblivious to these discrepancies. At one point, while discussing certain shortcomings in Appadurai's work on cultural globalisation, she laments:

> He makes no attempt to identify the processes that increasingly differentiate the power of mobile and nonmobile subjects. Indeed, he ignores the political economy of time-space compression and gives the misleading impression that everyone can take equal advantage of mobility and modern communications and that transnationality has been liberatory, in both spatial and political senses, for all peoples. This assumption is belied by a recent United Nations human-development report that the gaps between the rich and the poor within and between countries are at an all-time high. (Ong, 1999: 11)

Unfortunately the same criticism may be applied to Ong's own approach which treats political economy and culture as flipsides of the single sovereign. When one form of transnationality (economic) subsumes all manner of 'trans' effects (culture, citizenship, imagination) through a logic of embedding, then it becomes increasingly difficult to isolate the points of distortion in the force fields of the various categories. 'Trans', as an unresolved border condition, turns into a marker of privilege rather than being inflected differently for different cases. Falling through the gaps in this scheme are exactly those entities and effects that cannot fit into any of the given modes of the transnational. Consider this remark:

> If . . . we pay attention instead to the *transnational practices and imaginings* of the nomadic subject and the social conditions that enable his flexibility, we obtain a different picture of how nation-states articulate with capitalism in late modernity. Indeed, our Hong Kong taipan is not simply a Chinese subject adroitly navigating the disjunctures between political landscapes and the shifting opportunities of global trade. His very flexibility in geographical and social positioning is itself an effect of novel articulations between the regimes of the family, the state, and capital, the kinds of practical-technical adjustments that have implications for our understanding of the late modern subject. (Ong, 1999: 3)

Ong's study is patently concerned with the multi-territorial flexibility of a certain kind of subject – the taipan or elite businessman. She also makes it quite clear that the taipan's flexible subject position has to be seen in the context of a loss of territorial coincidence between family, state and capital accumulation. The outcome of the newly decentred relationship between the subject (flitting between territories), his family or families (living often in politically stable territories) and states (the multiple arenas of capital accumulation) is the variable identity of the multiple passport holder. While the passports seldom tell the whole story about the subject (his split allegiances, among other things), they do facilitate the taipan's shuttling back and forth between the multiple sites of business and family. Ong's choice of the Chinese diasporic entrepreneur to illustrate the workings of transnational capital and the consequent decentring of family, ethno-national and bounded identity regimes is based on a series of mimetic manoeuvres. Decentred regimes of capital, subject and family are informed by each other, engendering a mirrorwork of flexibility. The fault is not in the analysis per se (since the triadic relationship she describes is perfectly feasible), but in the manner in which the lived realities of the privileged bourgeois astronaut is taken to be representative of the late modern subject in particular and of transnational capital in general. The logic runs as follows. As a stage of late historical modernity, transnational capital engenders a new kind of social entity – namely, the late modern subject. By virtue of his flexibility in matters of business, family and citizenship, the ideal representative of the late modern subject is the elite businessman of the diaspora. This begs the following question. How is it that a miniscule but affluent proportion of the world's population comes to *represent* the late modern subject? By means of a mimetic correlation between flexible mobility and transnational forms of accumulation? But transnational forms of capital accumulation also facilitate unglamorous kinds of mobility: for instance, of guest workers, nurses, cleaners, drivers, street vendors, prostitutes, asylum seekers and refugees. Even more significantly, transnational capital creates stranded labour, whether it is active or semi-active labour in third-world sweatshops or masses of reserve labour in the fourth world. Are these stranded multitudes not late modern subjects simply because they fail the mimetic test of hypermobility? Or are they somehow even more representative of the effects of transnational capital? At what point, and through what logic of complicity, do *empowered* subjects turn into the *exemplary* subjects of late modernity? Gayatri Chakravorty Spivak's take on the transnational offers us a very different account of the phenomenon:

> What do I understand today by a 'transnational world?' That it is impossible for the new and developing states, the newly decolonising or the old decolonising nations, to escape the orthodox constraints of a 'neo-liberal' world economic system which, in the name of Development, and now 'sustainable development,' removes all barriers between itself and fragile

> national economies, so that any possibility of building for social redistribution is severely damaged. In this new transnationality, what is usually meant by 'the new diaspora,' the new scattering of the seeds of 'developing' nations, so that they can take root on developed ground? Eurocentric migration, labour export male and female, border crossings, the seeking of political asylum, and the haunting in-place uprooting of 'comfort women' in Asia and Africa. (Spivak, 1996: 245)

One outcome of the flexible and voluntary mobility of diaspora capitalists may be the involuntary mobility of certain sub-classes in the peripheries. A few pages later, Spivak draws an important distinction between the widespread effects of economic transnationality and population dispersions, noting that 'large groups . . . [especially subaltern women] subsist in transnationality without escaping into diaspora' (Spivak, 1996: 247). By separating the effects of transnational capital from diaspora flows, Spivak is able to point to the deleterious and contradictory effects of global capital for great masses of humanity. What are these multitudes if not the unfortunate subjects of late modernity?

Globalisation

Too many analysts simply amble through a system of alternating mirrors. In this system diasporas appear as transmigrants (flexible, border-breaching subjects) in the mirror of late modernity. Late modernity fixes the durational horizon for the appearance of transnational capital (flexible, border-breaching economic practices); the latter, in turn, mirrors the process that testifies to the spectre (or becoming-body, as Derrida would have it) of an integrated supranational economic system. Since the last – globalisation – is more or less a self-evident occurrence, an event no less, rather than a disputed category,[10] most critics feel no special need to elaborate on the relationship between globalisation, transnationalism and modern forms of social dispersion. This lack of engagement with discourses of globalisation forms the Achilles heel of diaspora criticism. The first point to make about globalisation is that it is a grossly overdetermined category, sparking much recent chatter, furore and antagonism.[11] In the first instance it names and constitutes a discourse on current macro economic events that find symptomatic expression in shifts experienced in the domains of culture, aesthetics, information, politics, the environment and so forth. Whether one is an adherent or a sceptic, it is beyond dispute that globalisation *refers* to an economic 'turn' whereby national forms of capital accumulation are being supplanted by transnational practices (such as the outsourcing of service industries) that herald an integrated world system. The dispute is not whether there is such a 'turn', but whether it might not be a recurrent phase within the intrinsically expansionist logic of capital. It has been argued, for instance, that in real terms the *belle époque* of 1890–1914 was far more global in scope than the present era (Held and McGrew, 2000: 19). It has also been argued that global capital is 'not some drastic new phenomenon but a historically explicable one whose peculiar forms are dependent on the specific series of crises that capitalism has engendered within and for itself in the continual process of revolutionising the means of production' (Smith, 1997: 21). This view accords with Marx-Engel's prediction that the bourgeois class is periodically obliged to revolutionise the instruments and relations of production, and thereby social relations in their entirety:

> The bourgeois cannot exist without constantly revolutionising the instruments of production, and thereby the relations of production, and with them the whole relations of society. Conservation of the old modes of production in unaltered form, was, on the contrary, the first condition of existence for all earlier industrial classes. Constant revolutionising of production, uninterrupted disturbance of all social conditions, everlasting uncertainty and agitation distinguish the bourgeois epoch from all earlier ones. All fixed, fast-frozen relations, with their train of ancient and venerable prejudices and opinions, are swept away, all new-formed ones become antiquated before they can ossify. All that is solid melts into air, all that is holy is profaned, and man is at last compelled to face with sober senses, his real conditions of life, and his relations with his kind.
>
> The need of a constantly expanding market for its products chases the bourgeoisie over the whole surface of the globe. It must nestle everywhere, settle everywhere, establish connexions everywhere. (Marx and Engels, 1978: 476)

Related to the issue of expansion is another concern. If globalisation is a dialectical phase of capital, then what is meant by global economic integration? Integration, a popular concept in neoliberal discourse, implies an equal participation of the parts in whatever whole that is generated, but plainly there is little chance of such an outcome in any system given over to the seizure of surplus. The point is that socio-economic and territorial disparities will persist simply because they are intrinsic to the system of capital accumulation. To contend, then, that the core–periphery dichotomy has been surmounted through globalisation (in that mega malls exist in India and sweatshops flourish in the United States) is to overlook the essential inequalities sustaining 'global class formations' (Visweswaran, 1997: 11) within specific territories. In a critique of Michael Hardt and Antonio Negri's *Empire*, Amin makes this point with formidable authority:

> In . . . [their] vision, transnationalisation has already abolished imperialism (and imperialism in conflict), replacing it with a system in which the centre is both nowhere and everywhere. The centre–periphery opposition (that defines the imperialist relation) is already 'surpassed.' Hardt and Negri here take up the commonplace discourse in which, since there is a 'first world' of 'wealth' in the 'third world' and a 'third world' of poverty in the first, there is no point opposing the first and third worlds to each other. Certainly there are wealthy and poor in India, just as in the United States, since we all still live in class divided societies integrated into world capitalism. Does that mean that the social formations of India and the United States are identical? Does the distinction between the active role of some in shaping the world and the passive role of others, who can only 'adjust' to the requirements of the globalised system, have no meaning? In reality, this distinction is more pertinent today than ever. In the earlier phase of contemporary history (1945–1980), the relations of force between the imperialist countries and the dominated countries were such that the 'development' of the peripheries was on the agenda, leaving open the possibility for the latter to assert themselves as active agents in the transformation of the world. Today these relations have changed dramatically in favour of dominant capital. The discourse of development has disappeared and been replaced by that of 'adjustment.' (Amin, 2005: 2–3)

Amin has also identified the thorny issue of the contradiction between national states, which are products of centralised economic practices and upholders of national interests, and the decentred forces of global capital that must either confront or court these supposedly outdated social and political apparatuses. Gary Teeple sees the stand-off in slightly more apocalyptic terms:

> Globalisation can be defined as the unfolding resolution of the contradiction between an ever expanding capital and its national political and social formations. Up to the 1970s, the expansion of capital was always as national capital, capital with particular territorial and historical roots and character. Afterwards, capital began to expand more than ever as simply the corporation; ownership began to correspond less and less with national geographies. Just as capital once had to create a national state and a defined territory, in the form of the transnational corporation (TNC) it has had to remove or transform this 'shell' to create institutions to ensure and facilitate accumulations at the global level. Globalisation is the close of the national history of the expansion of capital and the beginning of the history of the expansion of capital *sans* nationality. (Teeple, 2000: 9)

There are at least two grounds on which to quibble with this somewhat festive scenario. The first concerns the premature announcement of the death of the national state.[12] It is one thing to profess, as Amin does, that 'in the pair national/global the terms of causality are reversed: earlier the national power commanded the global presence and today it is the reverse' (Amin, 2004: 19), but quite another to declare the imminent demise of all nationalised forms. It serves no purpose to duplicate the neoliberal pseudo-utopian discourse of global economic integration, based as it is on the fable of a putative resolution of all antinomies, especially that between poor peripheries and rich cores. This was known as ideology in the old parlance, that is the attainment of consensus through a general submission to a fabricated imaginary. The second related problem pertains to the ideology of resolution, which, in the above discourse, appears to be an effect of transnational capital in its inexorable drive towards planetary integration that signals an end to the classical nation-state as we know it. But this account flies in the face of the contradiction within capitalist expansion so authoritatively mapped by Amin:

> Of course, by definition, the new globalisation erodes the efficiency of economic management by national states. However, it does not abolish their existence. Thus, it produces a new contradiction which, in my opinion, is insurmountable under capitalism. The reason for this is that capitalism is more than just an economic system; its economy is inconceivable without a social and political dimension, which implies a state. Until recently, the expansion of capitalism was founded on the coincidence between the space in which the reproduction of accumulation was determined and the space of its political and social management: the space of the central national state shaped the structure of the international system. Now, however, we have entered a new era characterised by a separation between the globalised space of capitalism's economic management and the national spaces of its political and social management. (Amin, 1997: 32)

It is Amin's opinion that the *crisis* between footloose capital and the bourgeois nation-state can only be overcome through the creation of social and political institutions truly global in scope.[13] This has yet to happen. Modes of capital accumulation, in other words, have assumed a global character but the surplus generated under the new system (heavily weighted in favour of finance or floating capital) continues to be seized by segments domiciled in a handful of powerful nation-states. Led by the United States, these nationalised segments maintain political, ideological and military hegemony over the global system:

> The dominant segments of capital indeed operate in the transnational space of world capitalism, but control of these segments remains in the

> hands of financial groups still strongly 'national' (i.e., based in the United States or Great Britain or Germany, but not yet in a 'Europe' that does not exist as such on this level). Moreover, the economic reproduction of the system is, today as yesterday, unthinkable without the parallel implementation of the 'politics' that modulate its variants. The capitalist economy does not exist without a 'state,' except in the ideological and empty vulgate of liberalism. There is still no transnational, 'world' state. The true questions, evaded by the dominant discourse on globalisation, concern the contradictions between the logics of the globalised accumulation of central capitalism's dominant segments (the 'oligopolies') and those governing the 'politics' of the system. (Amin, 2005: 2)

So built into the structure of global economic integration are inescapable paradoxes that attest to trends that go against the standard neoliberal account of globalisation. The dominant discourse of neoliberalism holds out the promise of greater global equity (via a system of deregulated industries, open markets, free trade agreements, etc.), but the economic practices of the core oligopolies constantly break this pledge.

If we were to accept (as I do) Amin's account of the contradictions that ghost globalisation and its multifarious discourses, then we would have to disavow any simple mimetic account of the relationship between the global economy and transnational practices. If the chief beneficiaries of unilateral globalisation (that is, one dictated by the G8 countries) are segments within the core western states, then it is reasonable to suppose that someone suffers. We know that the annual value of world trade is thirty to forty times lower than that of capital generated in financial markets (Amin, 1997: 97) (and we are not even including the estimated two trillion dollars generated through global money laundering), and that this excess is largely swallowed up by the United States to service its trade deficit[14] presently running at a massive $718 billion – an excess that could be invested, for instance, into developing the productive capacities and infrastructures of countless peripheries. These peripheries contain massive armies of reserve labour – that is, labour that has little chance of being put into economic circulation – which keeps distending as a consequence of the above practices. Globalisation, then, may be largely responsible for creating an immobilised army of reserve labour characteristic of the so-called fourth world. This is the brute logic of exclusion, not integration. Illegal forms of emigration may be the only sort of mobility left open to members of this stranded population. What is this if not the negative mobility of the outcast? Global economic practices, and this is the critical point, are capable of producing a bundle of contrary and anomalous effects – a paradox noted by far too few diasporists. Delinked capital does encourage certain transnational flows of people (legal, ephemeral or otherwise), and it would be foolish to deny this fact, but it also discourages such movements by systematically closing down options for peripheral populations. On the one hand we have the family-based, *guanxi*-oriented[15] networks of Chinese 'diaspora capitalists' (Lever-Tracy, Ip and Tracy, 1996: 21–40) spread over multiple territories (Hong, Kong, Taiwan, Indonesia, Macao, Malaysia, Shanghai, Australia, California, etc.) who enjoy a kind of hypermobility that has won them the tag of *taikongren* or astronauts; on the other, we have the garment industry workers of any number of peripheral states (not excluding China). The short-term employment and long-term immobility of this second group is a direct consequence of the predatory portability of transnational corporations. Time and again, whole segments of such low-waged, non-unionised workers are left high and dry in the national territory when the factories transfer to more congenial sites – congeniality being a matter of pragmatic economic (not enlightened political) reforms favourable to transnational corporations. These reforms usually include special provisions such as the granting of long tax holidays (thirteen years in some cases), freedom to repatriate profits, reduction in minimum wages, etc.[16] Based on the preceding example, it could be argued that the global circulation of capital leads, paradoxically, to less global integration of peoples and classes. By forcing peripheral states to enact trade and tariff policies (such as tax-free zones) that facilitate the transfer of capital to the industrialised core, while at the same time effectively impeding the mobility of less skilled peripheral labour (capital travels to semi-skilled labour and not the other way around), the long-term effects run counter to the discourse of globalists since the outcome is an expansion of the pool of stagnant labour in the peripheries. Incapable of generating the capital needed to reinvest in productive forces or basic infrastructure, these peripheries are further marginalised. But the contradiction does not end there. One of the few options available to the pool of inactive labour in the peripheries is emigration, more often achieved through illegal than legal means. In late December 2005, the BBC reported that 60 per cent of the workers in the service industries of North America were migrant Hispanics and that, in any given week, close to 10,000 Mexicans attempt to cross the border illegally in search of employment. Of the estimated eleven million undocumented persons residing in the United States, nearly 50 per cent are Mexicans. This negative mobility of labour finds an ambivalent response in the receiving country. Low-waged 'alien' labourers are economically necessary to the United States, but infringe on the rights duly earned by documented subjects – the same subjects who benefit from the services of underpaid workers (a significant proportion of domestic servants in Californian households are Mexicans) but who protest vociferously against their right to access social services. In a recent newspaper column, Tom Baldwin makes precisely this point:

> The paradox is that the illegal workers keep this shopping-mall-and-sunshine society going. Large parts of southern California would be unable to get out of bed without their help. The Mexicans do the jobs Americans spurn – lavatory cleaning, fruit picking and looking after rich white children. (*The Australian*, 1 March 2006: 8)

Holston and Appadurai note that nation-states in compact with managers of global capital exploit this ambivalence to the detriment of the workers. In short, there is a trade-off between nation-states out to attract capital investment and global economic institutions on the lookout for scab labour. This pact is manifested in new legal regimes designed to render 'significant segments of the transnational low-income labour force illegal by using the system of national boundaries to criminalise the immigrants . . . [the state] attracts for low-wage work' (Holston and Appadurai, 1996: 199).[17] According to this perspective, illegality is a tactic used by the nation-state in complicity with itinerant capital to beget a docile, non-unionised labour force that may be exploited through renewed threats of deportation. In recent times, this situation has descended to the level of tragi-comic farce where the double standard is the norm:

> On the US's southwestern border with Mexico, politicians are no longer sitting on the fence about illegal immigration. Instead, with elections looming, they are busy spending huge sums building real ones to stem the flow of an estimated 500,000 undocumented workers from Mexico each year.
>
> Federal funding of $US30 million . . . has just been allocated for completion of a third fence, running parallel with two barriers set up around San Diego in California over the past decade. A congressional plan to spend a further $US2.2 billion, extending the double-fence fortification 1287 km eastwards, awaits approval.
>
> But these are precisely the type of low-wage construction projects that the US usually gets Mexicans to do. Indeed, the Golden State Fence Co, which calls itself 'the top fence contractor in California,' was recently caught, for the second time in as many years, employing illegal immigrants. (*The Australian*, 1 March 2006: 8)

Once we accept that a series of irreconcilable contradictions exist at the first dimension of transnational economics, then the path from it to the second dimension of social relations and thence to the third dimension of cultural and aesthetic effects can hardly be straightforward. While diasporists have been able to trace the differences and contradictions within and between diasporas, seldom has this occurred in relation to the contradictions that haunt each dimension of the discourse on the synchronic plane. Some third scene diasporists have been able to paint a complex picture of the breaks between displaced populations on the historical horizon (that is to say, the diachronic horizon along which various diasporas gain visibility), but this complexity is usually absent when it comes to noting the contradictions that pervade the triadic interaction among *social formations*, *cultural effects* and *brute economic processes*. The problem is one of evasion arising from the fact that very few critics seek to analyse the workings of transnational or globalised capital. The upshot is that some fundamental questions remain unasked. Are we, for instance, really seeing some kind of radical transformation in the logic of capital accumulation? If yes, then how is it different from the classical modes of surplus seizure from embodied labour? Has post-Fordist capital based on market predictions and the exchange rates mechanism – the spectral economy – finally replaced the humdrum systems of surplus value generation and accumulation? Or is the spectral economy a symptom of an unravelling crisis in the world system? Since capital generated in the world's financial markets far exceeds that generated in world trade, does the labour power of the worker no longer matter? Or is this just another ideological ruse used in the ongoing seizure of surplus value? Is it true that delinked capital no longer relies on classically anchored modes of production for its daily proliferation? If so, how does the mad dance of self-spawning capital impact on the development of productive forces in the peripheries and on the masses in general? Is it true, as Žižek maintains, that spectral or finance capital pretends – and this represents ideology in its most uncanny form – that its work of self-propagation involves real people and material objects when, in truth, it functions purely on the level of abstract speculation sundered from concrete entities (Žižek, 2000: 15–16)? Has the information age, then, ushered in a new mode of surplus accumulation (via electronically unified trade in currencies and futures) or does it generate technological effects that somehow conceal the old dialectic of surplus value production and seizure?[18] Doubtless the domains of material production are no longer nationally based (German cars manufactured in India, Australian toys made in China), but should this new arrangement be taken to intimate a seismic shift in capital's structure or just an operational one? Is transnational or global capital, in other words, merely another way of describing a new strategy for the old game of surplus value acquisition, with the difference that *selected* groups from the peripheries have penetrated, possibly for the first time in the scheme of modernity, *at all levels but in different degrees* the hierarchy of social relations set up by the bourgeois political economy?

When not dodging such base-level questions, most diasporists prefer to go along with the idea that 'the transnationalisation of capitalism' involves 'the breakdown of national economies, and the creation of a more interconnected world economic system' (Jusdanis, 1996: 141), but the data needed to support this claim is typically absent. It could be argued, for instance, that workers from Kerala who flock to the Gulf States are lured there by auxiliary industries that rely on a relatively primitive mode of production (although the 'means' employed are certainly advanced), namely the extraction of crude mineral oil from the bowels of the earth; it could also be argued that the 80,000 Indo-Fijians who left Fiji after the political upheavals of 1987 and 2000 did so as scapegoats of a belated indigenous nationalism rather than as willing subjects of a hypermobile capital; further, it could be contended that it was not transnational capital but the surfacing of repressed nationalisms after the implosion of the socialist world system which produced the murderous doctrine of ethnic cleansing (in Kosovo, Bosnia and elsewhere), resulting in the deracination of stigmatised groups; and, finally, as Milton J. Esman shows, 'large-scale labour migration', whether legal or illegal, may be directly induced by vulgar demographics inasmuch as '[h]igh-income and growing economies', due to low birth rates, 'have a compelling need for labour' whereas '[l]ow-income economies with high rates of population growth generate large and chronic labour surpluses' (Esman, 1992: 3). All too precipitously, then, the transnational moment is invoked by diasporists as a mantra to prepare the ground for the engendering of 'models' that identify the features of one or another social formation or for expatiating on the hybrid texture of diaspora aesthetics. The overall point is that by treating the global economy as an established category rather than as an arena beset by controversies and contradictions, the implied links between the social, the aesthetic and the economic remain highly fraught and conjectural.

Arjun Appadurai and Disjuncture Theory

One diasporist who bucks the above trend by grappling with the enormously complex implications of globalisation on a number of fronts, not excluding the economic, is Arjun Appadurai. In a landmark essay, entitled 'Disjuncture and Difference in the Global Cultural Economy', he seeks to build a large-scale picture, almost as ambitious in scope as a world systems diagram, to explain the dynamics of globalisation. Insisting that we have entered a stage of modernity where 'the imagination has become an organised field of social practices, a form of work . . . and a form of negotiation between sites of agency ("individuals") and globally defined fields of possibility', he situates the material work of the imagination within the multi-nodal system (media, finance, culture, etc.) informing transnational networks. Just as political economy is a discursive practice (i.e. a material practice that is simultaneously a social discourse), so the imagination is a discourse that has material consequences on a global scale. The upshot is that the work of the imagination is seen to exert some sort of gravitational pressure (or effectivity) in the material arena which is already shot through with imagined and realised structures, desires, antagonisms, displacements and areas of contestation. The work undertaken by the imagination to actualise desires (nostalgic, prospective as well as invented) frequently runs up against other force fields, whether economic, ethnic, cultural, political, ideological or territorial. For example, the desire expressed by insurrectionist groups within Kashmir for an independent nation-state comes into collision with the multiply-determined *imaginaire* (or collective aspirations) of influential groups in Pakistan as well as India. For Appadurai, then, the so-called integrated world system imagined by globalists is sustained by certain internal disjunctures. These disjunctures are distributed across an epic field that includes technology, finance, ideology, culture, politics, ethnicity and information as well as the labour of the imagination. Appadurai calls this the 'new global cultural economy':

> The new global cultural economy has to be seen as a complex, overlapping, disjunctive order, which cannot any longer be understood in terms of existing centre–periphery models (even those that account for multiple centres and peripheries). Nor is it susceptible to simple models of push and pull (in terms of migration theory), or of surpluses and deficit (as in traditional models of balance of trade), or of consumers and producers (as in most neo-Marxian theories of development) . . . The complexity of the current global economy has to do with certain fundamental disjunctures between economy, culture and politics which we have only begun to theorise. (Appadurai, 1990: 6)

Essentially, there are five segments of analysis that comprise this system of disjunctures: ethnoscapes, mediascapes, technoscapes, finanscapes and ideoscapes. All these analytical segments assume a different shape, contour and implication whenever there is a change in context and viewpoint. Situational perspectives, whether first or third, matter greatly in the assessment of these segmented flows. Appadurai's segments are shapes-in-motion across a planetary field. Ethnoscapes denote the present pandemic of hypermobile persons and populations such as tourists, refugees, immigrants, guest workers and exiles. These travelling populations are altering 'the politics of (and between) nations to a hitherto unprecedented degree' (Appadurai, 1990: 7). The work of the imagination as it takes in the news and pictures of other worlds, other lives (fabricated or otherwise), plays a notable role in the actualities or fantasies of movement. Technoscapes, on the other hand, point to the intensification of transborder movements of material and intellectual technologies. One example is that of corporations from several nations operating in unison to set up high-tech industrial arenas in any number of developing countries even as these peripheries lose their software engineers to overdeveloped nations. In this fluid set-up, the reversal of technology transfers (i.e. material as well as intellectual) is forever on the cards. The transmission and reproduction, occurring in inestimable nanoseconds, of floating capital in the stock and currency markets of the world is captured by the term finanscapes, while mediascapes 'refer both to the distribution of the electronic capabilities to produce and disseminate information (newspapers, magazines, television stations and film production studios), which are now available to a growing number of private and public interests throughout the world, and to the images of the world created by these media' (Appadurai, 1990: 9). Finally, ideoscapes account for the ensemble of ideational terms around which states and those subversive of states organise their politics. It is the arena of competing ideologies based fundamentally around the battle over Enlightenment values and images of freedom, rights, democracy, sovereignty, etc. These values are no longer anchored to the master narratives of Europe and America, but form 'a loosely structured synopticon of politics . . . in which different nation-states, as part of their evolution, have organised their political cultures around different keywords' (Appadurai, 1990: 10).

After identifying the bundle of traits that define each of his segmented flows, Appadurai observes that the segments relate to one another in profoundly disjunctive and fortuitous ways. Although he does not express it in quite such terms, the image he has in mind is that of a series of minimally intersecting eccentric circles. Each circle has it own constraints and motivations but, on occasions, exerts a delimiting and constraining influence on the other circles: hence the overlapping portions. By and large, however, each circle maintains a radical autonomy that suggests the growing lacuna in the agential force one circle may exercise over another. Since each circle has its own independent intensity, *context* becomes vital for detecting the part it plays (ascendant or subordinate) in the largely *non-relational but fluid* behaviour that governs the system. So, for instance, Japan's receptivity to imported ideas and values (ideoscapes) and ability to export commodities (including technoscapes) to a diversity of cultures and markets bears scarcely any relation, deterministic or otherwise, to its legendary intransigence on matters of immigration (ethnoscapes). Likewise, the nationalist ideoscapes of certain transnational formations (such the Indian diaspora in the United States) may be fundamentally out of joint with its complicity in global finanscapes that act to weaken the sovereignty of nation-states. Appadurai provides further examples of such disjunctures:

> It is because labour, finance and technology are now so widely separated that the volatilities that underlie movements for nationhood (as large as transnational Islam on the one hand, or as small as the movement of the

> Gurkhas for a separate state in the North-East of India) grind against the vulnerabilities that characterise the relationships between states. States find themselves pressed to stay 'open' by the forces of media, technology, and travel that have fuelled consumerism throughout the world and have increased the craving . . . for new commodities and spectacles. On the other hand, these very cravings can become caught up in new ethnoscapes, mediascapes, and eventually, ideoscapes, such as democracy in China, that the state cannot tolerate as threats to its own control over ideas of nationhood and peoplehood. States throughout the world are under siege, especially where contests over the ideoscapes of democracy are fierce and fundamental, and where there are radical disjunctures between ideoscapes and technoscapes (as in the case of very small countries that lack contemporary technologies of production and information; or between ideoscapes and finanscapes (as in countries such as Mexico and Brazil, where international lending influences national politics to a very large degree); or between ideoscapes and ethnoscapes (as in Beirut, where diasporic, local and translocal filiations are suicidally at battle); or between ideoscapes and mediascapes (as in many countries in the Middle East and Asia) where the lifestyles represented on both national and international TV and cinema completely overwhelm and undermine the rhetoric of national politics . . . (Appadurai, 1990: 14)

At first sight the above account seems perilously close to the classical Marxist notion of the internal contradictions sustaining capitalist relations at the various levels of the economic, the social and the ideological. But this is patently not the case. Appadurai, in fact, shows no interest in dialectical procedures where movements are characterised by the reciprocal struggle among discrete sets of opponents, culminating in the utopian moment of resolution. His theory of disjuncture shuns the very idea of reciprocity based on the call and response mode of argument. One set of events may not summon up others in any purely relational or deterministic fashion. No cause-effect relation actually informs the macro system of segmented global flows in the time of late modernity. It follows that there can be no contradiction (only disjoint) between, say, Tonga's participation in space technologies (by 1992 the tiny island nation had been granted seven geostationary orbital parking spaces by the International Telecommunications Union) and its outmoded political system of hereditary constitutional monarchy. The technoscape is radically out of joint with the ideoscape.

Where Althusser bestows *relative or partial* autonomy to macro analytical categories such as politics, ideas and culture, Appadurai favours a form of extreme discontinuity. In the former, the partial autonomy of ideational structures is predicated on the economic mode operating as a motivational force in the last instance (Althusser, 1970: 99). Thus the pressure imparted by culture or politics or history on material events gets adjusted somewhere along the line by economic forces within any given situation. In Althusser's framework, which is conspicuously a disembedded one, the categories shape each other through their unequal intensities – or what he calls their '*degree[s] of effectivity*' (Althusser, 1970: 177) – with the economic exerting the most influence in the last instance. In short, variable pressure points of conjuncture (or determinisms) may be found within a largely disjunctive system. Appadurai's approach, by contrast, does away with the effectivity that allows one segment (human migration) to become fundamentally inflected by another (economics) *without* the displacing interference of a third factor (media images) or a fourth (political ideas) or a fifth (multinational technoscapes). To be sure, each fluid segment forms a terminally autonomous category locked in a disjunctive yet dynamic loop with the others. Where Ong imagines a system of tightly dovetailed categories in her embedded approach, Appadurai imagines a system of contingent global flows, or loops, where none of the segments link up except along random, eccentric and lateral pathways. This is the way of the rhizome as imagined by Deleuze and Guattari. Technocapes do not have a direct deterministic hand in shaping ethnoscapes or ethnoscapes in shaping finanscapes or finanscapes in shaping ideoscapes, and so on. But is there any room at all for 'limited' determination in this system of asymmetrical loops? Or are we being asked to surrender all thought of agency, influence and motivation? In reply, Appadurai observes that the arbitrary flows 'constellate into particular events and social forms' within specific zones or contexts. In these contexts, the segments begin to exhibit deterministic traits:

> Thus, while labour flows and their loops with financial flows between Kerala and the Middle East may account for the shape of media flows and ideoscapes in Kerala, the reverse may be true of Silicon Valley in California, where intense specialisation in a special technological sector (computers) and specific flows of capital may well profoundly determine the shape of ethnoscapes, ideoscapes and mediascapes. (Appadurai, 1990. 21)

So the disjunctive segments of labour and finance as they move about in the transnational context of Kerala and the Middle East may actively influence the shape and transmission of media images and political ideas in Kerala. Other combinations are to be had in the different context of Silicon Valley. In the above formulation, the intensities of each of the categories assume an active, passive, dominant or subordinate role according to the specific context. Economics, it follows, may not play an active or determining role in some contexts while it may well do in others. But if deterministic value moves about so freely and promiscuously from one category to another with every shift in context, how is it different from an *effect* obtained through the unpredictable permutation of fluid segments? Is there not a risk here that determinism forms the frothy wake left behind by the random constellation of analytical segments in a given context? This peculiar inversion testifies to the strong influence chaos and complexity theories have had on Appadurai's work. In chaos systems, random and tiny permutations give rise to patterns (such as the weather) that, due to the proliferation of incalculable variables, cannot be subject to laws of prediction over the long duration. In the well-known example of the butterfly effect even a slight variation in the wing activity of a Brazilian butterfly may (or may not) initiate a hurricane at some future time in faraway Tahiti. In short, there are no prior determining factors that account for any given pattern. Unstable permutations and strange attractors beget effects that may *seem* somehow determined. The problem of translation from numerical to alphabetical systems aside, the biggest drawback of applying chaos theory to social analysis is that the elements of motivation, action, culpability, morality and responsibility simply go out the window. Since a coin given to the local charity may just as likely save a child in Malawi as start a war in the Eritrea, the responsibility for what the coin does is no longer simply mine. My act of giving bears no relation to the coin which is a minute variable in an infinite series that generates unpredictable patterns. Since I have simply no way of predicting the consequences of my actions, I operate out of a realm of absolute amorality. Or take the example of capital accumulation. If my profit-making activity produces unpredictable results somewhere in the physical world (such as the slaughter of whales in the Antarctic or the eradication of malaria in Vanuatu), there is little sense in my switching over to social work because the consequences of this second activity would be just as egregiously unpredictable.

One way of overcoming the dangerous pitfalls of a chaos-based framework is through the identification of deterministic points that *secretly and asymmetrically* haunt all categories that make up a system. It calls for an approach where, for example, the interaction between an ethnoscape (say, a film audience) and a mediascape (the movie being screened) may disguise the effectivity exerted by a third factor (for instance, the diversity of ideological and cultural apparatuses informing the viewing process), which itself might camouflage certain uneven social relations determined by the last instance of economics. In this paradigm, which may be likened to the asymmetric relations between the dream content, the dream thought and the dream analysis identified by Sigmund Freud,[19] there is no simple correlation between the dominant position of a particular factor within the system and the issue of deterministic influence. An aspect that appears to be exerting a powerful influence in one context might not be doing so in the last count. The point may be illustrated with an example drawn from Appadurai:

> The transnational movement of the martial arts, particularly through Asia, as mediated by the Hollywood and Hong Kong film industries . . . is a rich illustration of the ways in which long-standing martial arts tradition, reformulated to meet the fantasies of contemporary (sometimes lumpen) youth populations, create new cultures of masculinity and violence, which are in turn fuel for increased violence in national and international politics. Such violence is in turn the spur to an increasingly rapid and amoral arms trade which penetrates the entire world. (Appadurai, 1990: 15)

In a series of moves that effectively undermines his own theory of disjunctures, Appadurai offers a classically mimetic account of causes and effects. The logic is quite straightforward: martial arts films (mediascapes) produce new youth cultures (ethnoscapes) that enact cinematic fantasies of masculine violence in the streets. These violent practices assume macro proportions since they fuel violent practices in the national and international arenas (ideoscapes). These large-scale arenas of violence form lucrative markets for arms traders (finanscapes) who, as the logic of loops would have it, disjunctively encourage the production of violent movies (mediascapes). The move from the humble youthful viewer in the cinema to the arms dealer in the war zone is too breathtaking for words. It will suffice to point out that the analysis simply ignores the complexities of viewer response to filmic discourses. Youthful viewers (no matter how lumpen) are just as likely *not* to read the martial arts film in the self-defining manner suggested by Appadurai. They may even read the violence ethically and didactically, which is to say as a warning against violent behaviour. Or they may enjoy the film purely for its artful callisthenics. They might even exercise the viewer's right to suspend disbelief, which disbelief (in the filmic world) gets re-engaged the moment they exit the cinema. Once the initial causal or mimetic link between films (mediascapes) and viewers (ethnoscapes) gets disrupted, the rest of the argument falls apart like a house of cards. The critical point here is that the issue of effectivity and determination is much more complex and clandestine than suggested by Appadurai. Let me clarify this point with a hypothetical case of my own. If a mill-worker from Bihar were to start desiring blonde women and fast cars after watching an action film on a communally owned video player, it may be that his infatuation in its overt form is only tangentially and superficially connected to the two objects in question. In fact, it is quite possible that the mill-worker has no actual interest in blonde women and fast cars. These objects may constitute displaced signs of life-worlds culturally, socially and economically unavailable to him. An economic content, I begin to suspect, lies buried in the affect inspired by the film. In order to test this discovery, I assess the impact of gender, culture, sexuality, race, religion and class in the organisation of his desire. What appeared at first to be a direct outcome of the film turns out to have multiple points of determination. While spread over a number of semi-autonomous terrains (gender, culture, politics, etc.), these points of determination exert different degrees and types of influence on the affect. Emboldened by my results, I redouble my efforts. I discover that the aforesaid semi-autonomous factors have acted on each other in complex ways. On the one hand a respect for the goddess Durga (whom the woman resembles) has curbed the worker's patriarchal tendencies; on the other, his sexual desire has been inflamed by Indian cultural aesthetics which equates lightness of skin with beauty. What's more, there is a third level of effectivity that impinges disproportionately on each of the semi-autonomous factors. I discover, for instance, that the worker trudges many miles to do the night-shift at the mill, that he rarely has sex with his wife because she works as a day-labourer and that the couple are scraping together a dowry for the marriage of their only child. The mill-worker's desire, then, shows clear links to a mode of transportation and to the radical sexual and financial independence of the blonde woman in the film. Since it is money that will allow him to take a bus to work, to put an end to his or his wife's drudgery (thereby freeing up time for sexual intimacy) and to meet his patriarchal obligations as a father, I come to the conclusion that his desire is determined in the last instance by economics. The worker's sense of the blonde woman's sexual and financial autonomy may also conceal a radical potential to subvert a social order that traps all three members of the family in a system of obligation and counter-obligation. It is precisely for this reason that the economic determinant is not the secret of secrets. What it does is to open up the space of revolutionary ethics for the worker (in that he may be able to critically assess the various strands of his desire), for the analyst (in that he or she may act as a conduit for the general potential for such forms of critical assessment) and for anyone seeking to destroy the iniquitous system of capital accumulation that provoked the desire in the very last instance.

Whatever the drawbacks of Appadurai's approach, he is one of the few analysts to have engaged with the socio-economic aspects of globalisation in a profoundly complex and original fashion.[20] His conclusions, no matter how disputable, are at least based on some sort of informed engagement with a grand discourse that forms the stepping stone for some fundamental assertions about transnational communities. Appadurai has recently suggested the possibility of a grassroots globalisation facilitated by Transnational Advocacy Networks (TANS) that may alleviate some of the worst excesses of globalisation from above (Appadurai, 2001: 1–21). Globalisation theory is beset with disagreements, hostilities and speculations and yet many diasporists insist on employing it as an uncritical launching pad for many of their assertions. Since they do not clear sufficient ground before expatiating on themes of migration, deracination, hybridity and deterritorialisation, the three concepts essential to diaspora criticism are also the most poorly explored.

Notes

1. David Held and Anthony McGrew observe that modern states eventually became nation-states, that is 'political bodies, separate from both ruler and ruled, with supreme jurisdiction over a demarcated territorial area, backed by a claim to a monopoly of coercive power, and enjoying legitimacy as a result of the loyalty or consent of their citizens. The major innovations of the modern nation-state – territoriality that fixes exact borders, monopolistic control of violence, an impersonal structure of political power and a distinctive claim to legitimacy based on representation and accountability – marked out its defining (and sometimes fragile) features' (Held and McGrew, 2000: 9).
2. Since they work mostly in western academies and since diasporas are endemic to bourgeois nation-states of the North, diasporists tend to overlook other types of nation and state formations in their commentary.
3. Prior to the Australian Federal Elections of 2001, the lead article in *The Weekend Australian* stoked the usual anti-diaspora paranoia/hysteria with the caption 'Our Open-door Borders: Fortress Australia Under Attack'. Losing even the semblance of journalistic dispassion, the article went on to discuss 'how guns, drugs and people [were] . . . swamping the nation's barely protected coastline'. Rather than desperate people fleeing terrible regimes in Afghanistan or Iraq, or poverty in South East Asia, asylum seekers were characterised as ruthless gunrunners and drug smugglers intent on violating 'the sanctity of our borders'. Needless to say, these interlopers were out to destroy the actual rather than the *imagined* fabric of Australian society. See *The Weekend Australian*, 25–26 August 2001. A few days later, the same paper ran a story on how the Norwegian freighter, *Tampa*, with its 'human cargo' of 438 asylum seekers (mostly Afghanis fleeing the Taliban regime) rescued from a dilapidated ferry, had been refused docking rights at Christmas Island by John Howard, the Prime Minister of Australia. Defending the severity of his stance, Mr Howard was quoted as having said: 'We appear to be losing control of the flow of people coming into this country . . . we have to take a stand.' See *The Australian*, 29 August 2001.
4. For a valuable account of the East India Company, see John Keay's *The Honourable Company* (1991).
5. In his magisterial study of Marx and Kant, Kojin Karatani notes that 'merchant capital attains surplus value from spatial difference' as opposed to industrial capital which 'attains surplus value by incessantly producing new value systems *temporally* – that is, with technological innovation' (Karatani, 2003: 10). In its early phase

the technological innovations of industrial capital allowed for nation-centred forms of accumulation, thus facilitating the shift away from merchant capital's heavy dependence on trans-territorial processes.

6. Noting James Clifford's advice not to foreclose definitional possibilities by taking the Jewish diaspora as the 'ideal type', Martin Baumann claims that this licenses 'scholars not to bother at all about the origin and coinage of the term. Thus, a rather free, arbitrary and often plainly metaphorical use of "diaspora" has emerged in recent years, "decomposing" in exactly the early Greek philosophical meaning the term's ability to encompass properly certain situations and relations . . . The currently predominant emphasis on the mournful experiences of exile, flight, and expulsion tells only half the story of the diaspora concept' (Baumann, 1997: 395).
7. For Balibar, this period of transition from primitive accumulation is characterised by the combination of independent elements into a new structure: 'In other words, the elements combined by the capitalist structure have different and independent origins. It is not one and the same movement which makes free labourers and transferable wealth. On the contrary . . . the formation of free labourers appears mainly in the form of transformations of agrarian structures, while the constitution of wealth is the result of merchant's capital and finance capital, whose movements take place outside those structures, "marginally," or "in the pores of society"' (Balibar, 1970: 281).
8. In their 'Introduction' to *The Politics of Culture in the Shadow of Capital*, Lisa Lowe and David Lloyd correctly highlight the contradictions permeating the neocolonial regime of transnational capital: 'We understand the transnational to denote the stage of globalised capitalism characterised by David Harvey, Fedric Jameson, and others as the universal extension of a differentiated mode of production that relies on flexible accumulation and mixed production to incorporate all sectors of the global economy into its logic of commodification. It is the tendency of such understandings of transnationalism to assume a homogenisation of global culture that radically reduces possibilities for the creation of alternatives, in confining them either to the domain of commodified culture itself or to the space that, for reasons of mere historical contingency, have seemed unincorporated into globalisation. It will be our contention to the contrary, that transnational or neo-colonial capitalism, like colonialist capitalism before it, continues to produce sites of contradiction that are effects of its always uneven expansion but that cannot be subsumed by the logic of commodification itself' (Lowe and Lloyd, 1997: 1)
9. The incident took place on Sunday, 11 December, at Cronulla Beach in Sydney.
10. Visweswaran also makes this point (Visweswaran, 1997: 11).
11. In their introduction to *The Global Transformations Reader*, David Held and Anthony McGrew provide a comprehensive summary of the debate between the adherents and sceptics of globalisation (Held and McGrew, 2000: 1–45).
12. Karatani argues that the trinity of nation, state and capital are essentially inseparable: 'One frequently hears today that the nation-state will be gradually decomposed by the globalisation of capitalism (neoliberalism). This is impossible. When individual national economies are threatened by the global market, they demand

the protection (redistribution) of the state and/or bloc economy, at the same time as appealing to national cultural identity. So it is that any counteraction to capital must also be one targeted against the state and nation (community). The capitalist nation-state is fearless because of its makeup. The denial of one ends up being reabsorbed into the ring of the trinity by the power of the other two. Countermovements in the past, such as corporatism, welfare society, and social democracy, resulted in the perfection of the ring rather than its abolition' (Karatani, 2003: 15–16).

13. Karatani locates the periodic eruption of crisis in the *salto mortale*, the leap of faith, underlying the credit culture of capitalism: 'Credit, the treaty of presuming that a commodity can be sold in advance, is an institutionalisation of postponing the critical moment of selling a commodity. And the commodity economy, constructed as it is upon credit, inevitably nurtures a crisis' (Karatani, 2003: 8).
14. Amin claims that the world has been in the midst of a period of economic stagnation for several decades and that this has given 'rise to a gigantic surplus of capital which finds no outlet in productive investment'. He adds: 'Under these conditions, the response of dominant capital to the situation is perfectly logical: priority is given to the management of this mass of floating capital. This management requires maximum worldwide financial openness and high interest rates. At the same time, the system allows the United States to maintain its negative position as it finances its deficit by draining the mass of floating capital; this is the only way for it to maintain its hegemony (by imposing the dollar as the international currency by default, and by sustaining an extremely high level of military spending)' (Amin, 1997: 34).
15. *Guanxi* refers to a 'network of particularistic ties' based on long-term reciprocity (Lever-Tracy, Ip and Tracy, 1996: 23).
16. Such economic reforms were, for instance, part of the package delivered by the new administration after the military coup of 1987 that saw the overthrow of the Bavadra labour government in Fiji. See Harrington (2000).
17. Baldwin cites Wayne Cornelius who makes the same point: 'Wayne Cornelius, of the University of California, San Diego, says that "far from being broken, the system is working very well for business" by providing an almost infinite and risk-free supply of low-cost, flexible and non-unionised labour' (*The Australian*, 1 March 2006: 8).
18. Paul Smith provides a persuasive account of the way apologists of capitalism have deployed discourses of global economy to distract from its age-old dependence on surplus value appropriation (Smith, 1997: 253–71).
19. See Sigmund Freud, *The Interpretation of Dreams* (1971).
20. Appadurai's disjuncture framework has been employed by many analysts, and most notably by Martin Roberts. Investigating the emergent world music 'as a new kind of commodity in the global marketplace of the popular music industry' (Roberts, 1992: 232–3), Roberts refutes the seductive argument that mass culture simply territorialises vernacular cultural forms by pointing to 'a complex process of *indigenisation*, whereby the interaction of global mass culture with local cultures

produces hybrid cultural forms which render simple oppositions between core and periphery problematic' (Roberts, 1992: 230). He goes on demonstrate how western musical forms have been assimilated into or vernacularised by 'non-western musical cultures'. To his credit, Roberts rarely loses sight of the commodity function of world music and refers to the 'six transnational recording companies (RCA, CBS, Time Warner, EMI, Polygram, MCA) and their subsidiary labels' that control the 'global music finanscape' (Roberts, 1992: 236). Furnishing relevant data, he also shows how multinational and transnational corporations, whose *modus operandi* is governed by shifting localities, disrupt nationally based economies where the raw material (music) gets disengaged from its cultural terrain (community, nation-state, region and so on) in the process of its reproduction (overseas recording studios) and consumption (first world markets). Roberts refuses, however, to see world music simply in terms of its commodity function; he acknowledges the ambiguous energy in cultural artifacts that can turn power against itself:

> On the one hand . . . the ideoscapes that world music articulates are co-opted as just another marketing strategy. Recognising a booming sector of the market, record companies and musicians alike have in recent years been jumping on the world-music bandwagon. The very idea of alternative, globally aware politics has been commodified: consumers are *sold* the idea that they are responsible, even participating in a form of cultural resistance, by the very system they are supposedly resisting . . . On the other hand, the implication of world music in the system of global capitalism allows for the possibility of turning that system against itself by using world music's mass cultural status as a kind of Trojan horse for disrupting the system from within, as sales from records, concerts, and tour merchandise are put to work, funding progressive political agendas, causes, and movements. (Roberts, 1992: 239)

While the last assertion may be mildly utopian considering the actual might of the corporate system the 'progressives' are battling, the general point about the way a cultural product can function antagonistically in spite of its co-optation tells us a lot about the elusive, anarchic character of the sign: whether it is sign musical, sign filmic or sign literary. This may, in turn, have a great deal to do with the aesthetics of affect that, in the final count, evades the commodity function but acts enigmatically on the consuming subject. It is on this threshold of inquiry that Roberts, unfortunately, terminates his stimulating account.

6

In Lieu of an Epilogue

In the introductory chapter, I referred to works that share in the nomination, diaspora, without recourse to generic memory and without the burdensome responsibility of participation. A simple titular nomination, what I shall refer to as extra-nomination, is held to be sufficient for any work to count as an exemplar of sorts. These emptily nominal studies, I suggested, upending Derrida's remark that genres are composed of works that participate without belonging, may be said to belong to the genre without actually participating in it. Wittgenstein, whose observation on family resemblances Derrida clearly has in mind, points out that the members of a family may share no common *features*, which is to say features identical to each and every member, and yet they will share a *face*. This important distinction implies that at some level the face exists outside the relational order because none of the features fits the face perfectly. It is precisely in this sense that the nomination – diaspora – incites generic statements (features) from the other side while evading them since no single statement quite matches its composite totality (face). With reference to our particular context, we may declare that none of the *featured* statements on diasporas can quite fit the *facial* nomination – diaspora criticism. Each one shares in the family face without belonging to it. Wittgenstein's choice of metaphor is, I think, no accident. The features that share a face, he implies, share it via the scene of the family. There can be, in other words, no sharing of the face – nomination – without some kind of participation in the scene of the family. Since there is no fundamental link between participation and belonging, the scene of the family is a relational not a natural one. Whichever statement or work enters into some kind of relation with the other statements or works making up the scene (and none may possess any features in common) will share in the face *without belonging to it*. By the phrase *without belonging*, I want to draw attention to (1) the certainty that the total statement will elude each featured statement that shares in the nomination (family face), and (2) the ever-present possibility of a statement (feature) migrating to other scenes or families as distinct from the present one of our example. So a statement on hybridity may participate in scenes that make up the different genres of classical biology (hybrid as cross-breeding), political science (hybrid as a parliamentary bill combining private and public characteristics), postcolonial studies (hybrid as structure of ambivalence within colonial discourse) and diaspora criticism (hybrid as a transnational form of identity). But what happens when a statement (or work) declines to participate in the relational scene of the family and yet professes titular membership? Since scene-based participation is a critical aspect of any genre, indeed is what gives it the total face that incites *as well as* eludes each feature, such titular statements exist outside the scene. They do not qualify as exemplars. They do not form the relations of non-identical features within the scene (family) that leads to the discovery of a shared face. Their profession to membership is, as a result, simultaneously gratuitous and arbitrary because the obligation (and it is precisely that, an obligation) to participate is not met. So that we leave no room for ambiguity, let me make this very clear. Extra-nominal statements identify with the nomination (family face) but admit of no relationship with the features, the other statements, that make up the scene. Since they do not constitute features in the first place, all claims to a shared face are founded on a whim. Radically isolated from the relational scene of features informing the family face, these statements belong without participating.

Saul Kripke's definition of the rigid designator will help clarify matters.[1] A rigid designator is any term with the self-referential and non-connotative property of a proper name. Even common or general names (such as cow or house) may, under certain conditions, perform the function of a rigid designator. Kripke observes that any name, 'if in every possible world it designates the same object' (Kripke, 1980: 48), may be described as such. The suggestion is that in any given epistemic situation, whether factual or counterfactual, actual or possible, the rigid designator retains a singular and fixed point of reference. No matter how a name shifts about from statement to statement, from factual to counterfactual worlds, it stares unflinchingly at its own navel and is unaffected by what surrounds it. Or, as Žižek notes, 'the reference of a name to an object cannot be grounded in the content of this name, in the properties it designates (Žižek, 2004: 123). It is my opinion that generic names function, more or less, as rigid designators. Whatever statement one might make about the novel, even to the point of denying that there is such a category, has little bearing on the singularity of the nomination. Wittgenstein notes that names are 'primitive signs' that resist analysis and recoil from definitions (Wittgenstein, 1981: 49). Names, even of genres, are primitive precisely because they retain a solipsistic interiority (face) that evades all possible statements (features) that they necessarily provoke within a given epistemic situation. So while any number of features (statements) shares in the family face (nomination), the face (nomination) itself is never reducible to any one of the features. The face is always seen intuitively, spectrally, since it is not the visible property of any one feature. It attests to the non-presence of what is present, and is therefore a spectre. It asserts its independence from all actual and possible features and, for this reason, acts like a rigid designator. The family face is no different from the idealised total statement that bears the name of the genre. An apotheosis of all possible features, the family face is reducible to none in particular. Likewise, in my view, the total statement may be said to be the apotheosis of all actual and possible statements, but reducible to none in particular. This irreducibility is what makes it a rigid designator. For any genre to count as such, however, the rigid designator has to incite an epistemic situation. This situation forms the scene where actual and possible, factual and counterfactual statements enter into relationship with each other, sharing a face that eludes each and every feature. Any statement or work that falls outside this epistemic situation (or scene) and yet claims kinship with the genre (family face) is extra-generic inasmuch as it fails to qualify as a participating feature. Such statements or works belong without participating in the genre.

It would be no exaggeration to profess that the number of works devoted to the study of diasporas has increased tenfold since the publication of *Modern Diasporas in International Politics* (1986). To their credit, a majority of these studies manage to lock horns, albeit some less feebly than others, with the major critical and methodological debates that have shaped the genre over the past two decades. On the one hand, there is Paul Spickard's intelligent but abortive aside on the strengths and flaws of the diaspora framework in his introduction to *Pacific Diasporas: Island Peoples in the United States and Across the Pacific* (2002), whereas on the other, we have Eva Østergaard-Nielsen's important inquiry into the distinction between diasporic and transnational approaches in *Transnational Politics: Turks and Kurds in Germany* (2003). Øivind Fuglerud's monograph on long-distance nationalism among the Tamil diaspora in *Life on the Outside* (1999) also rates a mention because of its sustained probing of the fundamental concerns of diaspora criticism: dislocation, militant trans-territorial nationalism, cultural reproduction and modernity. Ingrid Monson's introduction to *The African Diaspora: A Musical Perspective* (2003), which dwells on the musical legacy of the black Atlantic, performs the necessary groundwork in diaspora theory (Monson cites works by Andrew Apter, Jacqueline Nassy Brown, Khachig Tölölyan and, in particular, Paul Gilroy), thereby setting itself up as a feature sharing in the family face of the genre. A recent work by Elizabeth McAlister, entitled *Rara! Vodou, Power, and Performance in Haiti and Its Diaspora* (2002), makes an invaluable contribution to black ethnomusicology and to discussions on transnational popular culture. Karim H. Karim's *The Media of Diaspora*, an edited collection, takes an intimate look at the media effects (films, websites, music, chat groups, online magazines, television and so on) generated in diaspora and assesses their impact on transnational forms of subjectivity. The study also ponders the broader issues of citizenship, globalisation and the imagined community of nation-states. By tapping into current debates in the genre, all these studies gain admittance into the scene of relationality as non-identical statements (features) that share in the name (family face) of diaspora criticism. They each participate in the genre without actually belonging to it. The *not belonging* part of the statement may be explained in two ways. The first pertains to the fact that these works (as statements) participate in several genres at once and, consequently, *belong* to none in particular. For instance, Østergaard-Nielsen's monograph is officially part of a series in transnational rather than diaspora criticism, while Monson's edited anthology falls, according to its publisher, in the category of ethnomusicology *and* African-American Studies. The second concerns Wittgenstein's point about features and faces. The cited works behave like features that share a face (nomination), but the face corresponds to none of the features in particular. The participant features (works, statements) generate the family face (nomination) without ever belonging to it. As the impossible total statement, the face exists outside the relational scene of the participant features. In the reverse situation that I have identified as *belonging without participation*, the statements and works in question decline to enter the relational scene (or the arena of the family) and yet continue to profess some sort of membership. One consequence of the current popularity of diaspora studies is that an increasing number of works employ the titular nomination, diaspora, without actually participating in the relational scene[2] incited by the nomination. This should not be taken as a judgement on the intellectual worth of the works in question, but as an observation about genre as distinct from other forms of designation. Indeed, many of these extra-nominal studies contribute significantly (and sometimes brilliantly) to other domains and genres of scholarship, including ethno-history (Carmen Whalen and Victor Vázquez-Hernández's *The Puerto Rican Diaspora* comes to mind), cultural anthropology (Nancy Wellmeier's *Ritual, Identity and the Mayan Diaspora* is a case in point), and architecture (see Johannes Widodo's *The Boat and the City: Chinese Diaspora and the Architecture of Southeast Asian Coastal Cities*). In electing to bypass the theoretical debates that constitute the relational scene of diaspora criticism, however, these works yield up the right to form features sharing in the nominal – but forever elusive – face of the genre.

In most of these extra-nominal studies, the term 'diaspora' appears to hold little or no theoretical attraction for their respective authors. Rather than being the inciter of an entire critical discourse or, better still, the instigator of a whole new epistemic situation, the term serves as an auxiliary or fleeting sign that, reduced to its barest etymological sense, serves the interest of some other primary critical object. So it is that in her article, 'Colonialism, Citizenship, and the Making of the Puerto Rican Diaspora: An Introduction,' Carmen Whalen does not even pause to contemplate the methodological possibilities opened up by one of the pivotal concepts in her title (Whalen, 2005: 1–42). Indeed, the essay makes a notable contribution to the history of Puerto Rican labour migration to the United States, but it remains very much outside the sphere of diaspora criticism. The same holds for a number of other recent titles. In the preliminary remarks to his entertaining tome *Wherever Green is Worn: The Story of the Irish Diaspora* (2000), Tim Pat Coogan observes that, during his boyhood years, diaspora was known simply as emigration, but declines to investigate the implications of the change in terminology. He grasps that there has been an important semantic transformation, but does not interpret this as constituting a new epistemic situation. Essentially, then, he is unable to see that 'diaspora' ushers in a new framework that is fundamentally different from that of migration studies. Unacquainted with the three relational scenes of the genre, his study clearly belongs without participating. Such examples may be multiplied. In the introductory chapter to *The Greek Diaspora in the Twentieth Century*, Richard Clogg claims to have searched long and hard for critical works in the field but without luck; somewhat incredibly, he declares that he was 'struck by the relative paucity of writing about diasporas in general and about the Greek diasporas in particular' (Clogg, 1999: 3). Although the second part of his statement may quite possibly be accurate, the first plainly is not. At the time of the comment Gilroy's *The Black Atlantic* had been on the library shelves for some six years, Clifford's 'Diasporas' article had been doing the collegial rounds for five and the journal, *Diaspora*, had been churning out essays on the subject for just short of a decade. Clogg does make mention of Armstrong's early article on 'Mobilised and Proletarian Diasporas', but only to complain about the absence of comparative studies in the area. Again, he appears unaware of Sheffer's *Modern Diasporas in International Politics* (1986), Safran's controversial paper 'Diasporas in Modern Societies' (1991) and Cohen's overly ambitious *Global Diasporas* (1997). The 'paucity of material' argument enables Clogg to sidestep the unruly scene of features that share in the nomination (without, of course, belonging); the tactic also permits his project the luxury of belonging without participation. The same can be said for Michael Angelo's *The Sikh Diaspora* (1997), Nicholas Tapp and Gary Yia Lee's *The Hmong of Australia: Culture and Diaspora* (2004) and Michael A.

Gomez's *Reversing Sail: A History of the African Diaspora* (2005). Gomez, in particular, squanders the ideal opportunity to develop a transnational historiography by drawing on the works of Gilroy, Mercer, Hall and Edwards. He is not unaware of the studies put out by these scholars (he actually recommends Edwards' *The Practice of Diaspora* in his suggestions for further reading), but opts not to engage with the methodological issues they broach. Even more astonishingly, though clearly familiar with the work in question, he finds no use for the 'framework' discussions initiated by Elliott P. Skinner, George Shepperson, St Clair Drake and Joseph E. Harris in their respective contributions to the influential *Global Dimensions of the African Diaspora* (Harris, 1982). Still, he does appear to have an opinion on methodology:

> The study of the African Diaspora can be distinguished from the study of African Americans in the United States, or from other groups of African-descended persons in a particular nation-state, in that the African Diaspora is concerned with at least one of two issues (and frequently both): (1) the ways in which preceding African cultural, social, or political forms influence African-descended persons in their new environments, and how such forms change through interaction with non-African cultures (European, Native American, Asian, etc.); and (2) comparisons and relationships between communities of African-descended people who are geographically separated or culturally distinct. (Gomez, 2005: 2)

The trouble with the above proposition is that it fails to take stock of what has already been said on the matter. Hall's take on hybridity, Mercer's on dialogism, Gilroy's on the outer-national practices of the black diaspora and Edwards' concept of *décalage* (or time-space discrepancy) would have greatly expanded and enriched Gomez's highly rudimentary framework. In its published form, *Reversing Sail* constitutes an eloquent and significant introduction to the historical study of dispersed peoples of African origin but adds little to the genre of diaspora criticism.

Diaspora criticism, it is increasingly evident, has turned into a vibrant culture industry ceaselessly *defining* an object – diaspora – without becoming in any way *definite*. Extra-nominal studies form a vital part of the book market (since *titles* sell), but they do not participate in the relational scene of the genre. In my opinion the rapid proliferation of extra-nominal studies marks the high-point of the genre's impact on the popular imagination; paradoxically, however, it may also testify to the presence of a strain of exhaustion in the three scenes of exemplification that make up the nomination. The decline of the critical genre of postmodernism, to cite an analogous case, was directly proportionate to its soaring popularity in the public domain and its gratuitous expropriation by the popular media. No doubt this points to the paradox that haunts the very law that incites the generic event from its place of hiding. In its boundless desire to fix limits and to attain the definitional moment of the total statement, a genre is destined to keep overstepping set limits, rules and definitions.

As the rule is the want of a rule and the limit the want of a limit, it follows that the genre designation, the rubric, comes to be regarded, at least by those works not directly participating in its relational scene, as both empty and promiscuous. When this happens – and it usually happens to a genre at an advanced stage – it becomes possible for a breathtaking array of projects to share in the nomination *without any recourse to generic memory* and *without the burdensome responsibility of participation*. Such emptily 'nominal' studies, sundered as they are from the scenes of exemplification, *belong without participating* in the genre. And since participation without belonging best describes the genre, the reversal of this order may, in all probability, betray the first symptom of an imminent exhaustion.

It has been my intention, in this book, to think of critical domains in the context of genre theory. It is evident that diasporists hail from many different areas and disciplines and bring a variety of perspectives, apparatuses and idioms to bear on the study of diasporas. Karim notes that those involved in the enterprise hail from sociology, anthropology, human geography, migration, culture studies, political economy, communication and postcolonialism (Karim, 2003: 1). The paradox is that an essentially cross-disciplinary and cross-generic venture has spawned a new critical genre upheld by a series of competing exemplars. There is nothing strictly odd about this sort of development, since genres are composed of relational scenes where none of the participant features belong to the nomination. In effect, then, any statement assembled at the relational scene may participate in *several* genres at once without losing its place in a *particular* genre. It is the *peculiar* combination of features (none of which may have anything in common) at the relational scene which permits us to speak of *this* particular genre as distinct from some other. It is my view that diaspora criticism has experienced three scenes of exemplification, separated by epistemic 'turns' within the larger scene of the genre. Resulting from notable breaks between scenes, these turns are not strictly diachronic as they frequently coincide. The first of these I have called the scene of dual territoriality. The works and statements that participate here are primarily concerned with an ethno-national community caught between the stable coordinates of the hostland and the homeland. The second scene of situational laterality is based on a departure from this rigidly structuralist framework – a departure that remains stubbornly internal to the genre. Under the influence of post-structuralist theories, the second scene participants advance a framework that focuses on the unstable, crabwise movements of bodies, ideas, goods and information across multiple territories. Where the first scene diasporists put stress on the pressures exerted on diasporas by discrete national ideologies and shibboleths (whether of the homeland or the hostland), thereby generating a meat-in-the-sandwich approach (or, alternatively, the triadic relations schema), the second scene participants place emphasis on the being and becoming of deracinated subjects in specific situational contexts. Diasporas are no longer suspended between geopolitical ends and origins or between the imagined communities of here and there. Instead, by *differing* from other social entities and *deferring* their claims to territorial identification, they take on the characteristics of the detouring supplement. Generally speaking, they are considered to be at loggerheads with classical nation-state formations. Engaged in 'border' practices, they flout bounded forms, structures and affects. They are migrants yet exist 'beyond' and 'outside of' the usual definition of the term: hence 'transmigrants'. To get some purchase on the border condition of diasporas, the second scene participants work with the key concepts of hybridity, double consciousness, transnationalism, liminal zone, third time-space, mutilocality and hyphenated subjectivity. Responding to the worrying elision of historical differences within particular ethno-diasporas as well as between comparable ethno-diasporas, the third scene participants insist on specifying the archives. This leads to the institution of the 'historicist' turn that constitutes the most recent scene of the critical genre. Stress is placed on historical principles of differentiation. The third scene participants give special weight to the socio-economic context in which diasporas come into being. The specific diachronic character of the context creates fractures within a given ethnonym, so that one may no longer speak coherently and holistically of a single Chinese or Indian or African diaspora.

It has been my contention that diasporists rely on the conceptual trinity of modernity, transnationalism and globalisation in their pursuit of the ever-elusive total statement. They do this without properly addressing the viability of the economic relations that forms the underbelly of each of these categories. Instead of constituting the site of interrogation, transnational capital (used interchangeably with advanced modernity or globalised capital) serves as an untested point of departure for their statements on diasporas. This disinclination to participate in the economic disputes and discourses on globalisation results in the prevalence of a mimetic analytical approach where the category of transnational capital instigates the mirror category of transmigrants who, in turn, engage in transnational or hybrid cultural, ideological and aesthetic practices. There is little scope in this diagram for the paradoxes and anomalies within each of the categories or for asymmetric patterns of relations between them. Since the categories are mutually embedded in one version of this paradigm, it is sufficient to dissect the logic of one in order to illuminate the workings of another. On the other extremity, there is Appadurai's disjuncture theory where none of the categories act deterministically on any of the others. The relations between politics, economics and culture are deemed to be contingent and not governed by effectivity. In opposition to this radical discontinuity paradigm, I recommend the partial discontinuity framework where the semi-autonomous categories of culture, history and politics exercise a measure of effectivity, with economics exerting an influence in the last instance.

Finally, it is my opinion that diaspora criticism is at its strongest when taking stock of the varieties of historical continuity and rupture that exist (1) within and across the different diasporas, (2) within and across their cultural and aesthetic practices, and (3) between a single diaspora and its cultural and aesthetic creations. It is at its weakest as a conceptual field in its disinclination to address the hard economic issues of the day. The critical genre stands to benefit from a more rigorous encounter with the economic part of the scheme. It will also gain from developing frameworks that view the triadic relations between economic forces, social formations and cultural productions as grotesque, symptomatic and refractive rather than as verisimilar, unencumbered and mimetic. By its very nature a symptomatic sign – whether textual, social or economic – announces the presence of a trauma by disguising its proper name and territory. Criticism is obliged to lay bare the ruse.

Notes

1. In *Beyond Rigidity: The Unfinished Semantic Agenda of Naming and Necessity* (2002), Scott Soames affords a strong riposte to Kripke's theory of rigid designation. My understanding of Kripke's notion has to do with a certain quality of immanence that haunts all proper names.
2. I use the singular to include the three scenes discussed in the book.

Bibliography

Agamben, Giorgio (1999) *Remnants of Auschwitz: The Witness and the Archive*, trans. Daniel Heller-Roazen. New York: Zed Books.

Althusser, Louis [1968] (1970) 'The Objects of Capital', in L. Althusser and E. Balibar, *Reading Capital*, trans. Ben Brewster. London: NLB, pp. 71–198.

Althusser, Louis (1971) *Lenin and Philosophy and Other Essays*, trans. Ben Brewster. London: New Left Books.

Amin, Samir (1997) *Capitalism in the Age of Globalisation: The Management of Contemporary Society*. London: Zed Books.

Amin, Samir (2001) 'Imperialism and Globalisation', *Monthly Review*, 53, 2, pp. 6–24.

Amin, Samir (2004) 'U.S. Imperialism, Europe, and the Middle East', *Monthly Review*, 56, 6, pp. 13–33.

Amin, Samir (2005) 'Empire and Multitude', *Monthly Review*, 57, 6, pp. 1–12.

Anderson, Benedict (1991) *Imagined Communities: Reflections on the Origin and Spread of Nationalism*. London: Verso.

Anderson, Benedict (1994) 'Exodus', *Critical Inquiry*, 29, 2, pp. 314–27.

Anderson, Benedict (1998) 'Nationality, Identity, and the World-in-Motion: On the Logics of Seriality', in P. Cheah and B. Robbins (eds), *Cosmopolitics: Thinking and Feeling beyond the Nation*. Minneapolis, MN, and London: University of Minnesota Press, pp. 117–33.

Anderson, Perry (1992) *A Zone of Engagement*. London: Verso.

Angelo, Michael (1997) *The Sikh Diaspora: Tradition and Change in an Immigrant Community*. New York and London: Garland.

Appadurai, Arjun (1990) 'Disjuncture and Difference in the Global Cultural Economy', *Public Culture*, 2, 2, pp. 1–24.

Appadurai, Arjun (1996) *Modernity at Large: Cultural Dimensions of Globalisation*, Minneapolis: University of Minnesota Press.

Appadurai, Arjun (2001) 'Grassroots Globalisation and the Research Imagination', in A. Appadurai (ed.), *Globalisation*. Durham, NC: Duke University Press, pp. 1–21.

Appadurai, A. and C. Breckenridge (1989) 'On Moving Targets', *Public Culture*, 2, 1, pp. i–iv.

Armstrong, John A. (1976) 'Mobilised and Proletarian Diasporas', *American Political Science Review*, 70, 2, pp. 393–408.

Axel, Brian Keith (2002) 'The Diasporic Imaginary', *Public Culture*, 14, 2, pp. 411–28.

Badiou, Alain (2004) *Theoretical Writings*, trans. R. Brassier and A. Toscano. London: Continuum.

Bakhtin, M. M. (1981) *The Dialogic Imagination*, ed. M. Holquist, trans. C. Emerson and M. Holquist. Austin, TX: University of Texas Press.

Balibar, Étienne [1968] (1970) 'The Basic Concepts of Historical Materialism', in L. Althusser and É. Balibar, *Reading Capital*, trans. Ben Brewster. London: NLB, pp. 199–308.

Bambrough, Renford (1968) 'Universals and Family Resemblances', in G. Pitcher (ed.), *Wittgenstein: The Philosophical Investigations*. London: Macmillan, pp. 186–204.

Barthes, Roland [1977] (1990) *A Lover's Discourse*, trans. Richard Howard. Harmondsworth: Penguin.

Baumann, Martin (1997) 'Shangri-La in Exile: Portraying Tibetan Diaspora Studies and Reconsidering Diaspora(s)', *Diaspora*, 6, 3, pp. 377–404.

Baumann, Martin (2004) 'A Diachronic View of Diaspora, The Significance of Religion and Hindu Trinidadians', in Waltraud Kokot, Khachig Tölölyan and Carolin Alfonso (eds), *Diaspora, Identity and Religion*. London and New York: Routledge, pp. 170–84.

Bhabha, Homi (1990) 'The Third Space', in J. Rutherford (ed.), *Identity: Community, Culture, Difference*. London: Lawrence & Wishart, pp. 207–21.

Borradori, Giovanna (2003) *Philosophy in a Time of Terror: Dialogues with Jürgen Habermas and Jacques Derrida*. Chicago: University of Chicago Press.

Boyarin, Daniel and Jonathan Boyarin (1993) 'Diaspora: Generation and the Ground of Jewish Identity', *Critical Inquiry*, 19, 4, pp. 693–725.

Brah, Avtar (1996) *Cartographies of Diaspora: Contesting Identities*. London: Routledge.

Braudel, Fernand [1949] (1975) *The Mediterranean: And the Mediterranean World in the Age of Philip II*, Volume II, trans. Siân Reynolds. London: Fontana.

Butler, Kim D. (2001) 'Defining Diaspora, Refining a Discourse', *Diaspora*, 10, 2, pp. 189–219.

Carter, Donald (2003) 'Preface', in Khalid Koser (ed.), *New African Diasporas*. London and New York: Routledge, pp. ix–xix.

Chakrabarty, Dipesh (2000) *Provincialising Europe: Postcolonial Thought and Historical Difference*. Princeton, NJ: Princeton University Press.

Chambers, Iain (1994) *Migrancy, Culture, Identity*. London: Routledge.

Chow, Rey (1993) *Writing Diaspora: Tactics of Intervention in Contemporary Cultural Studies*. Bloomington and Indianapolis, IN: Indiana University Press.

Chuh, Kandice (1996) 'Transnationalism and Its Pasts', *Public Culture*, 9, 1, pp. 93–112.

Cleary, Joe (2002) *Literature, Partition and the Nation State: Culture and Conflict in Ireland, Israel and Palestine*. Cambridge: Cambridge University Press.

Clifford, James (1986) 'Partial Truths', in J. Clifford and M. George (eds), *Writing Culture*. Berkeley, CA: University of California Press, pp. 1–26.

Clifford, James (1992) 'Traveling Cultures', in Lawrence Grossberg, Cary Nelson and Paul A. Treichler (eds), *Cultural Studies*. New York and London: Routledge, pp. 96–116.

Clifford, James (1994) 'Diasporas', *Cultural Anthropology*, 9, 3, pp. 302–38.

Clogg, Richard (1999) 'The Greek Diaspora: The Historical Context', in R. Clogg (ed.), *The Greek Diaspora in the Twentieth Century*. London: Macmillan, pp. 1–23.

Cohen, Robin (1997) *Global Diasporas: An Introduction*. London: University College London Press.

Conner, Walker (1986) 'The Impact of Homelands Upon Diasporas', in G. Sheffer (ed.), *Modern Diasporas in International Politics*. London and Sydney: Croom Helm, pp. 16–45.

Coogan, Tim Pat (2000) *Wherever Green is Worn: The Story of the Irish Diaspora*. London: Hutchinson.

Davidson, Donaldson (1996) 'The Logical Form of Action Sentences', in R. Casati and A. Varzi (eds), *Events*. Aldershot: Dartmouth, pp. 81–95.

Deleuze, Gilles [1969] (1990) *The Logic of Sense*, trans. Mark Lester and Charles Stivale, ed. Constantin V. Boundas. New York: Columbia University Press.

Deleuze, Gilles (1995) 'L'Immanence: une vie . . .', *Philosophie*, 47, 6, pp. 3–7.

Deleuze, Gilles and Félix Guattari [1980] (1987) *A Thousand Plateaus: Capitalism and Schizophrenia*, trans. Brian Massumi. Minneapolis, MN, and London: University of Minnesota Press.

Derrida, Jacques (1976) *Of Grammatology*, trans. Gayatri Chakravorty Spivak. Baltimore, MD: Johns Hopkins University Press.

Derrida, Jacques [1967] (1978) *Writing and Difference*, trans. Alan Bass. Chicago: University of Chicago Press.

Derrida, Jacques (1992) *Acts of Literature*, ed. Derek Attridge. New York and London: Routledge.

Derrida, Jacques (1994) *Spectres of Marx*, trans. Peggy Kamuf. New York and London: Routledge.

Dostoyevsky, Fyodor [1864 and 1846 respectively] (2003) *Notes from Underground and The Double*, trans. Jessie Coulson. London: Penguin.

Edmondson, Locksley (1986) 'Black America as a Mobilising Diaspora: Some International Implications', in G. Sheffer (ed.), *Modern Diasporas in International Politics*. London and Sydney: Croom Helm, pp. 164–211.

Edwards, Brent Hayes (2003) *The Practice of Diaspora: Literature, Translation, and the Rise of Black Internationalism*. Cambridge, MA: Harvard University Press.

Ellison, Ralph (1967) *Shadow and Act*. London: Secker & Warburg.

Emberson-Bain, Àtu (1994) 'Backbone of Growth: Export Manufacturing and Fiji's Tuna Fish Wives', in À. Emberson-Bain (ed.), *Sustainable Development or Malignant Growth: Perspectives of Pacific Island Women*. Suva: Marama Publications, pp. 149–72.

Esman, Milton J. (1986) 'The Chinese Diaspora in Southeast Asia', in G. Sheffer (ed.), *Modern Diasporas in International Politics*. London and Sydney: Croom Helm, pp. 130–63.

Esman, Milton J. (1992) 'The Political Fallout of International Migration', *Diaspora*, 2, 1, pp. 3–41.

Foucault, Michel [1966] (1991a) *The Order of Things*. London: Routledge.

Foucault, Michel [1975] (1991b) *Discipline and Punish:The Birth of the Prison*, trans. Alan Sheridan. Harmondsworth: Penguin.

Foucault, Michel [1969] (1992) *The Archaeology of Knowledge*. London: Routledge.

Freud, Sigmund [1932] (1971) *The Interpretation of Dreams*, trans. and ed. J. Strachey. London: Allen & Unwin.

Fuglerud, Øivind (1999) *Life on the Outside: The Tamil Diaspora and Long Distance Nationalism*. London: Pluto Press.

Gabaccia, Donna R. (2000) *Italy's Many Diasporas*. London: University College London.

Gellner, Ernest (1991) 'Nationalism and Politics in Eastern Europe', *New Left Review*, 189, pp. 127–36.

Genette, Gérard (1992) *The Architext: An Introduction*, trans. Jane E. Lewin. Berkeley, CA: University of California Press.

Ghosh, Amitav (1989) 'The Diaspora in Indian Culture', *Public Culture*, 2, 1, pp. 73–8.

Gilroy, Paul (1987) *'There Ain't No Black in the Union Jack': The Cultural Politics of Race and Nation*. London: Hutchinson.

Gilroy, Paul (1993) *The Black Atlantic: Modernity and Double Consciousness*. Cambridge, MA: Harvard University Press.

Gomez, Michael A. (2005) *Reversing Sail: A History of the African Diaspora*. Cambridge: Cambridge University Press.

Goonewardena, Kanishka (2004) 'Postcolonialism and Diaspora: A Contribution to the Critique of Nationalist Ideology and Historiography in the Age of Globalisation and Neoliberalism', *University of Toronto Quarterly*, 73, 2, pp. 390–406.

Gramsci, Antonio (1971) *Selections from the Prison Notebooks of Antonio Gramsci*, trans. and ed. Quintin Hoare and Geoffrey Smith. New York: International Publishers.

Gupta, Akhil and James Ferguson (1992) 'Beyond "Culture": Space, Identity, and the Politics of Difference', *Cultural Anthropology*, 7, 1, pp. 6–23.

Hall, Stuart (1987) 'Minimal Selves', in *Identity: The Real Me*, ICA Documents 6. London: Institute for Contemporary Arts, pp. 44–6.

Hall, Stuart (1988) 'New Ethnicities', in *Black Film/British Cinema*, ICA Documents 7. London: Institute for Contemporary Arts, pp. 27–31.

Hall, Stuart (1990) 'Cultural Identity and Diaspora', in J. Rutherford (ed.), *Identity: Community, Culture, Difference*. London: Lawrence & Wishart, pp. 222–37.

Hall, Stuart (1992) 'The Question of Cultural Identity', in S. Hall, D. Held and T. McGrew (eds), *Modernity and its Futures*. Cambridge: Polity Press in association with Blackwell Publishers and The Open University, pp. 274–316.

Hall, Stuart and Tony Jefferson (eds) (1976) *Resistance through Rituals: Youth Subcultures in Post-war Britain*. London: HarperCollins Academic.

Harrington, Chris (2000) 'Fiji's Women Garment Workers: Negotiating Constraints in Employment and Beyond', *Labour and Management in Development Journal*, 1, 5, http://labour-management.anu.edu.au/volumes/prt/1-5-harrington.pdf.

Harris, Joseph E. (ed.) [1982](1993) *Global Dimensions of the African Diaspora*, 2nd edn. Washington: Howard University Press.

Hau'ofa, Epeli (1993) 'Our Sea of Islands', in E. Hau'ofa, E. Waddell and V. Naidu (eds), *A New Oceania: Rediscovering Our Sea of Islands*. Suva: University of the South Pacific, pp. 2–16.

Held, David and Anthony McGrew (2000) 'The Great Globalisation Debate: An Introduction', in D. Held and A. McGrew (eds), *The Global Transformations Reader: An Introduction to the Globalisation Debate*. Cambridge: Polity Press, pp. 1–45.

Helweg, Arthur W. (1986) 'The Indian Diaspora: Influence on International Relations', in G. Sheffer (ed.), *Modern Diasporas in International Politics*. London and Sydney: Croom Helm, pp. 117–29.

Hoerder, Dirk (2002) 'The German-Language Diasporas: A Survey, Critique, and Interpretation', *Diaspora*, 11, 1, pp. 7–44.

Holden, Philip (2002) 'Interrogating Diaspora: Wang Gungwu's *Pulse*', *Ariel*, 33, 3 & 4, pp. 105–29.

Holston, James and Arjun Appadurai (1996) 'Cities and Citizenship', *Public Culture*, 8, pp. 187–204.

Howell, Sally (2000) 'Cultural Interventions: Arab American Aesthetics between the Transnational and the Ethnic', *Diaspora*, 9, 1, pp. 59–82.

Ifekwunigwe, Jayne O. (2003) 'Scattered Belongings: Reconfiguring the "African" in the English-African Diaspora', in K. Koser (ed.), *New African Diasporas*. London and New York: Routledge, pp. 71–94.

Israel, Nico (2000) *Outlandish: Writing between Exile and Diaspora*. Stanford, CA: Stanford University Press.

Itzigsohn, José (2001) 'Living Transnational Lives', *Diaspora*, 10, 2, pp. 281–96.

Jameson, Fredric [1981] (1989) *The Political Unconscious: Narrative as a Socially Symbolic Act*. London: Routledge.

Jameson, Fredric (1991) *Postmodernism, Or, The Cultural Logic of Late Capitalism*. London: Verso.

Jusdanis, Gregory (1996) 'Culture, Culture Everywhere: The Swell of Globalisation Theory', *Diaspora*, 5, 1, pp. 141–61.

Karatani, Kojin (2003) *Transcritique: On Kant and Marx*, trans. Sabu Kohso. Cambridge, MA: MIT Press.

Karim, Karim H. (2003) 'Mapping Diasporic Mediascapes', in K. H. Karim (ed.), *The Media of Diaspora*. London and New York: Routledge, pp. 1–17.

Keay, John (1991) *The Honourable Company: A History of the East India Company*. London: HarperCollins.

Koser, Khalid (2003) 'New African Diasporas: An Introduction', in K. Koser (ed.), *New African Diasporas*. London and New York: Routledge, pp. 1–16.

Kripke, Saul A. [1972] (1980) *Naming and Necessity*. Oxford: Basil Blackwell.

Lal, Vinay (1999) 'The Politics of History on the Internet: Cyber-Diasporic Hinduism and the North American Hindu Diaspora', *Diaspora*, 8, 2, pp. 137–72.

Lamb, Sarah (2002) 'Intimacy in a Transnational Era: The Remaking of Aging among Indian Americans', *Diaspora*, 11, 3, pp. 299–330.

Landau, Jacob. M (1986) 'Diaspora and Language', in G. Sheffer (ed.), *Modern Diasporas in International Politics*. London and Sydney: Croom Helm, pp. 75–102.

Lavie, Smadar and Ted Swedenburg (1996) 'Introduction', in S. Smadar and T. Swedenburg (eds), *Displacement, Diaspora, and Geographies of Identity*. Durham, NC, and London: Duke University Press, pp. 1–25.

Lee, Christopher (2005) 'Diaspora, Transnationalism, and Asian American Studies: Positions and Debates', in W. W. Anderson and R. G. Lee (eds), *Displacements and Diasporas: Asians in the Americas*. New Brunswick, NJ: Rutgers University Press, pp. 23–38.

Lever-Tracy, Constance, David Ip and Noel Tracy (1996) *The Chinese Diaspora and Mainland China: An Emerging Economic Synergy*. London: Macmillan.

Linebaugh, Peter (1982) 'All the Atlantic Mountains Shook', *Labour/Le Travailleur*, 10, pp. 87–121.

Linebaugh, Peter and Marcus Rediker (2000) *The Many-Headed Hydra: Sailors, Slaves, Commoners, and the Hidden History of the Revolutionary Atlantic*. Boston: Beakin Press.

Lowe, Lisa (1996) *Immigrant Acts: On Asian American Cultural Politics*. Durham, NC, and London: Duke University Press.

Lowe, Lisa and David Lloyd (1997) 'Introduction', in L. Lowe and D. Lloyd (eds), *The Politics of Culture in the Shadow of Capital*. Durham, NC: Duke University Press, pp. 1–32.

Luibhéid, Eithne (2005) 'Introduction: Queering Migration and Citizenship', in Eithne Luibhéid and Lionel Cantú Jr (eds), *Queer Migrations*. Minneapolis, MN: University of Minnesota Press, pp. ix–xivi.

Lyotard, Jean-François (1984) 'The *Différend*, the Referent, and the Proper Name', *Diacritics*, 14, 3, pp. 4–14.

Lyotard, Jean-François (1989) *The Lyotard Reader*, ed. Andrew Benjamin. Oxford: Basil Blackwell.

McAlister, Elizabeth (2002) *Rara! Vodou, Power, and Performance in Haiti and Its Diaspora*. Berkeley and Los Angeles, CA: University of California Press.

Manalansan IV, Martin F. (1997) 'In the Shadows of Stonewall: Examining Gay Transnational Politics and the Diasporic Dilemma', in L. Lisa and D. Lloyd (eds), *The Politics of Culture in the Shadow of Capital*. Durham, NC: Duke University Press, pp. 485–505.

Manalansan IV, Martin F. (2005) 'Migrancy, Modernity, Mobility: Quotidian Struggles and Queer Diasporic Intimacy', in Eithne Luibhéid and Lionel Cantú Jr (eds), *Queer Migrations*. Minneapolis, MN. University of Minnesota Press, pp. 146–60.

Mann, Michael (1993) 'Nation-States in Europe and Other Continents: Diversifying, Developing, Not Dying', *Daedalus*, 122, 3, pp. 115–40.

Marx, Karl and Friedrich Engels [1872] (1978) 'Manifesto of the Communist Party', in R. C. Tucker (ed.), *The Marx-Engels Reader*, 2nd edn. New York and London: W. W. Norton, pp. 469–500.

Mercer, Kobena (1988) 'Diaspora Culture and the Dialogic Imagination: The Aesthetics of Black Independent Film in Britain', in *Blackframes: Critical Perspectives on Black Independent Cinema*. Cambridge, MA: MIT Press, pp. 50–61.

Mercer, Kobena (1994) *Welcome to the Jungle: New Positions in Black Cultural Studies*. New York and London: Routledge.

Minh-ha, Trinh T. (1990) 'Not you/Like you: Post-colonial Women and the Interlocking Questions of Identity and Difference', in G. Anzaldúa (ed.), *Making Face, Making Soul*. California: Aunt Lute Press, pp. 371–75.

Mishra, Sudesh (1996) 'Estranged and Estranging Bodies: Gazing on Caliban, or An Essay against Hybridity', *UTS Review*, 2, pp. 108–28.

Mishra, Sudesh (2002a) 'The Time Is Out of Joint', *Span*, 52, pp. 136–45.

Mishra, Sudesh (2002b), 'Diaspora Criticism', in Julian Wolfreys (ed.), *Introducing Criticism at the 21st Century*. Edinburgh: Edinburgh University Press, pp. 13–36.

Mishra, Vijay (1996a) 'The Diasporic Imaginary: Theorising the Indian Diaspora', *Textual Practice*, 10, 3, pp. 421–47.

Mishra, Vijay (1996b), '(B)ordering Naipaul: Indenture History and Diasporic Poetics', *Diaspora*, 5, 2, pp. 189–237.

Mishra, Vijay (2001) 'Diaspora and the Art of Impossible Mourning', in Makarand Paranjape (ed.), *In Diaspora: Theories, Histories, Texts*. New Delhi: Indialog, pp. 24–47.

Mishra, Vijay (2002) *Bollywood Cinema: Temples of Desire*. London: Routledge.

Monson, Ingrid (2003) *The African Diaspora: A Musical Perspective*. New York and London: Routledge.

Mukherjee, Bharati (1988) *The Middleman and Other Stories*. New York: Fawcett Crest.

Mullen, Bill V. (2003) 'Du Bois, *Dark Princess*, and the Afro-Asian International', *Positions*, 11, 1, pp. 217–39.

Nietzsche, Frederick (1976) *The Portable Nietzsche*, trans. and ed. Walter Kaufmann. Harmondsworth: Penguin.

Niovo, Edite (2002) 'Towards a Cartography of Portugueseness: Challenging the Hegemonic Center', *Diaspora*, 11, 2, pp. 255–75.

Ong, Aihwa (1999) *Flexible Citizenship: The Cultural Logics of Transnationality*. Durham, NC: Duke University Press.

Ong, Aihwa and David Nonini (1997) 'Chinese Transnationalism as an Alternative Modernity', in A. Ong and D. Nonini (eds), *Ungrounded Empires: The Cultural Politics of Modern Chinese Transnationalism*. New York and London: Routledge, pp. 3–33.

Østergaard-Nielsen, Eva (2003) *Transnational Politics: Turks and Kurds in Germany*. London and New York: Routledge.

Prashad, Vijay (2000) *The Karma of Brown Folk*. Minneapolis, MN: University of Minnesota Press.

Prashad, Vijay (2002) 'Countering Yankee Hindutva', *Frontline*, 19, 25, 7 December, http://www.hinduonnet.com/fline/fl1925/stories/2002/220005302800.htm.

Puar, Jasbir K. (1994) 'Writing My Way "Home"', *Socialist Review*, 24, 4, pp. 75–108.

Radhakrishnan, R. (1996) *Diasporic Mediations: Between Home and Locations*. Minneapolis, MN, and London: University of Minnesota Press.

Rai, Amit S. (1995) 'India On-line: Electronic Bulletin Boards and the Construction of a Diasporic Hindu Identity', *Diaspora*, 4, 1, pp. 31–87.

Ray, Manas (2003) 'Nation, Nostalgia and Bollywood: In the Tracks of a Twice-Displaced Community', in K. H. Karim (ed.), *The Media of Diaspora*. London and New York, Routledge, pp. 21–35.

Roberts, Martin (1992) ' "World Music" and the Global Cultural Economy', *Diaspora*, 2, 2, pp. 229–42.

Rouse, Roger (1991) 'Mexican Migration and the Social Space of Postmodernism', *Diaspora*, 1, 1, pp. 8–23.

Rubchak, Marian J. (1992) ' "God made me a Lithuanian": Nationalist Ideology and the Constructions of a North American Diaspora', *Diaspora*, 2, 1, pp. 117–29.

Rushdie, Salman (1988) *The Satanic Verses*. London: Vintage.

Safran, William (1991) 'Diasporas in Modern Societies: Myths of Homeland and Return', *Diaspora*, 1, 1, pp. 83–99.

Said, Edward (1978) *Orientalism*. New York: Pantheon Books.

Schwalgin, Susanne (2004) 'Why Locality Matters: Diaspora Consciousness and Sedentariness in the Armenian Diaspora in Greece', in W. Kokot, K. Tölölyan and C. Alfonso (eds), *Diaspora, Identity and Religion*. London and New York: Routledge, pp. 72–92.

Shapiro, Michael J. (2000) 'National Times and Other Times: Re-thinking Citizenship', *Cultural Studies*, 14, 1, pp. 79–98.

Sheffer, Gabriel (ed.) (1986) *Modern Diasporas in International Politics*. London and Sydney: Croom Helm.

Shepperson, George (1976) 'Introduction', in M. Kilson and R. Rotberg (eds), *The African Diaspora: Interpretive Essays*. Cambridge, MA: Harvard University Press, pp. 1–10.

Sinfield, Alan (1996) 'Diaspora and Hybridity: Queer Identities and the Ethnicity Model', *Textual Practice*, 10, 2, pp. 271–93.

Smith, Anthony D. (2000) 'Towards a Global Culture?', in D. Held and A. McGrew (eds), *The Global Transformations Reader: An Introduction to the Globalisation Debate*. Cambridge: Polity Press, pp. 239–47.

Smith, Paul (1997) *Millennial Dreams: Contemporary Culture and Capital in the North*. London: Verso.

Soames, Scott (2002) *Beyond Rigidity: The Unfinished Semantic Agenda of Naming and Necessity*. New York: Oxford University Press.

Sorenson, John (1992) 'Essence and Contingency in the Construction of Nationhood: Transformations of Identity in Ethiopia and Its Diasporas', *Diaspora*, 2, 2, pp. 201–28.

Spickard, Paul (2002) 'Pacific Diaspora?', in P. Spickard, J. L. Rondilla and D. H. Wright (eds), *Pacific Diaspora. Island Peoples in the United States and Across the Pacific*. Honolulu, HI: University of Hawaii Press, pp. 1–27.

Spivak, Gayatri Chakravorty (1996) 'Diasporas Old and New: Women in the Transnational World', *Textual Practice*, 10, 2, pp. 245–69.

Tambiah, Stanley J. (2000) 'Transnational Movements, Diaspora, and Multiple Modernities', *Daedalus*, 129, 1, pp. 163–94.

Tapp, Nicholas and Gary Yia Lee (2004) *The Hmong of Australia: Culture and Diaspora*. Canberra: Pandanus.

Tatla, Darshan Singh (1999) *The Sikh Diaspora: The Search for Statehood*. London: University College London Press.

Teeple, Gary (2000) 'What is Globalisation', in S. McBride and J. Wiseman (eds), *Globalisation and Its Discontents*. London: Macmillan, pp. 9–23.

Todorov, Tzvetan [1978] (1990) *Genres in Discourse*, trans. Catherine Porter. Cambridge: Cambridge University Press.

Tölölyan, Khachig (1991) 'The Nation-State and Its Others: In Lieu of a Preface', *Diaspora*, 1, 1, pp. 3–7.

Tölölyan, Khachig (1996) 'Rethinking Diaspora(s): Stateless Power in the Transnational Moment', *Diaspora*, 5, 1, pp. 3–36.

Van Den Berghe, Pierre L. (1976) 'The African Diaspora in Mexico, Brazil, and the United States', *Social Forces*, 54, 3, pp. 530–45.

Vertovec, Steven (1997) 'Three Meanings of "Diaspora", Exemplified among South Asian Religions', *Diaspora*, 6, 3, pp. 277–99.

Visweswaran, Kamala (1997) 'Diaspora by Design: Flexible Citizenship and South Asians in U.S. Racial Formations', *Diaspora*, 6, 1, pp. 5–29.

Wahlbeck, Östen (1999) *Kurdish Diasporas: A Comparative Study of Kurdish Refugee Communities*. London: Macmillan.

Wallerstein, Immanuel (1974) *The Modern World-System: Capitalist Agriculture and the Origins of the European World-Economy in the Sixteenth Century*. New York: Academic Press.

Weiner, Myron (1986) 'Labor Migrations as Incipient Diasporas', in G. Sheffer (ed.), *Modern Diasporas in International Politics*. London and Sydney: Croom Helm, pp. 47–74.

Wellmeier, Nancy J. (1998) *Ritual, Identity, and the Mayan Diaspora*. New York and London: Garland.

Whalen, Carmen Teresa (2005) 'Colonialism, Citizenship, and the Making of the Puerto Rican Diaspora: An Introduction', in C. Whalen and V. Vázquez-Hernández (eds), *The Puerto Rican Diaspora*. Philadelphia: Temple University Press, pp. 1–42.

Widodo, Johannes (2004) *The Boat and the City: Chinese Diaspora and the Architecture of Southeast Asian Coastal Cities*. Singapore: Marshall Cavendish International.

Wittgenstein, Ludwig [1922] (1996) *Tractatus Logico-Philosophius*. London and New York: Routledge.

Zenner, Walter P. (1983) 'The Jewish Diaspora and the Middleman Adaptation', in Étan Levine (ed.), *Diaspora: Exile and the Jewish Condition*. New York and London: Jason Aronson, pp. 141–56.

Žižek, Slavoj (2000) *The Fragile Absolute or Why is the Christian Legacy Worth Fighting For?* London: Verso.

Žižek, Slavoj (2004) 'The Parallax View', *New Left Review*, 25, pp. 121–34.

Index